INDIA-NIGERIA EXPERIENCE IN COMBATING TERRORISM

INDIA-NIGERIA EXPERIENCE IN COMBATING TERRORISM

EDITORS

Maj Gen BK Sharma, AVSM, SM** (Retd)

Brig Narender Kumar, SM, VSM (Retd)

EDITORIAL ASSISTANT

Mr. Gaurav Kumar

PENTAGON PRESS LLP

UNITED SERVICE INSTITUTION OF INDIA
NEW DELHI

NIGERIAN ARMY
RESOURCE CENTRE

INDIA-NIGERIA EXPERIENCE IN COMBATING TERRORISM

*Editors: Maj Gen BK Sharma, AVSM, SM** (Retd)*
Brig Narender Kumar, SM, VSM (Retd)

First Published in 2020

ISBN 978-81-942837-2-0

Published by
PENTAGON PRESS LLP
206, Peacock Lane, Shahpur Jat
New Delhi-110049
Phones: 011-64706243, 26491568
Telefax: 011-26490600
email: rajan@pentagonpress.in
website: www.pentagonpress.in

Printed at Aegean Offset Printers, Greater Noida, U.P.

CONTENTS

*

LIST OF TABLES, MAPS AND CHARTS

FOREWORD

Violent extremism has acquired new dimensions with technology and ideology as the most effective allies. The nature, targets and impact of terrorism have changed dramatically since the end of the Cold War. Terrorism is no longer a domestic phenomenon, it has assumed transnational linkages. The capacity to cause collateral damage by terrorist and insurgent groups is colossal. It affects relationship between the states and has the potential to trigger wars between them. The greatest threat to states today is from weaponisation of ideology, adaptation of technology by non-state actors and unleashing a war of perception. The objective is to destroy institutions of democratic governance and the idea of a nation state. Such an idea is against the development of modern states and empowerment of people. Therefore, states need to evolve a strategy to prevent subversion of masses and disruption of rule of law.

It is important to collaborate academically so as to develop an understanding of handling two diverse problems of Jihadi terrorism and insurgency/ militancy that may have its root in political, economic and religious subversion of a section of population. Unless there is conceptual understanding and cooperation among the nations that are threatened by this menace, it is not possible to defeat this idea. Thus it is in the best interest of the global community to develop institutional cooperation to share and work together to develop greater understanding of the conflict that requires shared strategy and belief for conflict resolution.

The joint publication by the United Service Institution of India & Nigerian Army Resource Centre will go a long way to set the stage for developing institutional relations and strategies to deal with violent extremism. This effort will assist the academicians, policy makers and professionals to learn from the experiences and good practices from each other. The large canvass that the scholars have covered will give a deeper understanding to even other countries, those which are victims of terrorism to understand nuances of counter-insurgency and counter-terrorism.

The views expressed by the authors are their personal views and in no way represent the stated views of the United Service Institution of India & the Nigerian Army Resource Centre. The lessons learnt and way forward suggested by the authors is for policy makers and respective security forces to consider while dealing with violent extremism.

New Delhi

Lt Gen PK Singh, PVSM, AVSM (Retd)
Director, USI of India, New Delhi

FOREWORD

The book, India- Nigeria Experience in Combating Terrorism is a welcomed publication for the two major reasons. First, it is a confirmation of the successful collaboration between the Armed forces of India and Nigeria over the years, which has translated to sharing of experiences on challenges of insurgency and terrorism. Secondly, it is a refreshing indication of the possibility of a South-South collaboration over the issues of mutual interest.

The book interrogates the challenges of terrorism and violent extremism confronting both the countries in particular alongside the general global dimensions. The varying experiences of the two countries and the efforts undertaken to combat the challenges are well chronicled. For instance the major Challenges facing Nigeria, the Boko Haram terrorism in the North East and militancy in the Niger Delta are given enough attention. Similarly, India's Punjab and the North East experiences are extensively examined.

Contributors cutting across the military consisting of both serving and retired officers, academia and security practitioners were carefully chosen. The various chapters assigned to them have been well researched and garnished with their vast personal experiences in the chosen areas of interest. Thus the lessons drawn from each topic are not only apt for the two countries or their respective regions, but the entire world.

It is expected that the momentum generated by this intellectual cooperation would be sustained and developed further. This book is a must read for serving and retired personnel of the armed forces of both the countries, and anyone involved in global security and defence studies.

Major General GA Wahab (Retired)
Director General
Nigerian Army Resource Centre
Abuja, Nigeria

INTRODUCTION

The spectrum of conflict is changing, state on state wars are becoming expensive and unaffordable due to lethality and the destructive nature of modern wars. The monopoly of the state over warfare is slowly diminishing and non-state actors are playing pivotal role in initiating hybrid and grey zone conflicts. Future warfare is ambiguous to understand, because contours of conflict are borderless and there are no defined boundaries between belligerent forces. The new era conflicts are giving space to states and non-state actors to operate in the same battle space to pursue their self-serving objectives. During the contemporary period, the war is played out at two levels—a trial of strength on the physical level, and a clash of wills on the psychological level. In the modern paradigm the primary objectives to wage wars are to bleed nations for a prolonged period, stunt growth and regime change by creating unsustainable conditions on the ground for the democratic institutions to function. Al Qaeda and Islamic State have made it possible to fight this war on the name of religion and ideology of Caliphate. Asia and Africa are most vulnerable due to radicalisation of impressionable youth owing to political, economic and social causes.

India and Nigeria are dealing with the religion based ideological terrorism, secessionist movements, insurgency due to economic reasons and political dissonance. Both nations have suffered economically and the conflicts are affecting internal harmony between the people of different faiths. The challenge to the governments on one side is to maintain harmonious relations between people of different ethnic background and faith and on the other side to maintain economic development and growth.

It is important to collaborate academically so as to develop an understanding of handling two diverse problems of Jihadi terrorism and insurgency/militancy in respective nations. The threat from home-grown violent extremists occurs with little or no warning because the perpetrators often strike soft targets with surprise. Unless there is conceptual understanding and cooperation among the nations that are threatened by this menace, it is not possible to defeat such ideas. Thus it is in the best interest of both nations to develop institutional cooperation to share and work together to develop greater understanding of the conflicts that require shared strategy and shared belief for conflict resolution.

The United Service Institute (USI) of India and the Nigerian Army Resource Centre (NARC) have taken an initiative to collaborate to document experiences and methodology of dealing with the terrorism and insurgencies in their respective nations. The overall objective of the joint study is to learn the lessons from the Indian and Nigerian experience of dealing with the violent extremism, insurgency and militancy. The joint study is divided into four parts. Part one dwells in "Ideological and Conceptual Construct of Violent Terrorism" in relations to India and Nigeria. The author from India has highlighted that violent extremists identifies four essentials in the conduct of their campaigns—human resources (to include extremists), war fighting wherewithal, finances and ideology. Application of security forces is a compulsion; however political intervention as early as possible is must for conflict resolution. The Nigerian scholars have highlighted that military is an inefficient instrument while dealing with ideologically driven violent extremism. Therefore, ideological, conceptual and military strategies will have to be combined to fight the violent extremism driven by an ideology.

The Part two has been devoted to "India's Experience in Dealing with Violent Extremism". At section 3 the author has highlighted that Pakistan has used terror and non-state actors as a state policy that is bleeding India militarily and creating social, political and economic disharmony in Jammu and Kashmir. Therefore, sole reliance on a security-centric approach will not help India win because Kashmir is also a battleground of perceptions and requires a whole of state approach. At section 4 the author has discussed rise and fall of militancy in Punjab. He highlighted the role of Pakistan in fuelling Punjab militancy in 1980s and states that the key to defeat Punjab militancy was sound politico-military strategy followed by precise kinetic operations, public support and proactive state administration. At section 5 the author has highlighted the complex nature of insurgencies in the Northeast of India. The insurgencies are against illegal migrants settled in Assam, secessionist movements of Naga tribes for Greater Nagalim and demand for sovereign state of Manipur. The Centre and State governments have adopted the strategy of engagement by suspension of operations and cease fire to end violent hostilities. Strategy of "Winning Hearts and Minds", sound rehabilitation of insurgent cadres and cooperation with the neighbouring countries has ensured peaceful environment to pursue enduring peace. At section 6 the author has decoded the genesis of Left Wing Extremism (LWE) and its threat to India. He has highlighted that the genesis of LWE lies in lack of development and disengagement of the tribal population with the state. The strategy of security for development is giving peace dividends and the area of influence of LWE is shrinking. At section 7 the author has highlighted India's approach to deal with radicalization. India's approach to pursue non-obtrusive forms of counter-radicalisation has succeeded and has managed to quell the number of radicals joining global terrorist ranks. Modernisation of madrasas and emphasis on education of vulnerable sections of the society has given good results. Counter-radicalisation and anti-radicalisation should be given greater emphasis since chances of reclaiming of an individual are far higher.

The Part three covers "Nigeria's Experience in Dealing with Violent Extremism". The author at section 8 has discussed evolution of Boko Haram and the ideological linkages inspired by unflinching religious belief of salvation through martyrdom. The strategy to deal with the threat to multi ethnic and multi-cultural society from a radical organisation can be best handled by adopting hard and soft options to erode support base of Boko Haram. The ultimate objective is to ensure peace by political consensus. The article of section 9 gives an overview of "Cross Border Linkages between Violent Extremist Groups Operating in Sahel Corridor, Chad Basin and North African States". The authors have given an overview of cross border linkages of violent extremist groups with identical ideology but with diverse objectives. The military approaches for countering violent extremism (CVE) in the Sahel has not yielded the desired results, therefore, it may be prudent to shift the strategy from purely military intervention to non-coercive CVE means, with an objective to prevent recruitment and countering of ideology of violence. The article at section 10 dwells on counter insurgency operations in the Lake Chad Basin. The author has highlighted the complex security threat to Lake Chad Basin and need for a Multi-national Joint Task Force (MNJTF) to undertake counter insurgency operations. The campaigns by MNJTF were successful and large number of towns and villages were liberated from the control of Boko Haram. The author at section 11 has discussed "Amnesty, Disarmament Demobilisation, Reintegration (ADDR) and Security Stabilisation in the Niger Delta". The author has carried out a critical review of ADDR and its success in Niger Delta. However, he is sceptical of enduring peace if economic reintegration fails or get disrupted. At section 12 the authors have eluded to the important issue of "Terrorism, Insurgency and the Quest for De-radicalization in Nigeria". The authors have examined the rising problem of radicalisation in Nigeria and the challenge a society faces to prevent youths becoming victim of this menace. The military method of coercion and deterrence to de-radicalise youth is unlikely to have enduring effects. However, a soft and structured approach of engagement, intervention, neutralization and rehabilitation of clients is likely to bear greater result.

The Part four lays down the lessons learnt and way forward to deal with violent extremism in India and Nigeria. The authors from both countries are unanimous in their opinion that violent extremism cannot be dealt purely by military strategy. It will require a whole of government approach with greater emphasis on soft approach or alternative methods of conflict resolution. Radicalisation is a threat to India and Nigeria and thus efforts should be made to put in place a structured approach to deal with radicalisation. Deliverance of governance, redressal of grievances and economic reintegration of the insurgents/ militant cadres is vital for restoration of peace.

The study is a milestone for future bilateral engagement between scholars and professional of NARC and the USI of India. It will facilitate policy makers to shape future strategies to deal with transnational terrorism and violent extremism.

CONTRIBUTORS

Lt Gen Ata Hasnain, PVSM, UYSM, AVSM, SM, VSM & Bar (Retd) is a former Indian Army officer. His last assignment in service was as the Military Secretary of the Indian Army. Prior to that, he commanded an Army Corps in the Indian state of Jammu and Kashmir. He is a Public Speaker, Strategic Analyst and Author.

Prof Usman A Tar (PhD) is Professor of Political Science and Defence Studies, and Head of the Centre for Defence Studies and Documentation, Nigerian Defence Academy.

Dr. Adejoh Sunday is a lecturer with the Department of Political Science and Diplomacy, Veritas University, Abuja. He has special interest in global governance and strategic studies.

Lt Gen DS Hooda, PVSM, UYSM, AVSM, VSM & Bar (Retd) is the former General Officer Commanding-in-Chief of the Indian Army's Northern Command.

Lt Gen Ghanshyam Singh Katoch, PVSM, AVSM, VSM (Retd), retired from the Army in 2016 as the Director General Perspective Planning. He is a Distinguished Fellow at the USI of India, and an elected member of its Governing Council.

Lt Gen Rameshwar Roy, UYSM, AVSM, YSM (Retd) is a former Army Corps Commander and Director-General Assam Rifles. He is a Distinguished Author and held the Chief of Army Staff Chair of Excellence at Centre for Land Warfare.

Dr P V Ramana is a former Research Fellow at IDSA. A student of South Asian studies, he works on the Naxalite-Maoist movement in India. He was awarded MPhil in 1996, and PhD in 1999 by Jawaharlal Nehru University, New Delhi.

Dr. Adil Rasheed is a Research Fellow at the IDSA. He is a political commentator and scholar of repute on issues related to radicalisation and violent extremism. He was a former Senior Research Fellow at the United Services Institution of India (USI).

Prof Kyari Mohammed is a professor of History and a former Vice-Chancellor of Modibbo Adama University of Technology (MAUTECH). He is one of Nigeria's leading scholars on the on-going Boko Haram insurgency and counterinsurgency.

Samuel Baba Ayegba is Research Fellow at the Centre for Defence and Documentation (CDSD), Nigerian Defence Academy, Kaduna.

Lt Gen Lamidi Oyebayo Adeosun is a serving seasoned infantry General with in-depth command, instructional and staff experience. His experience spans internal, ECOMOG and UN operations. He is a renowned veteran in the fight against Boko Haram insurgency.

Colonel S Inuwa is a serving senior officer with the Nigerian Army and a Research Fellow at NARC. His areas of research are armed conflict, disarmament, demobilisation and reintegration, post-conflict peace-building and reconstruction.

Dr. Hussaini Jibrin, PhD is a Lecturer in the Department of History and War Studies, Nigerian Defence Academy Kaduna, Nigeria. His main research interest is Military History and Defence Studies.

Zaharaddeen Sulaiman is a Lecturer in the Department of History and Security Studies, Umaru Musa Yar'adua University, Katsina. He is currently a doctoral student at the department of History, Usmanu Danfodiyo University, Sokoto, Nigeria. His research interest is on Religious History and Conflict Studies.

Maj Gen BK Sharma, AVSM, SM** (Retd) is the Deputy Director (Research) and Head Centre for Strategic Studies and Simulation (CS3) at the USI. He specializes in Strategic Net Assessment, Scenario Building and Strategic Gaming. He writes for professional journals and participates in national and international events.

Brig Narender Kumar, SM, VSM (Retd) is a Distinguished Fellow at the United Service Institution of India (USI). He has authored two books *Challenges in the Indian Ocean Regions and Response Options* and *Rise of China:*

A Military Challenge to India. He has authored more than 190 articles and chapter to various books and journals.

Dr. Fatima Akilu is a Nigerian psychologist in areas of Preventing and Countering Violent Extremism (CVE) and Counter-Terrorism. She is the Executive Director of Neem Foundation.

Ramatu Jaji holds MSc. in Internal Development from Sciences PO, Paris. She has been involved in peace- building interventions in Northeast Nigeria including research, dialogue and reconciliation, rehabilitation as well as reintegration of survivors of the Boko Haram insurgency.

PART I

IDEOLOGICAL AND CONCEPTUAL CONSTRUCT OF COMBATING VIOLENT EXTREMISM AND TERRORISM1

1

Ideological and Conceptual Construct of Combating Violent Extremism and Terrorism in India

Lt Gen Syed Ata Hasnain,
PVSM, UYSM, AVSM, SM, VSM & Bar (Retd)

ABSTRACT

India has a rich experience in dealing with violent extremism. It involves successes and failures from which many lessons have been learnt. Violent extremist movements in India have also been characterised as proxy wars sponsored by adversary nations. All such movements usually depend upon the employment of four essentials in the conduct of their campaigns—human resources (to include extremists), war fighting wherewithal, finances and ideology. Driving all these are well managed eco-systems and networks which remain embedded even as human resources are neutralised. They then act as pillars of resurgence each time the state efforts flag and the attention is diverted. This essay covers the Indian experience of dealing with violent extremism, especially in the state of Jammu & Kashmir (J&K) where for 30 years a separatist movement sponsored as proxy war has existed. It dwells on the challenges which security forces undergo and recommends early political intervention to prevent such movements becoming a sore for the nation.

Introduction

As a multi ethnic and multi faith developing nation, India has had its share of problems concerning violent extremism of different shades. In a multi-ethnic and plural society there is inevitably an inter-ethnic and inter faith competition for space due to limitation on resources, employment opportunities and scope for growth. When radical religious belief or alternative political ideologies which promote the use of violence to achieve ends are infused into the discourse violence becomes far more serious and difficult to contain; in fact sometimes assuming proportions of terrorism and irregular warfare. At the earliest after Independence India experienced separatist insurgencies of the North East which were neither religious nor carried any other ideological colour; they were purely separatist and political in nature. Irregular movements at that juncture had not experienced much infusion of ideology. This needs detailed examination and analysis. In practice, this makes national vulnerability to extremism and terrorism highly case specific, and involves intangibles that cannot be easily quantified.[1]

The Punjab separatist movement of the Eighties acquired a terrorist colour very early. Its religious ideological orientation was brought about to promote Sikh sub nationalism and violent extremism became the norm. Two more movements deserve a brief analysis. First, is the Left Wing Extremism (LWE) which at one time had swept through almost one third of India (today largely under control). It does not have a religious colour but carries an ideological imprint nevertheless; the much forgotten communist ideology of Mao Tse Tung, the Chinese leader. The LWE is largely based in India's tribal belt and has seen a revolt against the state for the lack of development and insufficiency of compensation for the extraction of minerals from the natural resource rich areas which coincide with the boundaries of the Red Corridor (the colloquial term for the area afflicted by the Maoist insurgency). Second, is Jammu & Kashmir (J&K) which since 1989 has witnessed a separatist movement, more appropriately termed as a proxy war; the latter because it's a border state with territorial issues involving a neighbouring state, Pakistan. India prefers to label this as a terrorist movement as no qualms have been displayed about the choice of targets for the extremist violence which is brought to bear against them. The turbulence in J&K would never have lasted long enough without the active support of Pakistan which has provided all the ingredients necessary to sustain such a movement.

Nature of Violent Extremist Movements in India

Violent extremist movements have some basic differences which may set them apart from the other. These could be historical reasons of the movement, the terrain of the region, level of foreign support, ideological base, whether a border related movement or a heartland one, and finally the ultimate intent it wishes to achieve (example—separatism or overthrow of the government or establishment of a dominant ideology). However, principally there are some commonalities between all of them.

- There is either a genuine or a contrived cause which drives all such movements. Keeping the cause alive and building on it is necessary for longevity and keeping the adrenaline flowing against the state. Building an environment of hate against the mother state is also essential. This has become much easier after the advent of the worldwide web and social media.
- A charismatic leadership is necessary, one that can inspire and sustain the focus. Many movements go off track with leaders getting hijacked by attractions for money and power. Bhindranwale (A Sikh militant leader) achieved this to a great degree in the Punjab separatist situation. Most of the violent extremist movements have had charismatic leaders. The proxy war in J&K has at times depended greatly on collective leadership and at other times inspiration from agencies in Pakistan. It has lacked a single personality although Syed Ali Shah (SAS) Geelani may be counted as a quasi-leader of the movement. Terrorist leaders such as Syed Salahuddin (Hizbul Mujahideen), Hafiz Sayeed (Lashkar-e-Taiyaba) and Masood Azhar (Jaish-e-Mohammad) have had a distinct influence over their individual terror groups. The coming of Burhan Wani, the 21 year old youth terrorist leader had a great effect on the violent extremist movement in South Kashmir. Worldwide, charismatic leadership has proven to be one of the major drivers of violent extremism. The targeting of Osama bin Laden by the US in 2011 finally diluted the effectiveness of the Al Qaeda to a great extent as Ayman Al Zawahiri has not been able to adequately fill the void. Well established leaderships are capable of taking great risk and planning terror acts with audacity and alacrity. Leaderships existing away from the geographical precincts of the region continue to drive movements due to the rise in facilities of communication technology.
- Four major ingredients go into initiating and sustaining violent extremism. The first is human resources. These include terrorists, local and foreign, rabble-rousers, clergy, youth, lawyers, teachers and university professors, local intellectuals and media personalities. They form a diverse set of entities that play their individual role in initiating and sustaining the movement. All have

to be intensely loyal to the cause and work towards garnering support of the nay-sayers and fence sitters in the same society.

- The second ingredient is the wherewithal which arms the extremists so that an element of awe, fear and caution is imposed upon the people and likewise on the government and the Security Forces (SF). Explosives, weapons and ammunition are essential. An additional element could be essential here—the explosives handler or the improvised explosive device (IED) doctor; or doctors.
- The third entity is finances without which nothing can progress. A movement will die out if there is little or no money. It is required for a range of activities; among them a few could be arrangement for safe houses, transportation, bribes, compensation to win hearts and even to pay the extremists a monthly allowance, sustenance of networks and Over Ground Workers (OGWs).
- The last and one of the most important ingredients remains ideology. It is the binder which brings disparate groups together. Religious ideology in current times is the most effective driver. It takes time to take hold and that could extend to even a transition of a generation. Kashmir is an excellent example where Pakistan consciously aimed at supplanting the plural and tolerant Sufi ideology by a more virulent form of Islam through the *Ahle Hadith* organization. With liberal funding the clergy of an indeterminate number of mosques were changed; the *Sufi* by the *Wahabi.*
- To ensure the success of each of the four ingredients above, violent extremist movements depend upon networks which are far and wide, diffused, extending across borders with communication links and employment of modern technology. The importance of networks for such movements lies in the fact that terrorists may be eliminated in large numbers but the movement must be sustained through infusion of more in the form of a pipeline. Plenty of safe houses ensures that extremists do not have to spend excessive time rooted to one or just a few locations and a degree of mobility exists at all times.
- Networks ensure that when a violent extremist movement suffers setbacks and a tactical pause may be necessary, they provide the continuity for resurgence. Many of these networks are run by OGWs. These could be common people who enjoy a degree of anonymity but work for the extremist cause from within.
- A very important part of the violent extremist movement in J&K

has been the extensive use of the media by the separatist elements. It needs to be understood that Indian democratic principles have hardly been compromised even while a 30 year long violent extremist movement which is really a proxy war, has raged. The media has been free to express its opinion without any restrictions. Much of the media is run by OGWs.

- A relevant element of any violent extremist movement such as that in J&K is the communication aspect or what may be called influence operations. As the sponsor state Pakistan has been adept at this, looking for and exploiting opportunities to turn the target population against the government and the SF. Human rights is one aspect which has been effectively employed as a manipulative tool to paint the SF red and promote the image of an occupation army. Pakistan has its Inter Services Public Relations (ISPR) which has mastered the technique of manipulation and perception management. ISPR has created an impression as if *Kashmiri Awam* and religion in Kashmir is in danger; as a result Pakistan has pursued a policy of continuous flow of terrorists into the Kashmir Valley. There are reports pointing out that Pakistan has sent about 150 to 200 locals of Pakistan Occupied Kashmir (PoK) to terrorist facilities for training in the last two months. These individuals are likely to be infiltrated into India to carry out attacks in Jammu and Kashmir, beef up the terrorist ranks and build up the local support base.[2]

The Indian Experience of Counter Violent Extremism

The United Nations has flagged the issue that, "In recent years, terrorist groups such as ISIL, Al-Qaeda and Boko Haram have shaped our image of violent extremism and the concern should be about how to address this threat."[3] In fact the message of intolerance—religious, cultural, social—has had drastic consequences for many regions of the world. Holding territory and using social media for real-time communication of their atrocious crimes, they seek to challenge our shared values of peace, justice and human dignity.[4] The broad description of the nature of extremist violence in India and in the region will be used as the model on which the narrative for counter violent extremism is built and exercised in India. The lessons learnt from on-going experience will be included as much as exposing some of the mistakes made by us.

The common belief among most ill-informed public is that the only and best form of counter violent extremism is to go after those who pick up arms against the state, eliminate or neutralize them, line up the bodies for a head count and the problem will disappear. It has never been that way in the past and nor will it ever be so in the future. Yet many governments the world over believe in the same when hit by the problem. The concept of counter violent extremism has to be based upon a set of principles extracted from the experience of many forces worldwide that have fought these movements and the experience of your own forces against movements in some parts of the country. They have then to be analysed and synthesized with the political, social, economic and geographical ground realities before a strategy can be drawn up. Professor Luttwak a famous defence policy expert said, "Insurgents do not always win, actually they usually lose. But their defeats can rarely be attributed to counterinsurgency warfare".[5] India has been practicing what Prof Lutwik advocated, as a result (Winning Hearts and Minds) WHAM and political initiatives are given prominence over military operations.

In most cases violent extremist movements commence with a big trigger event and exploit the effect of that unless state intelligence has been very effective. In the case of the Indian experience with J&K I would count the forced expulsion of the Kashmiri Pundit community (minority of four lakhs in a population of 70 lakhs) on 19 Jan 1990; an event often described as virtual ethnic cleansing, as a major trigger event which signalled the full weighted violent extremist movement. The majority population stood by even as their neighbours and friends from years were targeted. The initial state strategy is based upon immediate reaction which is usually an urge to employ counter violence to neutralize the extremists, arrest the rabble rousers and prevent mobs ruling the streets. However, in a sponsored proxy movement such as J&K the extremists and the sponsors can absorb the initial setbacks. Though counter-terrorism is seen by separatists and terrorist's sympathisers with negative perception, however, SF has little option than to employ controlled counter violence measures. Care should be taken at this juncture to prevent use of disproportionate force, as this becomes a millstone and a grey spot for the Government to defend later. Memories of out terrorising terrorists and their sympathisers are deeply etched and almost indelible.

It is important for the state to develop its aim or intent at an early stage and maintain it with some tweaking from time to time. A sample aim at the strategic level and applicable to a great extent at the operational level could be as follows:

> *'To mainstream the state/region of ..., or the people of ..., to the rest of the nation in the political, social, economic and psychological domains'.*

A catchy slogan should follow the strategic aim, example:

> *'Let national unity be the mantra of the new narrative'.*

The interpretation of the strategic aim at the operational level may be differently perceived and needs to be discussed by the highest commander, his operational staff and the operational level commanders and their staff. From this emerges the operational art that senior commanders will employ to draw up the tactical ends, ways and means in the employment of counter violence and other approaches towards achieving the strategic aim.

It is important for practitioners to appreciate the application of operational art to such an employment. It is vital to identify Centre of Gravity (CoG); sometimes there may be couple of CoGs or sub CoGs. Exemplifying this, the earliest identified CoG in J&K and in the North East was the population or the people of the region asking for secession from the country. If the people would be with India the extremists would all simply be renegades. However, if the SF lost the support of the people the very same renegades would be 'freedom fighters'; the tone and content of the separatist movement could be contingent upon how the population was treated by the SF and the state. Remember the age old adage—the extremist must be like a fish out of water, without any support from the public. As the counter violent extremist campaign progressed we strongly advocated the identification and inclusion of the 'Idea of Freedom' among the people as a sub CoG which needed to be addressed. 30 years after the campaign began one can now identify a third CoG which can be described as perception/narrative. Both the CoGs identified thus far were people centric which meant that even as intense operations were being conducted to neutralise the extremists, care was taken to ensure that the operations did not alienate the people. This cannot be taken to ridiculous extremes and as long as there is a balance in the employment of counter violence and the outreach to the people the purpose is met. Operational freedom should be curbed only to the level that operations should not be coercive towards the people, avoid atrocities at all costs, minimise collateral damage and create least amount of inconvenience to them.

It is important to train SF for the operations and give force protection through any legal measures that can be adopted. In India we cannot employ the Army for policing duties without special requisition by the civil administration and then too it has to be under magisterial control. To overcome this problem, both in the North East and in the J&K, India enacted the Armed Forces Special Powers Act (AFSPA). This empowered the Army sufficiently for a sustained campaign. Any force operating in an environment involving violent extremism requires two things to be clear. First is empowerment; this essentially means the power to conduct operations without reference to a civilian authority. Second is protection; in this case no soldier can be prosecuted for an act performed in the line of duty without specific sanction of the Central Government. No State Government can prosecute him; thus meaning limited immunity. AFSPA is valid in a district of the affected state if the district is declared 'disturbed' by an order of the Central Government. This legal empowerment has been considered an essential aspect of the campaign in both regions. However, such legal instruments must be drafted with great care lest they become the targets of international vilification by Human Rights organisations. The Indian AFSPA (1990) for example, was drafted in a hurry at a time when human rights were not such a sensitive issue. Today it is under severe criticism and may have to undergo revision without really changing the empowerment and legal protection to the soldiers performing mandated duties in Counter Insurgency/Counter Terrorism (CI/CT).

India has been flexible with its approach to violent extremism and always open to engagement and talks within the Indian Constitution. Ceasefire with one extremist group in Nagaland has helped negotiate a framework agreement. However, the Naga movement was initially supported by China as a proxy movement. Today the situation is different and tenuous but reasonable. In J&K the situation is different because proxy war conditions with the support from Pakistan have persisted. Through the mid Nineties (5-6 years after the outbreak of violent extremism) the Central Government followed certain principles which worked in favour of stabilisation. First was the effort towards political consensus. If a nation can achieve that a very major part of the battle is considered won. The government of Prime Minister Narasimha Rao (1991-1996) persuaded the political opposition to join hands to pass the 22 Feb 1994 Joint Resolution in Parliament declaring the entire territory of J&K as Indian and urging every Indian to aspire and work towards regaining illegally occupied by Pakistan and China. It was political diplomacy at its best displaying the unity of the people of India against the proxy efforts of Pakistan. Such gestures are essential whenever opportunities arise. Second, the Rao government also worked towards the early return of democracy to J&K irrespective of the initial turnout of the electorate. It proved to be an excellent decision, giving political power back to the people.

Third was the adoption of a mission called Operation Sadbhavna (Operation Goodwill) by the Indian Army with specific government funding for Military Civic Action (MCA) and the campaign towards WHAM. Sadbhavna was a runaway success providing succour to the people where government writ was under challenge or where the civil administration could not be as effective. The Army selected some key domains to focus on in its MCA. Among them were education, medical facilities, women empowerment, small scale infrastructure, national integration and later sports. The Army sponsored and funded 43 Army Goodwill Schools which are model educational institutions in the region. Units of the Army Medical Corps conduct special medical camps for the civil population free of cost to supplement the efforts of the civil medical authorities. Special 'medical bricks' with adequate medicines are released by the government for this purpose. Troops and officers should be sensitised and educated about the long term benefits of MCA. The primary focus of a counter-insurgency operation should be disengagement with the separatist movements and WHAM and not liquidation or elimination.[6]

To follow up on the idea of educating younger officers and troops, these operations if conducted without specific and focused training will become a recipe for disaster. The Indian Army opened specific battle schools for its troops likely to be deployed in J&K where special orientation packages were drawn up for training. Counter measures against IEDs were taught. Updated specific case studies of some operations with Do's and Don'ts are discussed to inculcate people friendly operations. Human rights were introduced as a subject very early. In the North East the Counter Insurgency and Jungle Warfare School was opened and is today an institution of international repute. As a rule all units under induction into operations have to undergo pre-induction training at these institutions, as full units. Individuals under separate induction undergo specially designed courses too.

The fourth measure towards humanisation of the operations was the Indian Supreme Court's set of Do's and Don't's to the Army in the conduct of operations under AFSPA. No operation is to be conducted without presence of reps of the civil police. Directions were passed to ensure that search operations in houses having women inmates were conducted only in the presence of women police officials or a member of the local clergy.

Essential Experience Based Advice on Conduct of Operations

Earlier in this essay it was emphasized that four domains make up the essentials of proxy war related violent extremism. These are human resources, war fighting material, finances and ideology. Most campaigns by SF around the world focus on the human resources to limit the number of extremists they have to encounter. This does not provide the means for lasting stabilization. In the Indian context a prime example of operational art in dealing with human resource was the construction of the continuous wire fence along the Line of Control (LoC) to aid in the counter infiltration efforts. It is a revolutionary idea implemented with zeal and pushed by the higher leadership which helped in achieving the objectives to prevent infiltration. It helped alter the mathematics of terror in J&K and reduced the residual strength of terrorists well below one thousand. Later it was further reduced to approximately 350 from a very high numbers over 5000. However, the elimination of this last 350 may prove more difficult unless a holistic approach is adopted to isolate the extremists. The stabilisation of violence has been achieved by the Indian Army many times only to see a surge revival prompted by triggers calibrated from Pakistan, induction of fresh leadership, funding and infusion of greater ideological content. All these need to be neutralised if a final success has to be gained. That can only be achieved by targeting the networks of the OGWs and what is called the eco-system which drives such violence. It is this eco-system which must become another sub or adjunct CoG and targeted with a focus. In J&K it is happening rather late but it is happening at last.

The media need not remain completely free to inspire separatism and must be harnessed towards the promotion of integration and mainstreaming. The media many times becomes a part of this eco-system. It is this field that our efforts have been found wanting primarily due to the lack of understanding of use of media for war of perception. The Army and other SF can target the terror groups and neutralize them but not the networks and other domains which are prevalent. For the latter it needs a 'whole of government' approach to achieve holistic stabilisation which can then lead to eventual peace. The quality of governance can play a major role in this in which government departments must be seen to be corruption free. The best and most experienced administrators need to be inducted into the government, deputed from other parts of the country if required.

The most challenging aspect of counter-terrorism is to fight ideological domains that give impetus to the violent extremism. First the SF themselves must be trained to be culturally sensitive and fully aware of local sensitivities. Rudimentary cultural education for troops and deeper research based knowledge for officers is essential. The essentials of Islam were never studied by the US troops in Iraq and Afghanistan until as late as 2010 when General Petraeus commenced the implementation of his Counter-

Insurgency (COIN) doctrine and introduced the concept of culture cards. The SF need to be comfortable and not remain alienated from the environment they serve in. At the second level the government has to adopt measures against the spread of radical ideology. Removing radical clergy and inducting moderate clergy over a period of time is one way. Adopting a professionally run social media campaign with information warriors backed by research teams is another. However, experiments with direct outreach through a campaign termed 'conversations without outcomes' may be adopted to directly interact with the population, especially the youth. The Army's everyday contacts can then be exploited by the political players through meetings under security provided by the Army. Officials of the district administration may similarly exploit the Army's outreach capability to interact with the public at the villages and small townships to satisfy the administrative needs which have suffered due to the endemic and long standing violence in some areas.

Conclusion

In conclusion one can summarize this essay with a few essentials which must become the mantra of any counter violent extremism campaign. The catch phrases are—articulation of the strategic and operational aims, balance between hard and soft power, identification of Centres of Gravity (CoG), targeting the eco-system, whole of government approach, use of operational art to draw up the tactical measures and identification of the right domains, targeting of extremist leadership and OGWs, training and orientation of the SF personnel to execute people friendly operations. There is also a need to make effective use of MCA (WHAM), employment of influence operations, David Galula had said, "The population represents this new ground. If the insurgent manages to dissociate the population from the counterinsurgent, he will win the war. Thus the battle for the population is a major characteristic of the revolutionary wars."[7]

NOTES

1. Anthony H. Cordesman, After the Caliphate: Factors Shaping Continuing Violent Extremism and Conflicts in the MENA Region, *Center for Strategic and International Studies*, May 6, 2019
2. Shaurya Karanbir Gurung, Pakistan sends 200 PoK locals to terrorist camps for training and infiltration into India, *The Economic Times*, August 09, 2019.
3. Plan of Action to Prevent Violent Extremism, A Report Published by United Nations office of Counter terrorism, Accessed from https://www.un.org/counterterrorism/ctitf/en/plan-action-prevent-violent-extremism on August 20, 2019.
4. Ibid.
5. Dr. David Kilcullen, Edward Luttwak's "Counterinsurgency Malpractice," Small Wars Journal.
6. Subir Bhaumik, Counter to the spirit of counter-insurgency, *The Hindu*, June 14, 2014.
7. Farnam Street, Counterinsurgency: Fighting Back, Accessed from https://fs.blog/2017/06/counterinsurgency/ on November 26, 2018.

2

Ideological and Conceptual Construct of Combating Violent Extremism and Terrorism in Nigeria

Prof. Usman A Tar and Adejoh Sunday

ABSTRACT

Violent extremism and terrorism are major national security threats that Nigeria is grappling with. The activities of Boko Haram terrorists have affected the security architecture of the country, threatened the sovereignty/territorial integrity of Nigeria and accounted for wanton loss of lives and properties which has eventually brought about Internally Displayed Persons (IDPs), refugee crisis and other forms of humanitarian crisis. It is the position of this paper that counter terrorism strategies in Nigeria has been militaristic and Military strategies are utterly insufficient instruments for combating violent extremism and terrorism. It further opined that Boko Haram is a jihadist group driven by ideological underpinnings, hence, the need to reconceptualise the ideological drivers of violent extremism and terrorism as strategies for combating them. It is a secondary research with the use of Ivan Pavlov theory of classical conditioning. In the final analysis it suggests among other things that ideological and conceptual constructs are potent strategies for combating violent extremism and terrorism in Nigeria.

Introduction

The phenomenon of terrorism and its impact on international security has been the focus of several works in social sciences and other related fields endeavour in recent times. Attempts have been made to examine the concept of, nature, impact and implication of terrorism as seen for instance in Lambert (1990), Schmid (1983), Williamson (2009), Wardlaw (1982), Kydd and Walter (2006), Steven (2002), Hoffman (1993).

The emergent threat of violent extremism, and in particular the global reach of terrorist recruiters, has impelled comprehensive changes in security arrangements both within and between states. This trend has strongly favoured governments expanding the powers and reach of the security sector with a view to enhanced intelligence gathering, disrupting networks and thwarting acts of extremist violence (Rosand, 2016).

Radicalism, violent extremism and terrorism, sit at the forefront of today's policy discussions, in both Arab and non-Arab states. The fear of these phenomena have instilled, their connection to wider tensions between and within religions, and how they have exposed a lack of social cohesion in seemingly resilient societies, have impacted communities in fundamental ways (Harper, 2018).

The degree of ideological commitment and indoctrination needed to 'justify' the use or threat of violence against civilians in a confrontation with a more powerful protagonist is significantly higher than for most other forms of violence widely practised by non-state actors. This high degree of indoctrination and the necessary 'justification' can only be provided by an extremist ideology. However, the fact that the ideological basis for terrorism may be provided by extremist ideologies of all types and origins—be it Maoism, anarchism, radical nationalism or Islamism does not mean that any such ideology is inherently linked to terrorism or automatically produces it (Stepanova, 2008).

In the mid-2010 yet another way of thinking about the relationship between radicalization and extremist behaviour surfaced. Radicalization was still understood as a process that culminated in the decision to join a violent extremist group, but one that was driven by certain 'push' and 'pull' factors. Push factors were largely understood as the negative social, political, economic and cultural drivers of individual decision-making, while pull factors were the positive characteristics or benefits offered by a group in exchange for participation (Bondokji Agrabi and Wilkinson, 2016). Violent extremism and terrorism have evolved and manifested in different forms in Nigeria. Though Boko Haram started as a non-violent group its ideology was extremist in nature. The state's initial high-handed, the extra-judicial approach and the increasing misery of the populace in the Northeast that called forth the need for a counter-narrative and imagery of the state in Nigeria. The approach of the government and its agencies in dealing with the perceived threat of Boko Haram in 2009 laid the groundwork for the emergence of the sect from the rubrics as a terrorist group. In addition, while socio-economic deprivation may not sufficiently explain the emergence and growth of Boko Haram, there is no gainsaying the fact that the increasing misery among the populace especially young people created the objective condition for the popularity of Boko Haram in the Northeast.

It is based on the above that this research attempts to investigate the ideology of Boko Haram with a view to developing conceptual and ideological constructs for combating violent extremism and terrorism in Nigeria.

Ideological and Conceptual Construct for Combating Violent Extremism and Terrorism in Nigeria

Combating violent extremism and terrorism in Nigeria requires an in-depth understanding of the ideological drivers of Boko Haram and an understanding of the concepts and context within which some Qur'anic verses manipulated by Boko Haram are used. Since ideology and conceptual construct are precipitators of violent extremism and terrorism, these variables can also serve as veritable strategy for combating violent extremism and terrorism in Nigeria. Violent extremism and terrorism situated within the context of Ivan Pavlov theory of classical conditioning clearly shows that extremism and Islamist terrorist activities are products of conditioning. Perpetuators of violence, extremist and terrorist, are people who have been mentally and psychologically conditioned to reason in certain manner. Indoctrination and radicalization are all products of conditioning. Terrorists and extremists have used and misused some verses of the Qur'an to reconfigure the thought patterns of people. Boko Haram is an Islamist terrorist organization with a claim to establish an Islamic caliphate and promote the teachings of Prophet Mohammed. Therefore, the ideological persuasion of Boko Haram is derived from their understanding and manipulation of Qur'anic verses to justify their actions and activities. Hence the need for an ideological and conceptual construct for combating Boko Haram in Nigeria.

Jihadi ideologues and group leaders craft their ideology by interpreting, reinterpreting or misinterpreting religion and politics. Ideology is used to attract and retain recruits as members, supporters and sympathizers. The personal history and worldview of an individual may make him or her more or less susceptible to a particular terrorist or extremist ideology (Gunaratna, 2007:21). Gunaratna further claimed that:

> *Ideology is a powerful message that motivates and propels ordinary human beings into action. Ideology, a dynamic and an evolving brief system, is created by the interpretation of events by ideologues. Ideology, not poverty*

> *or illiteracy, is the key driver of politically motivated violence. Ideology frames organizational structure, leadership and membership motivation, recruitment and support, and shapes the strategies and tactics adopted by the group (Gunaratna, 2007:21).*

Evidence suggests that Boko Haram has been very effective in using Islamic ideology to recruit, organize and sustain its battle against the Nigerian state. Boko Haram ideology is a spill over from the Sunni-Salafi doctrine that the "temporal proximity to Prophet Mohammad is associated with the truest form of Islam". On the other hand, contrasting approaches to returning to this original way of practicing Islam has given rise to Salafi jihadis that believe in the use of violence, even against other Muslims (Barkondo, 2014).

The Qur'an today is widely misused and misunderstood in respect of terrorism. For some extremist Muslims, it is misused to justify terrorism; its verses are quoted out of context to justify conflict as the permanent norm between Muslim and non-Muslims. And for some non-Muslims it is misunderstood as a book that preaches hate and calls for the killing of innocent people. Many Qur'anic verses are intentionally quoted out of their original meanings to suit the political and ideological agendas of individuals or groups whose objective is to disseminate fear and terror in the world (Schwartz-Barcott, 2004). As a result, "Qur'anic exegesis has become an ideological weapon employed by various socio-political powers to maintain or to change the status quo, a conservative weapon to maintain and a revolutionary weapon to change" (Abdul-Raof, 2010).

The concept of jihad is one that has been used and misused by most terrorist organizations including Boko Haram. The name Jama'atu Ahlis Sunna Lidda'awati Wal-Jihad which in English means "People Committed to the Propagation of the Prophet's Teachings and Jihad" clearly shows that its missions and activities are justified within the framework of jihad.

It is important to state at this juncture that, jihad is one most contested and most abused concept in Islam that has promoted the Islamophobic narrative that the religion is synonymous with terror. Some scholars have however attempted to conceptualize jihad within the context of the Qur'an and the Hadith of the prophet so as to debunk the argument that Islam is a religion of terror and to further claim that terrorism is anti-Islamic.

Islam is a faith and it by no means supports any kind of action that can be identified as terrorism, it rather prohibits it. To be sure, at issue is not a proper or an ill understanding of religion, but rather the on-going process of a religionization of politics and a politicization of religion leading to a jihadization of Islam in an invention of tradition (Helmut Anheier and Y. Raj Isar, 2007). The outcome is the ideology of Jihadism which is something else than the classical Islamic jihad. This is the basis of the ideological foundation of terrorism. Jihadists are people who perceived themselves as "True Believers" (Hoffer, 2002).

There were several Islamic clerics who attempted to disassociate Islam from Boko Haram by condemning their activities as un-Islamic. These set of preachers are also seen by Boko Haram as unbelievers and were killed. So many mosques have been attacked by Boko Haram on regular basis. One tends to wonder why Boko Haram is attacking Mosques when the worshippers are Muslims. The reason is simply that as far as Boko Haram is concerned any Mosques that preach against it are not preaching the true teachings of Islam and the prophet.

The above view is corroborated by Tibi (2008.110) when he says "Islamist terrorists do not perceive their actions to be irhab/terrorism, but rather jihadiyya/jihadism, i.e. a new interpretation of religious jihad being a duty/farida." To reiterate: In their self-proclaimed capacity as jihadists these Islamists believe that they act as the "true believers".

The Table 1 shows list of Islamic clerics killed by Boko Haram for not supporting their activities.

In view of the above Imam Kabir (in Adejoh, 2019) maintained that though many terrorist groups are described as 'Islamist' but they are not truly Muslims in the real sense of Islam. It is unfortunate that Muslims have become victims of Islamophobia because of the activities of some elements and the wrong notion of Islam portrayed by western media. He was of the opinion that true Muslims would not attack and kill human beings whether Muslims or non-Muslims. He further quoted (Qur'an, 5:32) which says that:

> *If someone kills another person—unless it is in retaliation for someone else or for causing corruption in the earth—it is as if he had murdered all mankind. And if anyone gives life to another person, it is as if he had given life to all mankind... Qur'an 17: 33 Also says: Do not take life, which God has made sacred, except by right...*

The Qur'an and the Sunnah of the Prophet also have elaborate rules prohibiting genocide or crimes against humanity, war crimes, the maltreatment and killing of war captives, the destruction of the environment, the killing of hostages, obeying unlawful commands and

Table 1: List of Islamic Scholars/Preachers Killed by Boko Haram

Sl. No.	*Name of Islamic Cleric*	*Islamic Affiliations*	*Location of Death/State*	*Period of Death/Year*
1.	Sheikh Ja'afar Mahmud Adam	Jama't Izalat al Bid'a WaIqamat as Sunna or 'Yan Izala	Kano State	April 2007
2.	Sheikh Bashir Mustafa	Not indicated	Maiduguri, Borno State	0ctober, 2010
3.	Ustaz IbrahiAhmed Abdullah Gomar	Not indicated	Maiduguri, Borno State	March, 2011
4.	Sheikh Goni Tijjani	Not indicated	Maiduguri, Borno State	May,2011
5.	Mallam Alhaji Abur	Not indicated	Maiduguri, Borno State	May,2011
6.	Sheikh Ibrahim Birkuti	Wahabbi	Biu, Borno State	June, 2011
7.	Liman Bana	Not indicated	Maiduguri, Borno State	August, 2011
8.	Mallam Dala	Not indicated	Maiduguri, Borno State	September, 2011
9.	Sheikh Ali Jana'a	Not indicated	Maiduguri, Borno State	October, 2011
10.	Mallam Mai Tatabara	Not indicated	Damaturu, Yobe state	February, 2012
11.	Modu Goroma (Arabic teacher)	Not indicated	Damaturu, Yobe state	February, 2012
12.	Sheikh Saina Alhaji Ajiya	Not indicated	Konduga Borno State	February, 2012
13.	Mohammed Alhaji Bukar	Not indicated	Maiduguri, Borno State	March, 2012
14.	Goni Mustapha	Not indicated	Maiduguri, Borno State	April,2012
15.	Usman Muhamme	Not indicated	Potiskun, Yobe State	May, 2012
16.	Sheikh Ibrahim Majim	Not indicated	Maiduguri, Borno State	July,2012
17.	Mohammed Alli	Shiite	Kano state	May, 2012
18.	Alarama Dan Gobobirawa	Not indicated	Potiskun, Yobe State	December,2012
19.	Mallam Sheriff	Not indicated	Ngamdu, Yobe State	May, 2013
20.	Alhaji Liman Bukar (Chief Imam)	Not indicated	Fune, Yobe State	August, 2013
21.	Sheikh Muhammad Auwal Adam Albani	Salafiyyah	Zaria, Kaduna State	February, 2014

Source: Akinola (2014.25 cited in Adejoh, 2019) in IFRA-Nigeria e-papers series, 2014, n°32

the use of child soldiers. Qur'an prohibits genocide or crimes against humanity by stipulating that 'if any one slew a person—unless it be for murder or for spreading mischief in the land—it would be as if he slew the whole people: and if any one saved a life, it would be as if he saved the life of the whole people' (Q 5 v 32.).

Drawing from the above, it is pertinent to note that one step towards combating violent extremism and terrorism in Nigeria is by combating the ideologies and reconceptualising the concepts upon which terrorism is propagated. This onus lies with the religious teachers, the Supreme Council of Islamic Affairs in partnership with the state. This will help to drastically reduce the level of recruitment of vulnerable minds. As part of this campaign some scholars and Islamic organizations have made efforts to combat Islamist terrorist by arguing and claiming that terrorist interpret the Qur'an out of context for their selfish ambitions.

The use of force in Islam is essentially defensive. In Q 22 v 39, it is stated that 'to those against whom war is made, permission is given (to fight), because they are wronged'. This was the first time that the Muslims were permitted to use force in the Qur'an. It was after the Prophet migrated to Madina. At that time, Muslims had been persecuted for 13 years (Shah, 2008:35). The above verse indicates that Muslims are only permitted to fight when they are wronged. Since it is in the passive, attacks must not be from Muslims as they can only respond to attacks. In Q 42 v 41, it is stated that 'But, indeed, if any do help and defend himself after a wrong (done) to him, against such there is no cause of blame'. Similarly, in Q 2 v 190, it is stated that 'fight in the cause of Allah those who fight you, but do not transgress limits; for Allah loveth not transgressors'. This verse reinforces the earlier verse. It was revealed a year after Prophet Muhammad migrated from Mecca to Madina (Shah, 2008.35).

As part of his contribution towards combating extremist and terrorist ideologies Adigun (2018) undertook an in-depth analysis of the ideology of Boko Haram both at doctrinal and practical levels. He then tests Boko Haram's radical ideology and practices against Islamic jurisprudence and international law and concludes that Boko Haram's ideology is inconsistent with the Qur'an and, more so, the interpretations of the Qur'an according to the Sunni Muslims, which Boko Haram claims to belong.

The above view as captured by Shah further gives credence to the argument that the ideology of Boko Haram is based on the falsification of Islamic principles thereby shading more light on the need to combat the ideology of Boko Haram. Since the Qur'an says children, women, the aged and the civilian community who are not engaged in war cannot be fought against why are all these categories of people victims of Boko Haram? All categories of people have been victims of Boko Haram regardless of age, faith, creed, sex etc. a lot of young girls have been kidnapped and either sexually violated or forced into marriage. Where is it in the Qur'an that permits sexual exploitation or forced marriage?

Killing Christians for their faith is un-Islamic. The use of child bombers is also un-Islamic. Taking women and girls (like the Chibok girls) as hostages by the group violates Islamic jus in bello. The marriage of Boko Haram captives to their tormentor is just to justify having sexual intercourse with them, and it is un-Islamic (Adigun, 2018.232).

Recognizing the extent of extremist ideologies tied to Islam and the degree of violence carried out in the name of Islam and for Islam vis a vis her campaign to combat extremist and terrorist ideologies, the Islamic Society of North America (2005.1) stated that:

> *As Muslims, we must face up to our responsibility to clarify and advocate a faith-based, righteous and moral position with regard to this problem, especially when terrorist acts are perpetrated in the name of Islam. Not because of external pressures or for the sake of "political correctness", but out of our sincere conviction of what Islam stands for... we must unequivocally condemn terrorism by stating: "Islam strictly condemns religious extremism and the use of violence against innocent lives. There is no justification in Islam for extremism or terrorism.*

Situating the activities of Boko Haram within the context of Islamic jurisprudence to combat its ideology (Adigun, 2018.230) says, the incompatibility of the Insurgent Activities of Boko Haram in the Light of Islamic Jus ad Bellum and Islamic Jus in Bello is obvious. He further summarised Islamic jus ad bellum as follows:

> *'The use of force in Islam is solely for defence. Even when it is to be used in defence, it must have been dictated by a situation of extreme urgency. This can be gleaned from the fact that the Prophet did not have recourse to the use of force until after 13 years of persecution. In fact, the Prophet had to leave Mecca and migrated to Medina so as to avoid persecution, which suggests that retreat may be the first rule before resisting attack. While acting in self-defence, Muslims must observe the principle of proportionality. Fighting in self-defence comes to an end whenever there is peace or when there is no more persecution. Where the other party shows the tendency of negotiating peace, then Muslims too should be willing to negotiate...Non-state actors cannot declare war in Islam. Boko Haram is a*

> *non-state actor and thus cannot declare war. This renders all their actions un-Islamic (Adigun, 2018.230)*

The proliferation of Islamic preachers, Islamic sects and schools vis-a-vis the content of their preaching play a major role in violent extremism and terrorism in North-eastern Nigeria for obvious reasons. Hence, regulating, preaching and establishment of Islamic school is pivotal to combating the ideological construct for terrorism and violent extremism as these constitute the platforms upon which vulnerable minds are radicalized or indoctrinated.

Islamic religious preaching is called Da'wah in Arabic, which means inviting both Muslims and non-Muslims to accept Islam. Scholars have defined it in different ways. It is 'an act of inviting people to accept Islam or to observe their religious obligations correctly'. The term 'comprises all acts of disseminating the knowledge of Islam through preaching, sermon and charity with a view of extending the idea of Islam on the one hand and to maintaining the true doctrine of the Oneness of Allah (Tauhid) on the other' (Modibbo, 2014:2-5).

Boko Haram has been able to recruit and radicalize as many followers as possible through preaching. This view was succinctly captured by Gunaratna (2007.22) when he pontificated thus:

> *"Using ideology, contemporary jihad groups recruit followers from a cross section of society- the rich, the poor, the educated and the less educated. To generate both recruits and support, they indoctrinate their potential and existing support base. Ideology is inculcated by disseminating it in the form of information or propaganda using lectures, speeches, pronouncements, writings, etc.... To counter terrorist ideology and to provide an alternative ideology, it is necessary to know its key ideologues, organizational structures, the evolving ideology, and the target audience—the community."*

In a similar vein, Walker (2012), also corroborated the argument by examining the role of teaching and preaching as conduit pipe for promoting violent extremism and the ideology of Boko Haram when he claimed that:

> *Boko Haram's religiously justified violent actions involving suicide bombings and mass murders. The promotion of suicide bombings can be found in the Salafi-jihadist beliefs, that death or martyrdom will be rewarded by Allah with a life after death filled with riches, glory, and many virgins. These suicide bombers are considered martyrs because they are dying for what they believe is the right cause in following the teachings of the Prophet. Even though many current Islamic scholars have detested this proclamation*

of suicide bombers as martyrs, Boko Haram indoctrinates its followers with such teachings and proclaims any other teachings that contradict as sinful and un-Islamic... (Walker, 2012.21).

Boko Haram began its campaigns with many locals, preachers and footmen who walk from village to village proclaiming the truth that Yusuf and Boko Haram stood for. It also uses trucks with speakers on the top that play the teaching and preaching's of Yusuf all throughout the streets of North-eastern Nigeria. Its evangelical approaches were non-violent and effective due to the lack of education in the area, it was easier to indoctrinate and persuade young followers (Barkindo, 2017). Of critical importance to the above subject is the increasing rate of Almajarai, a system of Islam tutelage, in northern Nigeria. A prominent thread in the explanation of the growth of Boko Haram and similar groups before it in the North is the massive number of young people under Islamic tutelage or the Almajarai system outside their homes.

Recognising the role of preaching in violent extremism and political instability, different states in northern Nigeria including Borno established religious preaching regulatory boards to design, draft and state the conditions upon which an individual or a religious sect can be allowed to preach publicly. On a general note, however, the functions of the religious preaching boards are to examine intending Islamic religious preachers and to issue preaching licence to those qualified. The laws of religious preaching boards criminalise preaching without a licence or violating the conditions of a preaching licence. In terms of spread, religious preaching boards are found in thirteen (13) states in northern Nigeria. Eleven (11) of these states have reintroduced the application of some aspects of Islamic laws in their domains. The religious preaching laws are designed to regulate Islamic religious preaching, but in some states like Bauchi, Plateau and Nasarawa, they have elements of general application. The composition of religious preaching boards is determined by the government, and in practice such compositions have mainly favoured dominant religious groups against minority religious groups (Garba, 2008.246)

It should be noted that Borno State had an Islamic religious preaching board law in place when the Boko Haram conflict started in the state. Borno State was the second state to enact a religious preaching board in northern Nigeria in 1977. The law was amended and replaced by the Islamic Religious Preaching Board Law of 1981. This was also amended and replaced by the Borno State Islamic Religious Preaching Board Law 2010 (as amended) in response to the Boko Haram conflict.

However, it is important to note that the regulation of religious preaching in some northern the northern states has been characterised by violence and state repression of minority religious sect in favour of dominant religious sects, and this has produced and continues to reproduce conflict. With the numbers of Islamic sects that exist in Nigeria such problem is bound to arise.

Conclusion and Way Forward

Nigeria has been grappling with series of security challenges ranging from armed robbery, kidnapping, ethno-religious conflicts, farmers-herders crisis, trans-border crimes just to mention but a few. However, in the fourth republic violent extremism and terrorism constituted the major security challenge facing nation. The emergence of Boko Haram has brought serious catastrophe to the state; loss of lives and properties, Internally Displays Persons (IDPs) and other humanitarian crisis. Terrorism in Nigeria cannot be attributed to a single factor as there are several variables responsible for its emergence ranging from economic, political, social and ideological reasons. Central to the argument of this chapter is the fact that ideological and conceptual construct plays a dualistic role as far as terrorism and violent extremism is concerned. As much as its serves as a springboard and driver for violent extremism and terrorism it is also a potent and viable strategy for combating violent extremism and terrorism.

Drawing from the foregoing conclusion, this chapter puts forward the following suggestions:

(i) To effectively combat violent extremism and terrorism in Nigeria the root causes of these phenomena should be identified and addressed promptly.

(ii) Ideological and conceptual construct are germane to counter-extremism and counter-terrorism. Hence, the Nigeria government should collaborate with scholars to identify and examine the ideological orientation of Boko Haram with a view to adopting an ideological approach in combating violent extremism and terrorism.

(iii) Violent extremism and terrorism are products of ideological radicalization and indoctrination majorly done using preaching and sermons. The Nigerian state and states with similar threat tendencies should establish functional Islamic regulatory boards to serve as watch dogs on the activities and contents of religious preaching and sermons.

(iv) The Supreme Council of Islamic Affairs has a major role to play as far as combating violent extremism and terrorism is concerned. Since Boko Haram claims to be anchored on Islamic ideologies, there is need for the council to regularly condemn the activities of Boko Haram by educating and sensitizing people on the true teaching and position of Islam.

(v) The Islamic colouration of Boko Haram has brought about Islamophobia in Nigeria manifested in forms of hate, prejudices and stereotypes against Muslims and Islam which if not checked can also bring about a new form of violent extremism.

NOTES

1. Abdul-Raof, H. (2010), Schools of Qur'anic Exegesis: Genesis and Development. London: Routledge.
2. Adejoh, S. (2019), A Perception study of Terrorism and Islamophobia in Nigeria and the Implications for National Security. Bing an unpublished PhD thesis submitted to the Department of Political Science and Defence Studies, Nigerian Defence Academy, Kaduna
3. Adigun, M. (2018), Boko Haram's Radical Ideology and Islamic Jurisprudence in John-Mark and Strydom (eds) Boko Haram and International Law Springer International Publishing, pp. 205-236
4. Akintola, E.O. (2017), Imperatives of Media Ownership by Nigerian Muslims Retrieved from www.vanguardngr.com/2018/01/muslim-scholars-advocate-fair-representa tion-islam-nigerian-media/ on the 2nd of February, 2018
5. Barkindo, A. (2014), Boko Haram: Ideology, Ethnicity, and Identity. https://institute.global/insight/co-existence/boko-haram-ideology-ethnicity-and-identity. Assessed on the first of April, 2019.
6. Barkindo, A. (2017), An Introduction to Boko Haram's Ideologues: From Yusuf to Shekau," Africa Research Institute, February 2, 2017. https://www.africaresearchinstitute.org/newsite/blog/introduction-boko-harams-ideologues-yusuf-shekau. Assessed 29th March, 2019.
7. Bondokji, N, Agrabi, L and Wilkinson, K (2016), 'Trapped Between Destructive Choices: Radicalisation Drivers Affecting Youth in Jordan', WANA Institute 2016.
8. Bondokji, N, Agrabi, L and Wilkinson, K (2016), 'Trapped Between Destructive Choices: Radicalisation Drivers Affecting Youth in Jordan', WANA Institute 2016.
9. Garba, A.S. (2008) Government Regulation of Freedom of Religion in a Democratic Society: Islamic Preaching Board Laws and Boko Haram in Nigeria in John-Mark and Strydom (eds) Boko Haram and International Law. Springer International Publishing 237-255.
10. Gunaratna, R. (2007), Ideology In Terrorism And Counter Terrorism Lessons From Al Qaeda in Aldis and Herd (eds) (2007), The Ideological War On Terror Worldwide strategies for counter-terrorism. London: Routledge, pp. 21-34.
11. Harper, E. (2018), Reconceptualising the Drivers of Violent Extremism: An Agenda for Child and Youth Resilience. Helping Children Worldwide and WANA INSTITUTE.
12. Helmut, A. and Isar, Y.R. (2007), The Cultural Economy. London: SAGE Publications Ltd.
13. Hoffer, E (2002), The True Believer. Thoughts on the Nature of Mass Movements, New York: Perenial Library.
14. Hoffman, B. (1993) "Holy Terror": The Implications of Terrorism Motivated by a Religious Imperative. Santa Monica, Calif.: RAND Corporation.
15. Kydd, A.H. and Walter B.F. (2006), The Strategies of Terrorism. International Security, Vol. 31, No.1, pp. 49–70.
16. Lambert, J. (1990), Terrorism and Hostages in International Law. Cambridge: Grotius Publications.
17. Modibbo, MS (2014), Proliferation of Islamic Da'wa (propagation) organizations in Plateau State 1948–2008. Unpublished PhD Dissertation University of Jos.
18. Rosand, E. (2016), 'Communities First A Blueprint for Organizing and Sustaining a

Global Movement Against Violent Extremism' The Prevention Project: Organizing Against Violent Extremism (2016) 8, and detailed comprehensively in Annex 4. 'Children and Counter-Terrorism' UNICRI (2016) 51;

19. Rosand, E. (2003), 'Security Council Resolution 1373, the Counter-Terrorism Committee, and the Fight Against Terrorism'. *American Journal of International Law*. Vol. 79, pp. 333-381.
20. Schmid, A. (1983), Political terrorism: A research guide to the concepts, theories, databases and literature. New Brunswick: Transaction Books.
21. Schwartz-Barcott, T.P. (2004), War, Terror and Peace in the Qur'an and in Islam: Insights for Military and Government Leaders. Carlisle, PA: Army War College Foundation Press, pp. 2–4.
22. Shah, N.A. (2008), Self-Defence in Islamic and International Law: Assessing Al-Qaeda and the Invasion of Iraq. New York: Palgrave Macmillan.
23. Stepanova, E. (2008), Terrorism in Asymmetrical Conflict: Ideological and Structural Aspects, SIPRI Research Report No. 23. Oxford: Oxford University Press.
24. Stevens, M.J. (2002), The Unanticipated Consequences of Globalization: Contextualizing Terrorism, in Stout, C.E. (ed.). Psychology of Terrorism, Vol. 3: Theoretical Understandings and Perspectives. Westport, CT: Praeger. pp. 31–56.
25. Tibi, B. (2008) Countering Ideological Terrorism. Defence Against Terrorism Review Vol. 1, No. 1, Spring, 101-136.
26. Tibi, B. (2005), Countering Terrorism als Krieg der Weltanschauungen, in: van Creveld, M and von Knop, K (eds), Countering Modern Terrorism. History, Current Issues and Future Threats (Bielefeld: Bertelsmann, 2005), pp. 131-172.
27. Walker, A. (2012), What is Boko Haram?, Washington: UNO Publication.
28. Wardlaw, G. (1982) Political Terrorism: Theory, Tactics and Counter-Measures. Cambridge: Cambridge University Press.
29. Williamson, M. (2009), Terrorism, War and international law: The legality of the Use of Force against Afghanistan in 2001. Farnham: Ashgate Publishing limited.

PART II

INDIA'S EXPERIENCE IN DEALING WITH VIOLENT EXTREMISM

3

Cross Border Terrorism and Proxy War in Kashmir: Evolving Strategy

Lt Gen DS Hooda, PVSM, UYSM, AVSM, VSM & Bar (Retd)

ABSTRACT

Kashmir conflict has internal and external dynamics that needs to be addressed separately. Key to deal with the cross border terrorism in Kashmir is to deny space to Pak proxies to operate with impunity. India would require a robust military strategy to deter Pakistan from indulging in Kashmir conflict. India also needs to constantly improve border management and upgrade border fence to smart fence. Radicalisation and disaffection of youth from the state cannot be wished away and needs to be handled by adopting a more pragmatic and rationale approach. A strategy for conflict resolution in Jammu and Kashmir must be a combination of political, social, psychological, economic, and security elements.

Introduction

On 14 February 2019, Adil Ahmad Dar, a resident of Pulwama in Jammu and Kashmir (J&K), rammed his explosive-laden vehicle into a convoy carrying personnel of the Central Reserve Police Force (CRPF). The blast killed 40 CRPF men, and this was the deadliest terror attack in J&K. In a video message released soon after the attack, Pakistan-based terror group, Jaish-e-Mohammed (JeM), claimed responsibility for the attack. Twelve days later, Indian Air Force jets struck a JeM terror camp at Balakot, inside Pakistani territory. Pakistan Air Force responded the next day by attempting to bomb Indian military targets along the Line of Control (LoC). The aerial skirmish that followed saw the downing of a Pakistani F-16 and an Indian MiG-21 fighter. For a few days, it looked as if the fighting would escalate, but international mediation resulted in calming of the situation.

The well-recognized factor is that despite international pressure, Pakistan continues to provide support for internationally recognized terrorist organizations such as JeM, the perpetrators of the devastation in Pulwama[1]. This incident reflects the complexities and dangers of the current state of the India-Pakistan-J&K triangle. A terror incident in Kashmir, carried out by a local owing allegiance to a Pakistani terror group, could spark off a conventional conflict between India and Pakistan. The ongoing insurgency in J&K has both a transnational and internal dimension. While the internal dimension cannot be ignored, the longevity of the 30-year-old insurgency owes a lot to the support it has received from across the border. That is why the conflict in J&K is also termed as a 'Proxy War' by Pakistan against India. Terrorists who enjoy safe haven in Pakistan cross the border to conduct attacks in India while religious groups in Pakistan recruit young men to join the jihad[2]. The terror groups involved in the proxy war in Kashmir have hijacked airliners, attacked India's parliament, and kidnapped and killed American and European tourists in Kashmir valley. In short, Pakistan's hands are far from clean[3].

Proxies and the Pakistan Army

The use of proxies has been a consistent strategy of the Pakistan Army ever since it was created out of the division of the British Indian Army in 1947. Two months after independence, thousands of Pakistani tribals, armed with the help of elements in Pakistan Army, invaded the state of J&K. Although Pakistan failed in its attempts to take control over the Kashmir valley, the 1948 ceasefire left approximately 37% of J&K under Pakistani control. Employing militant proxies offers Pakistan bargaining leverage and a cost-effective asymmetric strategy to counter India[4].

The 1965 war, initiated by Pakistan to free Kashmir from Indian control, was also preceded by the employment of irregular forces, led by Pakistani army officers. This plan, codenamed Operation Gibraltar, called for infiltrating several thousand Mujahideen into Kashmir, carrying out sabotage activities and fomenting a rebellion among the local population. Operation Gibraltar was a complete failure and resulted in a full-scale war between India and Pakistan.

As the decade of the 1980s was drawing to a close, a series of political blunders by India led to a steady deterioration in the law and order situation in Kashmir. By 1990, there was a full-blown insurgency in Kashmir, and thousands of youth were crossing the LoC into Pakistan Occupied Kashmir (POK) for arms and training. From POK, foreign fighters, freshly released due to the end of the jihad against the Soviets in Afghanistan, were infiltrating into Kashmir. Although the Pakistani Army was initially surprised by the scale of the uprising in Kashmir, they moved quickly to take control over it. In 1994, the Inter-Service Intelligence (ISI) agency formed the United Jihad Council, an umbrella organization of all the terrorist groups fighting in J&K. With this, the control over all the terrorist activities passed firmly into the hands of the Pakistani Army.

The levers that control the quantum of violence in the Valley lie not in Srinagar but in Islamabad. The successful marginalisation of any militant group that attempted to exercise strategic autonomy allowed the ISI to retain overall command of the proxy war[5]. Failure to anticipate that Islamabad would undermine the pro-independence movement and assist only those militants who favoured accession to Pakistan was the JKLF's big mistake[6]. As a result, ISI of Pakistan systematically strangulated pro Azadi terror groups and strengthened all those groups that were for merger of Kashmir with Pakistan. Today, the three main terrorist groups operating in J&K are the Hizbul Mujahideen (HM), Lashkar-e-Taiba (LeT) and the JeM. The latter two primarily take their recruits from Pakistan's Punjab province, and after training, these terrorists are infiltrated into J&K. It is for this reason that the number of foreign terrorists killed in the state has almost always outnumbered local terrorists; although the recent spurt in local recruitment could see a change in this trend.

The Last Decade (2009-2019)

A study of the insurgency in J&K in the last decade throws up some useful lessons in the handling of cross-border terrorism from Pakistan. The first half of the decade showed a steady improvement in the security situation in J&K. In 2009, the total fatalities in terror-related incidents dropped to below 500 for the first time. The trend continued till 2012 that saw only 117 deaths (data from South Asian Terrorism Portal). It was only towards the end of 2013 that there was a sudden spurt in violent incidents and a massive increase in ceasefire violations along the LoC.

Although there has not been any detailed analysis linking the J&K insurgency and the events happening inside Pakistan, there are some definite connections. In 2009, Musharraf had exited, and the Pakistan Army was heavily engaged in a fight against terrorists in the tribal areas bordering Afghanistan. The next few years would see the Pakistan Army under pressure, both internally and externally.

Relations with the United States (U.S.) were deteriorating as the Obama administration announced a surge in Afghanistan and ratcheted up its drone strikes in Northwest Pakistan. In 2010, drone strikes more than doubled over the previous year, and these were heavily criticized in Pakistan due to allegations of civilian casualties. Two further incidents brought the U.S.—Pakistan relations to a new low. In January 2011, Raymond Davis, a contractor with the American Central Intelligence Agency, killed two reportedly armed men in Lahore. This incident led to a diplomatic furore and widespread protests in Pakistan.

A more significant crisis occurred later in the year when U.S. Navy SEALs stormed a compound in Abbottabad on 2 May 2011 and killed the al-Qaeda leader, Osama bin Laden. This was a massive embarrassment for the Pakistani Army and a loss of credibility. It also led to a review of relations with the U.S. As reported by Steve Coll in his book "Directorate S," "By late May American intelligence reports showed that Kayani (Army Chief) and Pasha (Director-General ISI) had opened vigorous discussions about how to break off the relationship with America and reorganize around Pakistan's alliance with China."

By 2014, pressure had somewhat eased on the Pakistan Army. In Afghanistan, the NATO had handed over nationwide security responsibility to the Afghan forces, and President Obama had announced the withdrawal of U.S. troops to be completed by the end of 2014. The pull-out of foreign forces from Afghanistan was accompanied by a resurgence of the Taliban. As fighting intensified, Pakistan became a crucial player in the negotiations between the Taliban and the Americans.

Internally, the fight against terrorism in Pakistan was showing signs of success. After peaking in 2013, terror attacks and fatalities in violence were declining in Pakistan. This easing of pressure on Pakistan Army led them to refocus their efforts to destabilize J&K.

There was a five-fold increase in ceasefire violations from 114 in 2012 to 583 in 2014. Well-trained terrorist groups started infiltrating from Pakistan to attack security force camps. The first such attack was in September 2013 at the Hiranagar police station and an army unit at Samba. This was followed by attacks at Kathua (March 2014), Arnia (November 2014) and Mohra gun position (December 2014).

In the last few years, violence has steadily escalated in J&K and this is also mirrored in a sharp deterioration in the situation along the border. Following a terrorist attack on the Uri military garrison, India carried out 'surgical strikes' on terrorist camps in POK in September 2016. Ceasefire violations along the LoC have risen to approximately 3000 in 2018 and infiltration attempts continue to be made. The Union Minister of State for Home G Kishan Reddy informed the Parliament that nearly 400 terrorists infiltrated into Jammu and Kashmir in the last three years (2015-2018) and 126 of them have been killed by security forces[7]. Another worrying factor is that there are definite signs of the revival of militancy in the Doda-Kishtwar region. In the last decade, the area has witnessed rapid growth in the Madrasas and seminaries. As a result, intense radicalization has taken place which gets further accentuated by the susceptible nature of the communal-dynamics of the region.[8]

On 5 August 2019, the India Parliament bifurcated the state of J&K and abrogated the provisions of Article 370 that granted special status to the state. There was a swift and angry reaction from Pakistan, and it is more than likely that the coming days will see an intensification of Pakistan's proxy war efforts.

Strategy to Counter the Proxy War in Kashmir

The relationship between Pakistan and Jihadism cannot be understood without understanding the country's ideological dimension, the fact that it was created as the result of an idea[9]. Pakistan's adherence to an ideological nationalism based on Islam has allowed radical groups to propagate their message of Jihad without much hindrance[10]. Any strategy to deal with Pakistan's proxy war in Kashmir must necessarily combine the various elements of national power while also looking at aspects of the military strategy to deal with the transnational terrorist threat emanating from Pakistan.

Deterring Pakistan

The ideal strategy for India would be to deter Pakistan from sending terrorists into Kashmir. The success of a deterrence strategy depends on three criteria—capability, communication and credibility. It would appear that in the recent past, India has done enough to clearly communicate its intent to Pakistan that if it does not change its behaviour, there could be serious costs. There is a large conventional gap between the two militaries and the credibility of India's response has been validated through its cross-border actions against Pakistan's terrorist camps. Pakistan also finds itself under international scrutiny to cease support to terror groups, and its precarious financial situation could be exploited to further pressurize it to act against groups like the LeT and JeM. This will require a comprehensive and long-term strategy that combines diplomacy, international support, financial pressure, and, where needed, limited military action.

However, a word of caution is also necessary here. Pakistan remains a strategically important country, particularly for the U.S. and China. It is vital to the U.S. for a deal with the Taliban and a less than messy exit from Afghanistan. The Chinese need Pakistan as a counterweight to the growing power of India, which is the only country in Asia that is capable of resisting Chinese hegemony in the region. This encourages Pakistan to indulge in greater risk-taking behaviour against India.

The other issue with deterring Pakistan is that of perceptions. Pakistan Army remains obsessively concerned about appearing weak or inferior to its Indian counterpart. After studying six decades of Pakistani defence publications, Christine Fair observes in her book, "Fighting to the End: The Pakistan Army's Way of War," that Pakistani military writers establish that Hindus are "dishonourable, meek, pusillanimous, treacherous, and inequitable." Such a cognitive bias generally makes the success of deterrence somewhat unpredictable.

Military Pressure

The use of military force can put direct pressure on the Pakistan Army, which is the primary driver of terrorism in Jammu and Kashmir. The 'surgical strikes' of 2016 and the airstrike on Balakot have already shown the Pakistan forces in poor light. The Pakistan Army is also suffering a large number of casualties during ceasefire violations, a fact made evident when it refused to share with the Pakistani Senate the details of casualties in Indian firing along the LoC.

The Pakistani Army sees an element of success in the pursuit of its proxy war against India and will not abandon it quickly. Pakistan on the contrary will endeavour to revive terrorism in Central and North Kashmir. In addition leakage of terrorism South of Pir Panjal will be a setback to Indian Security Establishments. India must have an unpredictable military response to Pakistan's proxy war and calibrate it according to the scale and scope of Pakistan's reaction. Our actions must be well-thought-out so that we do not get drawn into an uncontrolled escalation cycle. After every Indian action, Pakistan will inevitably remind the international community about the danger of a nuclear war, but we must not get drawn into unnecessary rhetoric. Quick results must not be expected by employment of instrument of military power. Limited, but steady pressure will pay a higher dividend than single, spectacular actions.

Border Management

Offensive military strategies look attractive but in transnational insurgencies, the defensive aspects, including a strong border management posture, are more important. Regular infiltration of terrorists from Pakistan has been a significant factor in the sustainment of the conflict in J&K. These terrorists are better trained than locals, provide the leadership, and are immune to the 'hearts and minds' campaign. Paul Staniland, in his article titled, "Defeating Transnational Insurgencies: The Best Offence is a Good Fence," writes:

> *"History indicates that the best policy combination for neutralizing the transnational component of an insurgency is containment. A mixture of border defences, marginalization campaigns promoting nationalist propaganda, and law enforcement/intelligence initiatives that undercut diaspora networks is the most likely to succeed at the lowest cost. Such containment policies are not as sexy as bold offensives, telegenic aerial bombing, or high-profile crisis diplomacy, but they are extremely effective at precisely slicing the sinews of transnational insurgent power."*[11]

The preventing of infiltration from the Jammu region was one of the key reasons that this area has been largely free of terrorism, barring few attacks on the security forces camps. Due to terrain and weather constraints, the border management posture has not been as effective in Kashmir, where infiltration is still continuing. Even if the number of Pakistani terrorists in Kashmir is low, they provide a psychological link to show that the country is backing the so-called 'freedom struggle' in Kashmir. An essential component of the containment strategy is a system of defensive barriers along the border. India does have an 'Anti-Infiltration Obstacle System' in J&K, but it needs a major upgrade in quality and technology. A 'smart fence' has been in the works for some years and needs to be quickly put in place.

Managing the Internal Dimension of Conflict in J&K

While Pakistan is engaged in a proxy war in Kashmir, it is also a fact that there is an internal dimension to the conflict. There is a section of the youth in Kashmir valley that is alienated, radicalized and willing to pick up the gun. Political steps to address the problem have been tentative and half-hearted, and the latest move to bifurcate the state will be seen as an attempt to stifle the Kashmiri identity.

A strategy for conflict resolution in Jammu and Kashmir must be a combination of political, social, psychological, economic, and security elements. WHAM remains at the heart of this strategy. Many noted experts have identified collective memories of past traumas, fear of the future among societies, and the salience of ethnic identity as drivers of conflict. These sentiments must be addressed through a healing touch.

In the past, India has always adopted a policy of negotiations and political accommodation to deal with insurgencies among ethnic minorities. This will also be the correct approach for J&K. It is also vital that a compelling narrative is put in place by the government to show that it genuinely cares for the people of J&K. It is only when the population of Kashmir is convinced about the sincerity of the government that we can start building a path towards peace. An improvement of the internal situation in Kashmir will make it much more difficult for Pakistan to find popular support in Kashmir to continue with its proxy war.

Conclusion

The use of proxies has been an accepted norm in all forms of warfare. However, while armies generally use proxies as an adjunct to their conventional forces, Pakistan Army uses terror groups as the main element of their strategy in contesting India. In Kashmir, Pakistan-sponsored terror groups have been attempting, since the past thirty years, to force India to negotiate with Pakistan on the future status of J&K.

In the recent past, India has shown much greater resolve to forcefully deal with Pakistan's proxy war in Kashmir. This resolve must now result in a comprehensive strategy that combines military pressure and effective border management with diplomatic efforts to internationally isolate Pakistan as a state sponsor of terrorism. It is also crucial that we find ways to address the internal dimension of the conflict in J&K. This will remove much of the justification that Pakistan gives for continuing its support to the Kashmiri cause'. Sole reliance on a security-centric approach will not help India win because Kashmir is also a battleground of perceptions. Also, State needs to act more forcefully against extremist organizations instrumental in radicalizing young minds, such as Jamaat-i-Islami and Ahl-i-Hadith.[12]

NOTES

1. Sameer Lalwani and Emily Tallo, Drivers, Decisions, Dilemmas: Understanding the Kashmir Crisis and its Implications, War on the Rocks, February 20, 2019.
2. Max Frost, Pakistan Prepares to Fight India for Kashmir, *The National Interest*, August 08, 2019.
3. Ibid.
4. Lalwani, N1.
5. Prem Mahadevan, A Predictive Analysis of the J&K Militancy, *CLAWS Journal* Winter 2008, p. 148.
6. Ibid.
7. Nearly 400 terrorists infiltrated into J-K in 3 years, government tells LS, PTI, *The Economic Times*, July 16, 2019.
8. Abhinav Pandya, View: Militancy in Kashmir not yet over, *The Economic Times*, July 29, 2019.
9. Husain Haqqani, Our Jihad Adiction, Hudson Institute, Accessed from https://www.hudson.org/research/10945-our-jihad-addiction on September 09, 2019.
10. Ibid.
11. Paul Staniland, Defeating Transnational Insurgencies: The Best Offense is a Good Fence, *The Washington Quarterly*, Winter 2005-06, p. 31.
12. Pandya N8.

4

India's Conflict Resolution in Punjab

Lt Gen Ghanshyam Singh Katoch, PVSM, AVSM, VSM (Retd)

ABSTRACT

The Conflict in Punjab from the early eighties to the mid-nineties was an insurgency that degenerated into a terrorist movement which ultimately made it lose its support base. Its genesis like many insurgencies was the perceived fear of the Sikh people that being a minority in India they would lose their identity. This fear was used by political parties to create constituencies to garner votes. The accompanying discontent and infighting were used by Pakistan as an opportunity to strike at arch- rival India. However, over a period of about 12 years the secessionist violent movement was defeated. This article studies the conflict resolution in Punjab to draw lessons for combating similar insurgencies.

Introduction

India has been engaged in several counter-insurgency operations since its independence.[1] One can say that when a new country comes into existence which has several minority ethnicities within it, such conflicts are unavoidable. This is the process of nation-building. The US had to do this in the form of its Red-Indian wars, the UK had to do it in Scotland much earlier and in Northern Ireland later, the Russians have been heavily engaged in it in its trans-Caucasian region and so has been China, in Tibet and Xinjiang. In India's case some insurgencies—notably the one in Nagaland which is also called "the mother of all (Indian) insurgencies"—have been long lasting and though subdued, continue to simmer because of certain aspirations being unfulfilled. The insurgencies in Mizoram and the Punjab have been success stories. This article studies India's insurgency resolution strategy in Punjab and examines the factors which led to its successful resolution.

The Punjab Insurgency

The Punjab insurgency originated in the late 1970s through the militant Sikh ethnicity and religion based nationalist Khalistan[2] movement seeking protection of Sikh beliefs, which were viewed as likely to be subsumed within the Hindu Indian identity. In the 1980s the movement had developed into a secessionist insurgency, especially under a militant religious leader Jarnail Singh Bhindranwale. Electoral politics have traditionally wooed community leaders to garner votes. In Sikhism as in some other religions, temporal and religious authority is accepted in one person or body. Bhindranwale was hence courted initially[3] but when he became secessionist the State realised the danger and sought to restrain him. Pakistan which looks for chinks in India's armour had seized the opportunity and began providing sanctuaries, training and weapons to the Sikh militants who had rallied around Bhindanwale. The violent insurgency consumed 21,469 lives before it was comprehensively defeated in 1993.[4]

Birth of the Violent Khalistan Movement

In the 1972 Punjab state elections, the Congress party had defeated the Sikh religious political party the Akali Dal[5]. To regain political space, the Akalis in 1973 convened a meeting at a shrine at Anandpur Sahib demanding greater autonomy for the Sikhs. The Congress government considered the demand of the secessionists and rejected it. Bhindranwale at the same time was also being used by the Akalis "as a card against the government to be able to dictate its terms"[6] as he had supported the Akali demand of Khalistan, the Sikh homeland. Later he decided to achieve it through coercion and violence because of which he received prompt support from the spy agency Inter-Services Intelligence (ISI) of Pakistan, to wage a violent conflict with the Indian State. In 1983 in order to escape arrest, Bhindranwale, along with his militant cadre moved into the vast Sikh shrine, the Akal Takht. This is located inside the Golden Temple sanctorum which is the holiest seat of the Sikh shrines. As the level of illegal activities, killings and violence unleashed by Bhindranwale from the sanctuary of the Akal Takht increased, on 1 June 1984 the Indian army was ordered to remove him from the shrine as the State police was unable to do so, because by now he was known to have built up a formidable armoury inside the shrine. An operation called "Blue Star" was launched to remove him and the armed militants from the Golden Temple complex. On 6 June Bhindranwale died in the operation. The operation was initially started with small arms, with very restrictive rules of engagement given to the army. However, as the heavily armed and entrenched militants who had been trained by a retired Sikh army general—who had been cashiered from the army on disciplinary grounds—inflicted heavy casualties on the security forces, heavier weapons were used. These weapons caused extensive damage to the shrine. This caused outrage among the Sikhs and increased the support for the Khalistan Movement. Four months after the operation, on 31 October 1984, Prime Minister Mrs Indira Gandhi was assassinated in vengeance by two of her Sikh bodyguards. Public outcry over Gandhi's death who was a revered leader, led to the killings of Sikhs in anti-Sikh riots. These events in turn had a snowball effect and gave a great spurt to extremism and violence in Punjab.[7]

Rise of Militancy

Post Operation Blue Star and the anti-Sikh riots the extremist groups grew in numbers and strength. The financial funding from a sympathetic and prosperous Sikh diaspora in US, UK and Canada, sharply increased. Other sources of income for the militants were bank robberies, kidnapping, ransom and extortion.[8] Indira Gandhi's son and political successor, Rajiv Gandhi who had become the Prime Minister after Mrs Gandhi's assassination, tried unsuccessfully to bring peace to Punjab through various political initiatives but failed.

The extremist violence had started with targeting of a Sikh sect, the *Nirankaris* who were considered "Tankahiyas" or non-believers (in the same manner that *Ahmediyas* are considered 'non-believers' by radical Islamists). By 1985, the situation in Punjab had become highly volatile; several mass killings of Hindus took place to induce an exodus out of the Punjab. By March 1986, the Golden Temple was back in control of an extremist Sikh organisation called the *Damdami Taksal*. This was followed by attacks on the state and central government administrative bodies and the Hindus. Ultimately the Sikh terrorists also targeted other Sikhs with opposing viewpoints.

Decline and Demise of Violent Extremism in Punjab

Between 1987 and 1991, Punjab was placed under President's rule, in other words it was governed by the federal government appointed Governor. Elections were eventually held in 1992. In spite of poor voters turnout the Congress party managed to establish the government in Punjab. Mr Beant Singh a dynamic political leader was chosen as the Chief Minister of the State. This government authorised the State police chief Mr KPS Gill, a Sikh police officer with a hands-on experience of dealing with insurgency, to implement a vigorous counter militancy strategy. The aim of this strategy was to destroy the roots of the violent movement in Punjab by targeting the leadership and rolling up the support base. Till then the Punjab Police was targeted by the militants and even some of the police personnel had lost their family members to the militancy. Aug 1992 saw the most savage wave of killings of police families. In just a few days 60 family members of policemen were killed.[9] This appears to have been a tipping point. This led to loss of public support for the militants among the majority Sikh population. The militancy was decimated by synergised application of the army and Punjab Police. Three things worked in favour of combating militancy in Punjab at this stage. First, was the loss of public support to militants, second, there was no interference in execution of counter militancy strategy put in place by Mr KPS Gill and third, synergised application of army and police in counter militancy operations became the norm. The political leadership displayed missionary zeal to end the reign of terror under the decisive leadership of Mr Beant Singh who was later assassinated by militants in 1995 through a car bomb.

Factors which Aided Resolution

The following are the main factors which in unison created an environment in which terrorism in the Punjab became weaker and was then eliminated:

The Demographic and Political Profile. Sikhs make up only 2 per cent of India's population but form 55-60 per cent of the population of the Punjab, with Hindus forming 36-45 per cent.[10] This profile of Punjab was against the success of terrorism. Of the Sikhs, 20% of Sikhs with roots in Punjab were settled in other parts of the country. The leaders of the largest Sikh political party, The Akali Dal, had some reservations with respect to the movement. Many Sikhs even within Punjab did not support it.[11] Punjab was among the most prosperous states in India in the 1980's where the Sikhs having large landholdings and an industrious nature had made huge agricultural output gains from the 'Green Revolution'. After 1965 till the early 1980s, high yield seeds had been introduced with help from the US based Rockefeller foundation. Nor were the Sikhs discriminated in any manner whether to practise or proselytize their religion. The Sikhs are considered a martial race and were a community with one of the highest representations among the military and police officers and men in the country. In other words, poverty and discrimination which fuel insurgencies were absent. What was present was third party foreign support from Pakistan. This was sufficient to fuel insurgency when the government forces were not prepared. After the initial gains made through coercion and induced fear, the militants were unable to sustain their ground swell and were decimated when public support dwindled due to excesses and synergised operations by security forces.

Strengthening and Modernization of Police and Security Forces. At the start of the violence, security forces were ill equipped to deal with violence in terms of their strength and weapons vis-à-vis the militants. The latter armed by Pakistan had a fair proportion of AK-47 rifles. The army had the 7.62 SLR[12] and the police had the World War II, .303 Lee Enfield rifle. However, realizing the gravity of the crisis, the state and central governments made concerted efforts to modernise the police. The strength, transport, weapons and equipment of the police were improved.[13] AK series of weapons, bulletproof vehicles, modern communication equipment and other wherewithal was inducted for the police. The state government recruited more policemen. The strength of the Punjab police in 1989 was 35,000 personnel.[14] It rose to 70,000 by 1993. Defence analyst Rostum K Nanavatty quotes, "it was the revitalising of the police leadership; upgradation of the police stations; improved intelligence collection and sharing of intelligence [between the army and police] and integration of security forces operations which brought about change."[15] The police department created new police districts. The Punjab police commandos were raised and trained in counter-insurgency methods of operations. The army and paramilitary forces joined the state police and in the early 1990s; the army had close to 15,000 troops and 40000 Central Armed Police Force (CAPF)[16] constables were engaged in the anti-militant operations.

Strengthening Anti-Terrorism Laws. Many strict terror and criminal laws were introduced in the state to curb terrorist activities, such as Essential Services Maintenance Act (ESMA), Maintenance of Internal Security Act (MISA), National Security Act (NSA), Armed Forces Special Powers Acts, Disturbed Areas Act, and Terrorist and Disruptive Activities Act (TADA). The enactment of various laws and acts provided teeth to the counter militancy forces to operate without fear of prosecution while discharging the legitimate duties. Laws were used as potent weapons that led to evaporation of ground support and over ground workers could be detained under MISA.

Counterinsurgency by the State. The police used every possible strategy and tactic to crush militancy. These included static and mobile check posts, focal point patrolling by day and night, and cordon and search operations based on specific intelligence in built-up areas and general intelligence in areas like the *Mand.*[17] People who were either related to or supported the terrorists or were providing information to the militants about the movements and activities of the security forces were arrested under the new laws. This while cutting off support to the militants also provided valuable intelligence. The State gave the police a 'free hand' to carry out counter- insurgency operations after 1991 when the whole of Punjab was declared a 'disturbed' state. This gave extensive powers to the security forces to deal with the situation. An effective step was the order of the Director General of Police issued on 30 August 1989 promising police personnel handsome specific rewards, such as quick promotions for the apprehension/liquidation of 53 specifically dreaded militants.[18]

Peoples' Resistance to Terrorists and Support to Police and Administration. The people were sandwiched between firm handling by the security forces and oppression by terrorists. However, as the security forces started gaining the upper hand the militant's support base started eroding. By now people had realised that militancy would lead to economic and cultural downswing that may not be easy to recover from. There was a conscious decision by the masses to cut short the logistic and financial support to the militants. Besides individual or familial resistance, there were many instances of organised collective resistance against the militant organisation. Awareness campaigns in the form of rallies and public demonstrations were organised by social organisations and political parties.

President's Rule. India has resilient and vibrant democracy; however, at times the democratic process can be coerced by use of violence, and the population can be prevented from exercising their franchise. The suspension of State government and imposition of direct central government rule in a State when there is grave internal threat is through President's Rule imposed under article 352 & 356 of the Indian constitution. Here the representative of the President in a State—the Governor—assumes direct control including maintenance of law and order and administration of the state. Along with other enabling laws he is then empowered to restore order. The provision of Governor's Rule can be applicable for six months and extended when required, through constitutional amendments. Through a cumbersome procedure, in President's rule in Punjab was extended up to five years which enabled the security forces to quell the insurgency in Punjab. This was done at the height of the insurgency, in the periods 10 October 1983 to 29 September 1985, and from 11 June 1987 to 25 February 1992. The second period of nearly five years was decisive in ending the conflict.

Border Barrier. From 1988 the Border Security Force started creating an illuminated border fence barrier on the international border with Pakistan in Punjab, and by 1992 had completed it. This greatly curtailed the movement of militants across the border with Pakistan.

Lessons Learnt

The following were the lessons learnt from the successful defeat of the insurgency in Punjab:

Mass Base Erosion. It is important to erode the mass base of the militants through a concerted government campaign to rebuild grassroots democracy. The security forces therefore must know the process of peace building. The government administrative machinery must be able to restart functioning at the earliest. Civic actions in such situations start with the army when the civil administration is completely marginalised by the militants. Thereafter it must progressively become a civil government function. The acceptability of a healing balm applied by the force which is fighting the militants is low in areas which are pro-insurgent people. This is because the locals out there would have lost their kith and kin who had taken to the gun, and also on account of some collateral damage which is inevitable.

Local Police as the Lead Agency. In counter insurgency/terrorist operations the local police should assume the lead role as soon as their writ is re-stablished by the army, and their equipment and training has been upgraded. Once this stage is reached the CAPF and the Army units employed in operations even if taking on the burden of operations must create the perception of the local police being the lead and paramount agency in the operations. This improves the morale and standing of the local police and their effectiveness. This in turn—as actionable intelligence improves, and militants start getting eliminated or apprehended—creates a snowballing effect in effective CI operations and leads to the defeat of the militants. In doing all this, it is important that some local policemen whose kin have joined militancy or those who have sympathies with the militants, or their cause, must be segregated or discreetly removed from sensitive duties.

Perception Management of the Misdeeds of Terrorists. The atrocities by the terrorists or their misdeeds and misbehaviour need to be highlighted by the media through perception management. This has a decisive impact in lessening the sympathy that they often earn from the people by being son of the soil. The mass killings of some Hindus by militants attracted adverse publicity and were deplored even by the Sikh community. Similarly, attempts to demoralise the Punjab Police by targeting their families which became known to all policemen through the media, galvanised the police to seek retribution and strengthened their resolve to defeat the insurgency.

Intelligence. The intelligence gathering apparatus should operate in complete synergy with other sister organisations and the forces which are required to undertake counter militancy operations. These intelligence agencies should be enabled technologically and financially so that they are able to optimise their efforts to gain actionable intelligence. There, is a requirement of having joint interrogation and joint intelligence tasking so that efforts are not duplicated.

Protection of Important Persons/Sources/Installations. This can be done by creating Village Defence Committees and Special Police Officer schemes. Bridges and communication infrastructure which enable quick movement need to be secured so that the movement of security forces is not hindered. Population control and infrastructure security should not lead to harassment of population.

Night Operations. The militants generally prefer to move or conduct their operations in hours of darkness. The security forces need to be proficient in night operations. In this, equipping them with modern night vision devices (equipment which is difficult for the militants to obtain) can give the security forces an edge in night operations.

Targeting of Leaders. After the initial initiative had been wrested from the militants, it was important to target the terrorist leadership. "Instead of wasting resources on every petty criminal and opportunist who had joined the terrorist ranks, the available manpower and infrastructure was focused disproportionately on the leaders, the planners and the ideologues of the movement."[19] This broke the morale of the terrorist cadres and slowly the pipeline of new recruits dried up.

Deliberate Operations. While conducting operations in built up areas there is a requirement to carry out detailed assessment and planning for an accurate intelligence picture. This is very important to avoid collateral damage. In Punjab, Op Blue Star was characterised by haste under political directions. In 1984 the army was sent [into the Golden Temple] with needless haste, virtually blind "that resulted in both the unnecessary loss of [both civilian and army] lives and excessive damage to various building within the shrine".[20] Another operation, (Op Black Thunder) to flush out the terrorists who had reoccupied the Golden Temple was planned in detail and carried out by specialised commandos over ten days in May 1986. The militants were rooted out with 41 being killed and 200 surrendering with only minor damage to the shrine.

Conclusion

It is important to revisit history to adopt best practices in counter-insurgency and counter terrorism operations. Punjab militancy could be brought under control by precise kinetic operations, public support and able support of the state administration. It can be stated without doubt that the actions of the state and the support of the central government, combined with resistance of the rural Sikh population and the efforts of democratic forces resulted in complete eradication of insurgency-related violence. At the same time it is pertinent to say that the defeat and decline of the Punjab militancy was dependent on some factors which will not be available in all cases of counter-insurgency. The demography, the terrain, the position of Sikhs in Indian society and government are factors which may not exist in other insurgencies in India. The press and social media is a common factor in all counter-insurgency conflict resolution situations. In Punjab, the press remained vigilant even suffering physical casualties in the process. It did not submit to the terror threats and played its role and remained steadfast in its responsibilities towards the state and the people. Presently, a nascent 'Khalistan' movement remains in Pakistan or and some foreign countries where radicals have taken refuge. In conclusion, it must be said that the lack of an ideological perspective and a loss of common people's trust were the key factors in the defeat of militancy in the Indian state of Punjab.

NOTES

1. Hamish Teleford, Counterinsurgency in India: Observations from Punjab and Kashmir. *Journal of Conflict Studies*, [S.l.], Aug. 2001. ISSN 1715-5673. Available at: https://journals.lib.unb.ca/index.php/JCS/article/view/4293/4888. Accessed: 01 Apr 2019.
2. The translation of the word is "Land of the Pure". 'Khalis' is a Persian word meaning pure which has found its place in Urdu or Hindustani.
3. Kirpal Dhillon, *Identity and Survival, Sikh Militancy in India, 1978-1993* (New Delhi, Penguin India: 2006), p. 81.
4. Anant Mathur, Secrets of COIN Success Lessons from the Punjab Campaign, *Faultlines*, Vol. 20, January 2011. Available from http://old.satp.org/satporgtp/publication/faultlines/volume20/Article2.htm. Accessed Jun 02, 2019.
5. This is an abbreviated term for the full name of the party the "Shiromani Akali Dal" (Supreme Eternal Arm).
6. Satyapal Dang, *Terrorism in Punjab* (New Delhi, Gyan Publishing House: 2000), p. 47.
7. Sergei DeSilva-Ranasinghe, Counterinsurgency in India: Lessons from the Punjabi Insurgency—Interview, *Eurasia Review*, Dec 24, 2012, Available at https://www.eurasiareview.com/24122012-counterinsurgency-in-india-lessons-from-the-punjabi-insurgency-interview/, accessed Jun 02, 2019.
8. Dang, pp. 74-75.
9. KPS Gill, p.106.
10. Refworld, UNHCR, Canada: Immigration and Refugee Board of Canada, *Punjab Human Rights Update*, 1 January 1994, available at https://www.refworld.org/docid/3ae6a83b1c.html [accessed 2 June 2019]
11. Harish K Puri, Paramjit Singh Judge, Jagrup Singh Sekhon, *Terrorism in Punjab, Understanding Grassroots Reality* (Delhi, Har Anand Publications: 2007), p.113.
12. It was only after the setbacks against AK-47 armed militants in Srilanka and Kashmir that the Indian army shed its semi-automatic and cumbersome SLR which was ill suited for fleeting engagements in an unconventional war against militants and inducted the versatile, light and automatic AK-47.
13. KPS Gill (ed.) Terror and Containment Perspectives of India's Security (New Delhi: Gyan Publishing House: 2001), p. 37.
14. Ibid. p.106.
15. Rostom K Nanavatty, *Internal Armed Conflict in India: Forging a Joint Civil-Military Approach*, (New Delhi: Pentagon Press, 2013), p. 77
16. The CAPFs employed in Punjab were the Border Security Force (BSF), The Central Reserve Police Force (CRPF) and the Indo-Tibetan Border Police (ITBP).
17. *Mand* is a 600 sq km riverine and mostly marshy area with thick elephant grass spread over the Ferozepur, Amritsar, Kapurthala and Jalandhar districts of *Punjab*. Being the few forest like areas in Punjab it was used by militants for refuge and training.
18. Puri et al, p. 118.
19. Sergi De Silva, op cit.
20. KPS Gill, Punjab, The Knights of Falsehood (New Delhi: Har-Anand Publications: 1997), p. 96.

5

Insurgency in India's North-East: Options and Strategy for Conflict Resolution

Lt Gen Rameshwar Roy UYSM, AVSM, YSM (Retd)

ABSTRACT

This paper deliberates upon the complex subject of insurgency in India's Northeast and suggests options and strategies for conflict resolution. In terms of connectivity and communication, the Northeast poses a unique challenge to India for many decades, and its turbulent geopolitical history adds to the quandary. Factors aiding the complexity of the region are ethnicity, economic viability, and governance. Over the decades, the situation reached a point wherein the insurgency got institutionalised, allowing them to hibernate as well as proliferate similar sentiments across the region. The prolonged existence of various militant/insurgent groups in the North-eastern states are used as constant leverage with the Indian government to extract aid and funds with little or no accountability when it comes to spending and implementation of schemes. The symbiosis between the respective state governments and insurgent groups need to be addressed holistically in order to address this deep-rooted threat to India's overall security and stability.

Introduction

The partition of India in 1947, and the creation of East Pakistan (now Bangladesh), ended the natural connectivity of the North-eastern states with the outside world, through the Bay of Bengal. This created a claustrophobic environment for the entire population of this region, which is surrounded by China, Myanmar and Bangladesh. The Siliguri corridor link with Mainland India can at best be termed as a cartographic relic of the British decolonisation process.[1] The Siliguri corridor stretches for 200-km and is between, 17 to 60 kilometres metres wide. The strategic significance of this narrow corridor is due to proximity to Chumbi Valley of Tibet Autonomous Region (TAR). Another important geographical factor that makes it more critical is the reason that this corridor is sandwiched between Nepal in the West, Bangladesh in the South, Bhutan in the East and TAR in the North.

The Northeast, however, has always posed a challenge in terms of connectivity, whether through land, sea, air, or even the electronic media. The region has remained isolated, as also insecure in many ways, since Independence. The British too, seemed to have found it difficult and unwise to integrate this region with the Indian mainland due to lack of financial viability and other constraints of management and treated it more like a buffer zone. They justified this isolation for 'anthropological' reasons respecting tribal sensitivities. They made all out efforts to, apparently, protect the 'Hill People' from the ills of development so as to preserve their cultural identity, customs and traditions—an idea that seems to have persisted until recent times. However, that did not stop them from spreading Christianity in these areas, particularly Nagaland and Mizoram, even at great personal risk.

Brief Historical Perspective

The seeds of insurgency had been sown in Nagaland even before independence making it the oldest insurgency in India. Therefore, it is described as the 'Mother' of all insurgencies in the North-eastern states. The British had found it convenient to protect these areas with the Inner Line Permit. However, the spread of Christianity and establishment of modern political, administrative, and educational institutions created an educated, elite class amongst the 'Nagas'. In 1918, these Naga elites with the help of the British officials formed a Naga Club that slowly evolved into a political voice of the fragmented Naga tribes.

In 1935, the then Government of India Act designated the Naga Hill districts as "excluded areas" wherein the Nagas could maintain their tradition, culture and lifestyle, with little interference from the federal or provincial governments. This ultimately led to the formation of the Naga National Council in 1946, which appealed to the British authorities as well as the Indian political leadership to grant them independence. After considerable persuasion a Nine-point Agreement was signed in June 1947, between the Naga leaders and Akbar Hydari, the then governor of Assam, wherein it was agreed that for ten years following this agreement, the Nagas would be free to decide their own future.[2]

In fact, in 1952, the Nagas even boycotted the first general election in independent India. A few years later, in 1956, the Naga militants under the leadership of Phizo secretly formed the Naga Federal Government (NFG) with around 1,500 armed guerrilla fighters.[3] This started the so called 'freedom struggle for Greater Nagaland' better known as 'Nagalim'. The Indian government in a reactive approach first sent in the Army to control the insurrection and subsequently, Nagaland was given the status of an Indian state in 1962, within the existing boundaries of the state.[4] But the Naga problem has remained unresolved till date.

On August 3, 2015 a Naga Framework Agreement was signed between the National Socialist Council of Nagaland (NSCN), Issac Muivah (IM), the strongest faction and the Ministry of Home Affairs (MHA), the details of which have not been declassified as yet.[5] But it did indicate the possibility of enhancing the scope of talks to include more Naga political groups for building a broader consensus. There are significant Naga tribes such as Angamis, Aos and Konyaks whose interests are not represented by the NSCN (IM). The fact of the matter is that Muivah is a Thangkul from Manipur and his tribe has virtually no presence in Nagaland. Similarly, Issac Swu represents just one faction of the Sema tribes, while the Konyaks constitute the single largest tribe represented by the NSCN, Khaplang (K).[6] The dream of a greater Nagaland 'Nagalim' has given way to the idea of shared sovereignty, though what this means in real terms is difficult to define, but any redrawing of the boundaries of the state of Nagaland is highly unlikely. The adjoining three states of Assam, Arunachal Pradesh, and Manipur are against any move to redraw geographical maps or existing state boundaries, to create a greater Nagaland/Nagalim as per the demands of the Naga leadership.

It should be understood that 'Naga' is a generic term for a group of over 34 major tribes, who inhabit not only the boundary areas along and within Nagaland, but also some hilly regions of the adjoining states of Assam, Manipur and Arunachal Pradesh, and some parts of Myanmar as well.[7] Therefore, any meaningful settlement of Naga problem, will require a consensus solution approved by all Naga tribes.

The famine in Mizoram following the flowering of the bamboo in 1966, gave rise to insurgency in the state under leadership of the Mizo National Front (MNF), the erstwhile Mizo National Famine Front (Political Wing) and the Mizo National Army (MNA). But this rebellion was very successfully controlled by the Indian Armed forces for nearly two decades. A Peace Accord was finally signed on June 30, 1986, on two conditions—

the MNF would eschew violence and the talks would take place within the framework of Constitution of India. Mizoram was granted full statehood in February 1987. The deal also saw Laldenga the leader of MNF, becoming the interim chief minister of Mizoram. Nearly a year later in 1987, he contested the state's first assembly elections and won. However, internal friction led to a split in the party and his government fell in 1988 without completing its full term of five years. He died two years later of lung cancer.

It was around the same time that two other states, Tripura and Manipur, also got engulfed in the armed struggle against the Indian state. The basic issue was the fear of local population of getting overwhelmed by influx of Bengalis, as also because minority communities in the states were being suppressed by the migrant population. This is the primary reason for the ongoing armed struggle against India being waged by these states.

Manipur got statehood in 1972, while Tripura was already a state. The Indian government kept on giving in to the demands for dividing the states in the Northeast on 'ethnic' considerations, rather than their economic viability and ease of governance. This not only allowed insurgency to fester but it led to a growing sense of insecurity amongst large sections of population, resulting in number of insurrections. Not surprisingly, India's problem got multiplied and complicated manifold as time went by. There was a brief respite during 1971 war with Pakistan, when Bangladesh was created out of East Pakistan.

Soon after, Assam slid into insurgency because its local population felt threatened by migrants from Nepal and the newly created Bangladesh. The agitation was spearheaded by United Liberation Front of Assam (ULFA), and was soon taken over by All Assam Students Union (ASSU). In 1985, after six years of bloodshed and turmoil a peace agreement was signed with the Indian government, but it has been uneasy peace (negative Peace). Factional fights continue to erupt between various smaller tribes in the area and innocent civilians continue to be killed by ULFA, in spurts.

Later on even Arunachal Pradesh got dragged into insurgency, more by default than design, due to its geo-strategic location. Most of the insurgent groups in the Northeast started using this state as a transit route and for safe camps—particularly its border districts of Tirap and Changlang, that border with Myanmar.

Transition from Insurgency to Terrorism

The transition from political disaffection to insurgency and then to terrorism requires profound study. We still continue to use the term 'insurgency' in the Northeast and elsewhere in the country. This transition from 'insurgency to terrorism' was bloodiest in the Punjab province (A North Indian State) particularly after *Operation Blue Star* (An operation conducted by Security Forces to flush out Sikh militants from the religious places) in 1984.

The basic reason for this was India's weak enforcement of the law of the land and the incapability of the state machinery to prosecute the terrorists/criminals. These law breakers could not be prosecuted owing to lack of evidence and because people did not come forward to testify against the insurgents/terrorists out of fear. Under such circumstances the political leadership found it convenient to hand the situation over to the security forces to absolve themselves of accountability. This has since become the norm in fight against terrorism from the late nineties till today. We also started using the term Counter Terrorists- Operations (CT Ops) in Jammu & Kashmir and Northeast thereafter.

The other major driver of this trend has been the communication technology, which enhanced state's capability to monitor, locate and eliminate these terrorists in much shorter time span. While the security forces themselves became less and less vulnerable to terrorists' attacks; unprotected and unsuspecting civilians became soft targets of terrorism world over. Human rights groups and globalisation further helped the cause of terrorists by giving them publicity which furthered their cause, justified or otherwise. Incorporation of technology in Counter-Insurgency/ Counter-Terrorism (CI/CT) operations added new dimension to state's capability to tackle insurgency and terrorism.

Institutionalisation of Insurgency in the Northeast

The reality and bitter truth in the contemporary context is that the existence of various militant groups has got institutionalised. Not surprisingly, the North-eastern states use it as leverage to extract more aid and funds from the central government, with reduced accountability. It has led to a mutually beneficial relationship between the respective state governments and the insurgent groups, with most of them sustaining themselves by means of the aid and schemes of the central government. Although not proven on ground, many contracts for various development projects are obtained by front-end organisations affiliated to the various active/dormant insurgent groups.

Tripura State: A Contextual Case Study

The peace prevailing in Tripura should serve as an example of how enduring peace can be achieved in India's North-east. Insurgency in Tripura began with the formation of militant group National Liberation Front of Tripura (NLFT) in March 1989 and its armed wing, All Tripura Tiger Force in 1990. It had its ups and down, but there was a steep decline in insurgency from 1996-98 after which it tapered off completely.[8] The major lessons to be learnt from this case study are:[9]

- A strong and well thought out conflict resolution mechanism.
- A responsible, efficient, credible and responsive state administration.
- A credible surrender policy and rehabilitation system for the surrendering rebels.
- Zero tolerance for excesses by the security forces, combined with psychological operations.
- Proactive and dynamic participation of the people.
- Civil society and government agencies working in tandem to maintain peace during the periods of negotiation and rehabilitation of insurgents.
- Tripura has not been under the Armed Forces Special Powers Act since 2015 and therefore could well become the key reference point for conflict resolution in the Northeast.

Consistency in Policy a Cornerstone to Deal with Insurgencies

It is most important to ensure "consistency in policies" of the federal and state governments. Both governments should be on the same page while dealing with the insurgencies. The insurgency in the North-eastern states should not be considered in isolation, but as a social, political, economic and security problem. Attempts to deal with issues in these states, on a case-to-case basis for the sake of expediency and entering into different arrangements with different insurgent groups at different times with varying conditions, not only sends mixed signals to the militant groups but, also encourages them to carry out their activities with impunity. So the government of the day needs to have an all-inclusive, coherent integrated, as also consistent policy to deal with this issue.

What has also been learnt with experience is that the talks with insurgent groups must not be held, for cease fire agreements (CFA) or suspension of operations (SOO) without imposing at least one pre-condition—i.e., the surrender of their weapons to the security forces. The failure to do this has resulted in the revival of militancy and insurgency, time and again at the cost of peace. More importantly, it has impacted security forces' operations and morale.

It needs to be clearly understood that these groups come to the negotiating table only when the pressure of sustained operations by the security forces, threatens their existence. It is during this phase that the insurgent groups desperately seek a 'break time' to regroup and reorganise their cadres and the struggle. The Indian government has been known to believe in buying time so as to tire out and break up the insurgent groups. This actually appears to have worked at times, but it has never translated into any concrete gains for the state in the long run.

Good Neighbourly Relations: A Key to Peace in the Northeast

The core issue of tackling insurgency in the North-eastern states has to be based on ensuring the speedy and proactive improvement of relations with India's immediate neighbours particularly Bhutan, Bangladesh and Myanmar. India's tackling of insurgency in Assam is a case in point. *Operation All Clear* was launched by the Royal Bhutan Army (RBA) in 2003 to uproot ULFA insurgent camps from Bhutanese territory. It broke the back of ULFA as an organisation.[10] Improving relations with Bangladesh also resulted in the closing down of sanctuaries for the ULFA. The Bangladesh government displayed great resolve in ensuring that the ULFA groups from Assam and insurgents from Tripura were also denied safe havens to operate against the Indian states. The improved relations with both countries have ensured continuous pressure on the insurgent groups, with the result that the leadership that was operating from outside the state, has been neutralised.

The insurgent safe havens and camps in Myanmar still remain a problem for India. This is primarily because of dense forests and difficult terrain with limited accessibility. Myanmar has cooperated with India to a great extent, but the porous border and hostile terrain provide sanctuary to the insurgents. Moreover, insurgents do not remain static but keep shifting camps to avoid being raided by the security forces from India and Myanmar.

Options and Strategies for Conflict Resolution in North-East

Today, India seeks a peaceful environment for the inclusive development of the region. The instability persisting in the North-eastern states, one way or another, over the past seven decades calls for a relook at the policy followed by successive Indian governments i.e., fatigue factor and maintaining an incident free environment. The panacea for all problems for long has been to let the security forces deal with the insurgency.

This approach needs to change now, mainly because insurgent groups are no longer being driven by the 'Just' cause for which they initially started the movement. There is no popular support from the masses and extortion rackets and fear-driven movement have been going on in the Northeast for far too long. Today, the Indian government is in a much stronger position to deal with these groups than before. Therefore, the insurgent groups operating in the Northeast have been reduced to terrorist outfits fighting for survival rather than for any viable cause.

India does not have the luxury of tiring out these groups to settle the issue. The vibrant democracy in India and the North-east has redressed most of the grievances but the bane at the moment, is corruption and delivery of governance.

It is more and more critical to develop India's North-eastern region at a faster pace to address its vulnerabilities in the east, particularly with regard to China. Conflict resolution in the North-east is imperative for the Act East Policy to succeed. Therefore, the Indian government needs to formulate its policies for the North-eastern states on the following lines:

- Surrender of arms and weapons as a pre-condition for peace talks.
- Operations by security forces to continue unless the insurgent groups surrender.
- A comprehensive and implementable rehabilitation package.
- Enhancing the capacity and capability of the state security apparatus, including state armed police forces, so that the Army can be pulled out of all these states and the AFSPA can be lifted.
- Develop these states as viable self-sustaining economic entities to prevent them from becoming economically sick.
- To adopt a comprehensive and all-inclusive developmental model for these states with better accounting for the 'fund flow' from the central government.
- Improved connectivity within the Northeast and rest of India.
- Relentless operations against those who continue to use violence as a mean to pursue their own agenda.

Conclusion

It must be accepted that regardless of the government at the centre, a consistent Indian policy for conflict resolution in the Northeast is mandatory. There should be strict preconditions for talks with insurgents along with a good governance model.

Huge investment in infrastructure, particularly surface connectivity and the power sector is the need of the hour. The Northeast has the potential to become an agriculture and industrial hub centre, thus restrictions on the acquisition of land and employment of skilled labour from outside need to be removed. The Northeast is rich in natural resources that can be put to optimum use for the betterment of people as also for the entire nation. This will also help in connecting India to its eastern and South Eastern neighbours as part of our Act East Policy.

NOTES

1. Ankit Panda, "The Siliguri Corridor is terrifyingly vulnerable artery in Indian Geography," *The Diplomat*, November 8, 2013.
2. H Srikanth and CJ Thomas, "Naga Resistance Movement and Peace Process in the Northeast India," *Peace and Democracy in South Asia*, Vol. 1, No. 2, 2005, p. 60.
3. Subham Dutta, "The Naga Movement: A Brief Chronological Understanding," *IOSR Journal of Humanities and Social Science, vol. 21, no. 5,* May 2016, pp. 37-40.
4. Srikanth et al., n. 2.
5. Sangeeta Barooah Pisharoty, "Revealed: RSS Draft Plan for Nagaland Accord," *The Wire,* January 19, 2018.
6. Rupak Chattopadhyay, "The Challenge of Peace in Nagaland," *Forum of Federations,* Vol. 5, No. 2, March/April 2006.
7. Ibid.
8. DN Sahaya, "Triumph Over Insurgency," *The Statesman,* July 5, 2017.
9. Ibid.
10 Namrata Goswami, "An Assessment of Insurgencies in Assam, Manipur, and Nagaland in 2009," Institute of Defence Studies and Analyses, April 5, 2010.

6

Left Wing Extremism in India's Tribal Heartland and the Conflict Resolution Strategy

Dr. PV Ramana

ABSTRACT

India's Maoist movement is on the decline. It is at the present largely concentrated in tribal inhabited areas of the country. The Maoists have established their own governments in their strongholds. The Indian government is taking various measures to wean the people away from the Maoists. These initiatives have been well received and have to an extent succeeded in integrating of the tribal population into the main stream. Good governance and development are winning over a population that was disengaged from the state.

Introduction

The Naxalites of the Communist Party of India (Maoist), [CPI (Maoist)], Maoists, in short, presently have a presence in 90 districts across 11 states in India. Previously their presence was noticed in 126 districts. Their objective is to capture state/political power through armed struggle.

The underground cadre strength and support base of the Maoists is dependent upon the demography of a place. Thus, in undivided Andhra Pradesh[1] the largest number of cadres were from the Backward Classes (BCs), followed by Scheduled Castes (SCs) and Scheduled Tribes (STs). The Maoist movement, to a large extent, is presently concentrated in the tribal (adivasi[2]) regions of Chhattisgarh, Odisha, Jharkhand and parts of Bihar, West Bengal, Andhra Pradesh and Telangana. Of the 90 affected districts, violence has been reported in 60 districts. The list of Maoist affected districts is as per the table below:

Table 2: Maoist Affected Districts, 2019

State	*Districts*	*Number*
Andhra Pradesh	East Godavari, Guntur, Srikakulam, Visakhapatnam, Vizianagaram, West Godavari	6
Bihar	Arwal, Aurangabad, Banka, East Champaran, Gaya, Jamui, Jehanabad, Kaimur, Lakhisarai, Munger, Muzaffarpur Nalanda, Nawada, Rohtas, Vaishali, West Champaran	16
Chhattisgarh	Balod, Balrampur, Bastar, Bijapur, Dantewada, Dhamtari, Gariyaband, Kanker, Kondagaon, Mahasamund, Narayanpur, Rajnandgaon, Sukma, Kabirdham	14
Jharkhand	Bokaro, Chatra, Dhanbad, Dumka, East Singhbhum, Garhwa, Giridih, Gumla, Hazaribagh, Khunti, Koderma, Latehar, Lohardaga, Palamu, Ramgarh, Ranchi, Simdega, Saraikela-Kharaswan, West Singhbhum	19
Kerala	Malappuram, Palakkad, Wayanad	3
Madhya Pradesh	Balaghat, Mandla	2
Maharashtra	Chandrapur, Gadchiroli, Gondia	3
Odisha	Angul, Bargarh, Bolangir, Boudh, Deogarh, Kalahandi, Kandhamal, Koraput, Malkangiri, Nabrangpur, Nayagarh, Nuapada, Rayagada, Sambhalpur, Sundargarh	15
Telangana	Adilabad, Bhadradri-Kothagudem, Jayashankar Bhupalpally, Khammam, Komaram-Bheem, Mancherial, Peddapalle, Warangal Rural	8
Uttar Pradesh	Chandauli, Mirzapur, Sonebhadra	3
West Bengal	Jhargam	1
Total		90

Source: Lok Sabha, Unstarred Question No. 401, February 5, 2019.

Maoist View of the Adivasi (Tribal)[3]

Forests are 'strategically important' for the Maoists owing to their relative inaccessibility[4]. Way back in the 1980s, Kondapalli Seetharamaiah, the founding general secretary of the Communist Party of India—Marxist-Leninist (People's War), PW for short, the predecessor of the CPI (Maoist), made an in-depth field study of Bastar and identified Abujhmad (Unknown Hill) as the Force Headquarters (FHQ) of the rebels[5]. To gain and retain control over forest areas the Maoists necessarily need the support of the inhabitants—the tribal population or adivasis. Therefore, the Maoists have paid special attention to them and their grievances.

The Adivasis constitute about seven per cent of India's population. Their economy, social system and cultural characteristics are significantly different from the rest of the population. The Maoists claim that most

Adivasis, are in the process of becoming nationalities as an overwhelming majority of them are among the most suppressed and repressed sections of the Indian society. A vast majority of Adivasis have been deprived of their land and other traditional means of livelihood without being provided with any alternative source of income. The Maoists claim:

> *The forest produce and mineral resources, which were traditionally in their possession, are being forcibly taken away by the imperialists, the CBB (Comprador Big Bourgeoisie), the feudal classes, money lenders and usurers, unscrupulous traders, bureaucrats, and other exploiters mainly from outside, resulting in the disintegration of their traditional economy. The mining, quarrying, other industrial activity and building up of big dams devastated lives and livelihoods of the adivasis. Moreover, they have been neglected socially, culturally and politically.*

The neglect of adivasi-inhabited areas by successive governments, has enabled the Maoists to involve large sections of the Adivasi population to become part of their so-called new democratic revolution (NDR). The Maoist, "prepare soldiers and leaders" from among the adivasis. Nevertheless, the Maoists have themselves admitted in an internal document, that they have largely failed in grooming leaders from among the tribal population.

The Maoists envisage organising the adivasis "on the basis of their political, economic, social, cultural, lingual and educational issues by ensuring them political autonomy". In line with this thinking, the Maoists have mobilised the tribal population by organising them into various mass organisations, also known as *sanghams*. A bird's eye view of these organisations is given below:

Dandakaranya[6] Adivasi Kisan Mazdoor Sangh (Dandakaranya Tribal Farmers & Labour Association)

Originally formed in 1981 in the Khammam district of Telangana state, the Dandakaranya Adivasi Kisan Mazdoor Sangh (DAKMS) is a semi-secret organisation. Sometime during 1983 its activities spread to the Bastar region of Dandakaranya in Chhattisgarh where it has a presence in almost every village in the area[7]. The issues around which DAKMS organises struggles from time to time include:[8]

- Protection of the self-respect of Adivasis
- Opposition to religious conversions.
- Protection of the land rights of Adivaisis.
- Distribution of the surplus lands of Zamindars.

- Privatisation and the entry of MNCs in Dandakaranya
- Dispossession and displacement owing to the launching of major projects.
- Ending forced marriages and social evils.
- Better wages for beedi/tendul leaf collectors, bamboo fellers, etc.
- Development of Bastar region, etc.

It has been reported that their rallies attracted huge audiences sometimes ranging around 10,000 to 37,000[9].

Krantikari Adivasi Mahila Sangh (Revolutionary Tribal Woman Association)

Krantikari Adivasi Mahila Sangh (KAMS) acquired an independent status of its own in 1987; before which they formed part of the Dandakaranya Adivasi Mahila Sangh (DAKMS)[10]. With the overarching objective of increasing the participation of tribal women, as the name suggests, KAMS espouses women's issues. These centre around:[11]

- Abolition of child marriages.
- Putting an end to forced marriages.
- Fight against the practice of 'Gotul' (common dormitories
- Equal rights for men and women in all spheres, including property
- Fight against male domination.
- Fight against superstition.
- Fight against all forms of discrimination and for protection from state violence.

Dandakarnya Adivasi Chhatra Sangh (Dandakarnya Tribal Students Association)

Dandakarnya Adivasi Chhatra Sangh (DAKCS) is a body of students and takes up issues relating to them. Launched in 1997, DAKCS is known to have organised struggles for the:

- Proper implementation of mid-day meal government scheme
- Provide free text books, disburse scholarships, implement schemes for providing free breakfast in welfare hostels, as well as better amenities to students and develop infrastructure such as school and hostel buildings.

In its wake, committees were said to have been formed at the school and hostel-level, and its members imparted 'political education'.

Krantikari Adivasi Balak Sangh (Revolutionary Tribal Children Association)

Krantikari Adivasi Balak Sangh (KABS) is believed to have been founded in 1998 in South Bastar and spread to several other areas in Dandakaranya in the space of a year. At different points in time, there have been contradictory reports about this organisation. At times, there were reports that the organisation functioned for a few years, but was wound up later. But, going by the list of Maoist organisations and affiliates proscribed by the various state governments, this organisation continues to exist in some form or the other, at least in Chhattisgarh and Odisha.[12] According to a well-known authority on the Maoists, KABS serves the purpose of 'intelligence gathering' for the Maoists.[13] It is said that KABS members keep a close watch on the entry and movement of 'strangers' and security forces in their areas. It is also believed that children provide logistics support when a squad visits a village.

Generally, KABS members are indoctrinated and taught about protecting the environment and keeping it clean and green. They are inculcated with discipline and encouraged to keep away from social evils and bad habits in order to lead a good life.

Janatana Sarkar (People's Government)

After having wrested control of these areas, the Maoists established their own government known as Janatana Sarkar.[14] More importantly, the Maoists have crushed feudal structures within the tribal society, and have, thus, empowered the adivasis.[15] Janatana Sarkar undertakes development works in Maoist strongholds. In a booklet entitled *New Peoples War in Dandakaranya*, published in 2000,[16] the then PW explained the relationship between development work and their movement as follows:

> *A Base Area, besides certain military aspects, would (and must) necessarily have a self-sufficient economy, without that, it can neither sustain itself, nor can it provide the ever growing needs of the party and people's armed forces. The enemy seeks to crush a Base Area not only by the force of arms but even by economic blockades.*

Development work is undertaken through various committees. These include: Vidya (education) Committee; Fish Committee (collective farming of fish); Health Committee; Pranthiya Vyvasaya Sangam (Regional Agriculture Committee); Forest Protection Committee; Vanji Society (grain bank); Panchayat Committee for arbitration; Credit Societies; Library Committee; and Sports Committee.

State Response[17]

In order to counter the Maoist challenge, the union government framed a National Policy and Action Plan in 2015. This envisages:

> *... a multi-pronged strategy involving security related measures, developmental interventions, ensuring rights & entitlements of local communities, etc*[18] *[and public perception management].*

Security Response

The union government shares intelligence with the governments in the various affected states, coordinates between the states, assists the state governments in imparting training to their respective police forces and conducts periodic review/coordinating meetings with the affected States.

The union government has initiated a scheme known as Security Relayed Expenditure (SRE) Scheme. This scheme has evolved over a long period of time and new elements of financial assistance have been added. Under this scheme, the union government provides funds to state governments for:

- Expenditure incurred for training and operational needs of state police forces and other security forces.
- Victim reassurance, i.e. payment of compensation to the family of civilians/security forces killed in Maoist violence; compensation for property of private individuals damaged in Maoist violence.
- Compensation for Maoist cadres and leaders who surrender to the authorities to join the mainstream as per the policy existing in that State.
- Expenditure incurred for community policing and village defence committees.
- Central Armed Police Forces (CAPFs), for augmenting infrastructure as well as for hiring helicopters for relief and rescue (evacuation), of injured personnel.
- The CAPFs to undertake Civic Action Programmes to win the trust of the local population in their areas of operation.
- Special Infrastructure Scheme and Fortified Police Stations to strengthen the State police forces.

Development Response[19]

As part of development response the union government has initiated an Integrated Action Plan (IAP), which subsumed the earlier Backward

Districts Initiative (BDI), and is now known as the Special Central Assistance. The main objective of the scheme is to fill the critical gaps in public infrastructure and services, which are urgently required.

The union government has initiated a Roads Programme in two phases—RRP-I[20] and RRP-II[21] for improving road connectivity in rural and Adivasi areas.

The Union government has initiated LWE Mobile Tower project in two phases to augment mobile connectivity in rural, remote and Adivasi areas. 2,335 towers have been erected in phase-I, while 4,072 are being erected in phase-II. This programme, much like the RRP, has dual benefits. While it increases connectivity for the populace, it also assists the security forces and has, therefore, been an irritant for the Maoists leading violent resistance and destruction.

Media Plan

As part of the Union government's public perception management (PPM) initiative, a media plan has been put in place. This programme includes Adivasi youth exchange programmes, radio jingles, documentaries and posters and pamphlets depicting Maoist violence and destruction of public property. This is essentially to counter Maoist propaganda and their mischievous actions of 'misguiding' the people.

As a result of these various initiatives in the various affected states, the Maoist presence and influence has significantly diminished. From a high of 160 districts in 2006[22], Maoists have been confined to 90 districts in 10 states, as of 2019[23]. Also, there has been a drastic reduction in the violence committed by the Maoists. The incidents of Maoist violence and fatalities have come down, while fatalities among Maoists remain high. The table below illustrates the Maoist violence profile:

Table 3: Maoist Violence Profile

Years	*2009*	*2010*	*2017*	*2018*
Incidents	2258	2213	908	833
Civ killed	591	720	188	173
SF killed	317	285	75	67
Maoists killed	220	172	163	225

Source: Adapted from Lok Sabha, Unstarred Q No. 489, June 25, 2019.

What Else Can be Done?

There is a need to have a long term action plan to integrate the tribal population with the mainstream and reintegrate the Maoists with the state. Some measures that could go long way for ensuring peace in the region are as under:

- Attend to the problems of the people in their everyday life Prevent tribal land alienation; improve health care and educational facilities to increase their accessibility and efficient delivery.
- Improve the purchasing capacity of an Adivasi (tribal) family by ensuring higher levels of income through organic farming, livestock and beekeeping.
- Save the Adivasi population from the vicious grip of money lenders.
- Speedy rehabilitation of displaced and dispossessed farmers from their land owing to the setting up of industries, mining or construction of dams, etc.
- Provide alternate sources of income before displacing Adivasis.
- Make administration responsive and accessible to the tribal population.
- Ensure full utilisation of funds allocated for Adivasi development without diversion to other regions of the state.
- Improve communication facilities and connectivity.
- Assist in procuring quality seeds and encourage organic farming.
- Ensure smooth functioning of educational institutions and provide career counselling for the meritorious students.
- Pay special attention to programmes for empowering women and youth.
- Create centres of excellence and cultural hubs to promote tribal culture.

Conclusion

The Maoist challenge will be defeated by the joint efforts of the Union and State governments. The various measures being adopted are evidence of the declining strength and influence of the Maoists and the rising success of the government.

NOTES

1. Andhra Pradesh was bifurcated in 2014 June and a new state of Telangana was created.
2. The Maoists refer to the tribal population as adivasis.
3. This section is largely based on internal documents of the Communist Party of India Maoist (CPI [Maoist]) and documents of its predecessor, Communist Party of India—Marxist-Leninist (People's War), popularly known as PWG, read during a field visit to Hyderabad, June 2019, and interviews with senior police officers, Hyderabad, June 2019.
4. Interview with Dr M Malakondaiah, former Director General of Police (DGP), Andhra Pradesh, Hyderabad, July 4, 2019.
5. *Ibid*. Abuz Maad (Unknown Hills) is a hilly-forest region stretching across Narayanpur district in Bastar region of the Central Indian State of Chhattisgarh and Gadchiroli district in the Western Indian State of Maharashtra. The highest leadership of the Maoists is believed to be residing here.
6. As per the *Encyclopaedia Britannica*, the Dandakaranya, physiographic region is in east-central India. Extending over an area of about 35,600 square miles (92,300 square km), it includes the Abujhmar Hills in the west and borders the Eastern Ghats in the east. The Dandakaranya includes parts of Chhattisgarh, Odisha, Telangana, and Andhra Pradesh states. It has dimensions of about 200 miles (320 km) from north to south and about 300 miles (480 km) from east to west.
7. Interview with a senior IPS officer, Raipur, April 2017.
8. *Ibid*.
9. P V Ramana, "Front Organisations of CPI (Maoist)," *IDSA Fellow Paper*, April 21, 2017, unpublished.
10. Interview with a senior IPS officer, Raipur, April 2016.
11. *Ibid*.
12. *Times of India*, New Delhi, May 2, 2018; *Economic Times*, New Delhi, May 16, 2016; *Economic Times*, May 5, 2009.
13. Interview with Mr K Srinivas Reddy, Editor, *Telangana Today*, Hyderabad, July 1, 2019.
14. Janatana Sarkar translates into English as 'People's government'. For a detailed description of Janatana Sarkar, as envisaged by the Maoists, please see P V Ramana, *Understanding India's Maoists: Select Documents*, New Delhi: IDSA-Pentagon Press, 2014, pp. 226-43.
15. Interview with a former high-rankling leader of the CPI (Maoist), February 16, 2013.
16. An internal document of the PW read during a field visit to Hyderabad, June 2019.
17. This section is largely based on information provided on the website of Ministry of Home Affairs, from time to time. The initiatives mentioned here have been culled from the author's personal databases and information available at https://mha.gov.in/division_of_mha/left-wing-extremism-division, as on September 2, 2019.
18. Lok Sabha, Unstarred Question No. 401, February 5, 2019.
19. The schemes/programmes mentioned here those designed exclusively for Maoist affected districts. Besides these, there are a plethora of development schemes and programmes that are implemented across the country, such as housing, rural electrification, protected drinking water, employment guarantee, free education and various pension schemes/incentives, etc.
20. This is officially known as Road Requirement Plan-I (RRP-I). Of the intended 5,422 km of roads to be laid, 4,809 km have been already been completed.

21. This is officially known as Road Connectivity Project-II (RRP-II). Under this programme 5,412 km of roads and 147 bridges are to be constructed at an estimated expenditure of Rs 11,725 cr. This programme is in various stages of progress at different places.
22. P V Ramana, "Policy of Wink and Fudge", *Indian Express*, New Delhi, September 23, 2006.
23. Please see Table 1.

7

India's Approach in Dealing with Radicalisation

Dr. Adil Rasheed

ABSTRACT

As global jihadist groups, such as the ISIS rise from the ashes of defeat in West Asia, they are looking at the vast population of the Indian sub-continent for new blood. Until this time, Indian security forces have mainly fought these forces at the operational and tactical levels, but the ideological challenge posed by these transnational actors, whose militant religious orientation is different from Indian schools of Islam and needs to be parsed and countered effectively. The good news is that India's effective and non-obtrusive forms of counter-radicalisation have been producing good results and have managed to quell the number of radicals joining global terrorist ranks. The prevailing debate is, will the present approach continue to prove effective or is there need for an upgrade?

Introduction

Terrorism has often been called a diabolical form of communication and strategic experts often read such acts of indiscriminate violence as non-verbal/non-intractable forms of political messaging. In fact, the intended targets of terrorism are not just the hapless victims of their attacks, but the people at large and the institutions of governance that are under attack.

The targeting of innocent worshippers in the early morning of Easter Sunday in Sri Lanka on 21 April 2019, which claimed over 250 lives,[1] was one such form of violent messaging that not only announced the rise of ISIS from the ashes of its defeat in Syria and Iraq, but also made its statement of intent about shifting its operations to a hitherto less explored region—the Indian subcontinent.

In fact, ISIS' subsequent announcements of forming a so-called 'Wilayat Al Hind' (its fictitious province in India)[2] and the appointment of a new leader (a certain Abu Muhammad Al Bengali)[3] to lead its charge in India and Bangladesh validate this dubious messaging. There are a variety of reasons for the growing attention of global jihadist organizations to focus their operations on South Asia now, which only accentuates the need for India and its neighbours to be wary of the rising threat.

Shift in Terror's Cost-benefit Analysis

To begin with, the depleting ranks of Al Qaeda and ISIS—following the decimation of their core bases in the Arab world and even Afghanistan—has increased their need for finding fresh blood in the immediate vicinity. Unfortunately, India with its second largest population of Muslims in the world, surrounded by four predominantly Muslim states in the region—Afghanistan, Pakistan, Maldives and Bangladesh—provides an attractive catchment area for global jihadist groups to swell their ranks.

The present political and socio-economic conditions in the region—with high rates of unemployment, communal angst and polarization of society—provide the right conditions for greater resonance of the radical message, even as the young Muslim generation is getting exposed to the murky world of social media and insular chat rooms. In addition, the socio-political payoff in terms of the long term damage and fissures that a terrorist attack could cause to the social fabric to derive more recruits and stronger bases in future has further incentivised terrorist groups to strike at the seams of countries in the subcontinent. This is clearly in evidence from the level of communal acrimony and violence witnessed in Sri Lanka after the dreadful attacks. For a long time, security experts believed, global jihadist organisations (Al-Qaeda and ISIS) were not so keen on targeting the subcontinent for a variety of reasons.

Being Salafi-Wahhabi in orientation, global jihadists had to engage in a turf war with Pak-backed Hanafi-Deobandi terror groups (like the Taliban) already active in the region since the 1990s, with whom they have fundamental doctrinal differences. Thus, Al-Qaeda could never subsume independent-minded Taliban into its Salafist fold, even though many of its leaders like Abu Qatada and Abu Musab Al Zarqawi did not accept the Taliban emirate as Islamic due to doctrinal differences.[4]

Even ISIS (which is more hard-line in its religious orientation than Al Qaeda) has found it difficult to convert Hanafi terror groups in Af-Pak region and Kashmir to its brand of jihadist Salafism. Thus, global jihadist groups never found greater doctrinal discordance with potential jihadist allies in other parts of the world than they have in this region.[5] This is one of the main reasons that radicalization of Al-Qaeda and ISIS has not found much resonance in a largely Hanafi India,[6] and is only more resonant in some southern provinces of the country as well as in states like Maldives and Sri Lanka, which have a sizeable Ahl-e-Hadeeth and Salafi population.

In addition, Al-Qaeda and ISIS never found India as critical to their global campaign against the West-led international order. Since the time of Bin Laden's fatwas of jihad in late-1990s, global jihadists identified 'crusading' Western powers as their primary adversary and have tried to gain religious legitimacy by projecting themselves as prophesised forces that would wage an apocalyptic war with the Christian West. India does not figure prominently in this narrative. Even, the recent Sri Lanka attacks were directed primarily against Christian worshippers and many Westerners staying in big hotels.[7] Moreover apart from gaining Indian recruits, India has offered little strategic value to global jihadists.[8] From the beginning, Al-Qaeda and ISIS have targeted failing Muslim states, to carve their own areas of influence. Therefore, they have preferred to focus more on countries like Iraq, Syria, Yemen, Afghanistan, Pakistan, Libya, Somalia etc. to spread their ideology through violent extremism.

India's vigilant security agencies, a largely law-abiding Muslim population and a strong secular social fabric have hardly allowed global jihadists any prospect of growth. However, as there is growing tension between neighbouring countries in the region and societies are getting increasingly polarized in the name of religion, the cost-benefit analysis of the wily terrorist groups is changing the earlier equations of profit.

Countering the Global Jihadist Narrative

For a long time, militaries and security agencies in the region focused primarily on the security aspects of the threat and did not care to understand the ideological literature that was fed to radicalize potential recruits to jihadist organizations. The Jihadist agenda is too complex to be understood by reading elementary literature on the subject or listening to the views of security experts to get to know the real strategic objectives of Jihad. It requires profound understanding of idea of Jihad as interpreted by different radical organisations. Whatever is relevant to the Al Qaeda may be at cross purposes to the ideology of ISIS.

However, the time has come to scan through an entire body of literature of Salafi-jihadist scholars, who have given a new meaning to the term 'Jihad' and introduced hitherto unknown concepts in Islamic theology in order to wage an indefinite and asymmetrical form of warfare against the entire international order. It is this literature, which radicalizes the views of young, impressionable minds, which needs to be countered.

When one looks into the origins of modern globalist jihad, one finds it to be the militant offshoot of the radical ideology of political Islam which emerged in the Arab world in the early 20th century, mainly out of the Salafi-Wahhabi movement. Having suffered failures at each stage of its political and violent campaigns, this movement introduced even more virulent and radicalized concepts to gain more potency in its extremist worldview and strategic thinking. Thus, global Jihadism has kept evolving a more strident and sharper strategic ideology for sustained transnational and asymmetric warfare against the humanist and liberal socio-political and economic international order for achieving its end state in a Salafist global caliphate.

Be it non-violent extremist groups like Hizbut Tahrir, or global jihadist organizations such as Al-Qaeda and ISIS, both have principally emerged out of a collective pool of Salafi-Wahhabi post-modern interpretation of the world, which provide a largely similar alternative to the modern social, political and economic way of life. The young, rebellious and impressionable mind is naturally drawn to any new alternate theories to existing socio-political systems. It is partly for this reason that many educated youth fall into the spell of this new variant of Islam and even end up accepting it's more radical and violent extremist ideas.

The main ideologues of Salafi jihadism that have created lot of literature to radicalise and spread this socio-political movement include Syed Qutb, Taqiuddin Nabhani, Ibn Taimiyya, Mohammad Farag, Abu Musab Al Suri, Abu Muhammad Al Maqdisi, Abu Bakr Naji, etc. Salafi jihadist organizations use a canon of books to radicalize young impressionable minds, such as *Al-Ahkam Al-Sultaniya* by 10th century Islamic theologian Abul Hasan Al-Mawardi as a basis for the theoretical reconstruction of an Islamic polity state and the ideal Caliphate. They indoctrinate their ranks with books on jihad by 14th century scholar Ibn Nuhaas, the body of work by controversial theologian Ibn Taimiyyah and Muhammad ibn Abdul Wahhab, etc.

The Economic System of Islam by Taqiuddin Nabhani[9] is often used by jihadist scholars as reference and it gives the details of so-called 'inherent structural anomalies' of the modern 'debt and speculation driven' financial system and calls for the replacement of the 'exploitative' fractional reserve system of banking with a 'non-usurious' model of 'Islamic finance'.

However, the principal inspiration for global jihadism to this day remains Syed Qutb's seminal book *Milestones (Ma' alim fi al-Tariq)*,[10] which speaks of the alleged incompatibility of Islam with the ideals of nationalism, capitalism and socialism and seeks the violent overthrow of most Muslim potentates. For firebrand ISIS recruits, Abu Bakr Naji's *Management of Savagery*[11] provides instructions for using barbarity, terrorism and a protracted state of war to whittle down Western armies in a protracted war of attrition, while lone wolf terrorists find the online book of Abu Musab Al Suri '*Call to Global Islamic Resistance*'[12] a useful reference.

Much of this radical literature, often accompanied with manuals on combat training and other propaganda material (like the ISIS' slick magazine *Dabiq*, Al Qaeda's *Inspire* and Hizbut-Tahrir's *Khilafah*), is easily accessible in the English language on the Internet. Much of the jihadist literature provides a lot of material on conducting lone wolf attacks and making weapons out of everyday products available in the market.

When it comes to India, the country gets an additional dose of terrorist hogwash from Pakistan-based terror groups, the writings of Talibani ideologues and incendiary articles published in online Urdu newspapers like *Al-Qalam* as well as e-magazines, such as Wyeth that foment insurgency in the Kashmir valley.

Having scanned through the foundational literature of global jihadism, it is important that Islamic scholars around the world develop effective counter-narratives against the poison of such incendiary texts. Many scholars in India, both theological and strategic experts, have currently started producing literature to counter the ideological challenge posed to impressionable minds in the country. There is also an attempt to devise ways for disseminating counter-narratives through effective strategic communication programmes to reverse the metastasizing menace of terrorism. However, it has to be admitted that the process has started very late in the day and there are few successes to write home about when it comes to counter-narrative messaging in the country.

India's Non-obtrusive Approach

When it comes to reversing the process of radicalization, India has so far adopted a nuanced, unobtrusive approach. The central government has thus far given enough latitude to provincial administration and state police to carry out counter-radicalisation and de-radicalisation programmes in keeping with the nature and sensibilities of each region at a given time and has avoided imposing any singular set of measures. However, there have reportedly been plans drawn by the central government to introduce a set of clearly articulated, standardised set of programmes, but such reports still lie in the realm of speculation.

Here, it is also important to differentiate the process of Islamist radicalization in the state of Jammu and Kashmir from the rest of India. From the Indian perspective, the problem related to the state of Jammu and Kashmir is not caused by religious radicalisation per se, but is a politically motivated seditious campaign conducted by the state of Pakistan against the country—an unfortunate vestige of India's partition in 1947. Thus, the political and social dynamics of the Kashmir problem has more elements to it than conventional jihadist radicalization.

In any case, the alert yet cautious approach of the Indian security agencies is to avoid over-reaction to the threat of radicalisation by conducting counter-radicalisation programmes in such a manner so as to avoid undue focus and politicisation of such endeavours. Thus, the effort of security agencies have been to isolate, localise and de-politicise operations so that no particular religious community feels unduly targeted. On the contrary, the attempt is to make the vast majority of the affected community a willing contributor towards solving the relatively few incidents of radicalisation and terrorism.

Thus, Indian security agencies have so far engaged families of suspects, community leaders and elders, religious preachers and imams as well as civil society members in the process of counselling, apprehending, de-radicalising and wherever possible rehabilitating suspects in order to contain the problem, without allowing sensitive matters to spiral out of control.

Curiously, Indian security agencies have preferred to employ sociological approaches instead of purely security-centric measures towards counter-radicalisation and have employed social, theological, psychological and cultural means for defusing the problem without taking recourse to heavy handed measures. As part of its de-radicalisation measures, Indian security agencies have initiated post-surrender and post-detention programs,[13] such as:

- Ideological or religious counselling,
- Vocational education,
- Recreational and psychological rehab,
- Behaviour modification programmes,
- Drug de-addiction centres,

- Personality development centres for youth,
- Inter-religious or inter-communal discourse programs,
- Post-release surveillance and care, as well as
- Involvement of family members and civil society to foster rehabilitation etc.

In this regard, the state of Maharashtra has launched an effective de-radicalisation programme[14] and has reportedly reclaimed many individuals affected by ISIS indoctrination. The programme is said to focus on the four aspects of the individual, family, religion and psychology and seeks to bring about a lasting change in the individual's belief system.

In the state of Jammu and Kashmir, attention is being given to reclaim drug addicts who often become victims of terrorist designs. Various other states, such as Andhra Pradesh, Telangana, Karnataka, Kerala, Tamil Nadu, Gujarat, Assam, Jammu and Kashmir, Delhi, Uttar Pradesh and Madhya Pradesh have been running their own counter-radicalisation programmes, which involve innovative and effective, multi-vector approaches.[15] The Indian government has also introduced schemes for greater engagement with communities affected by the scourge of radicalisation, their religious and political organizations, civil society, educational centres (schools and colleges), research and social activist groups.

Various prison programmes have been devised to prevent radicalisation, as well as to de-radicalise offenders etc. through religious and psychological counselling, vocational and other rehabilitation programmes. Greater inter-communal interaction through the hosting of literary and poetic symposiums, sporting events etc. is being conducted. Inter-communal housing schemes to prevent ghettoization and polarisation of communities have also been initiated.[16]

As stated above the government has also started research for developing effective counter-narratives and strategic communications measures, as well as for formulating appropriate legislative measures. Steps are also being taken to clampdown on drugs trafficking and to bust the linkages of drug addiction and radicalisation.

However, there is room for improvement when it comes to tackling economic and social prejudice and inequalities, speedy dispensation of justice, as well as cracking down on the funding of certain radicalizing groups in the country. There is also a need for:

- Launching counselling programmes for parents over raising their adolescents,

- Opening help lines for psychological counselling of the adolescents and teenagers,
- Providing career guidance and employment opportunities for the youth.

Apparently, there is historical evidence to prove the correlation between increase in youth population, also known (as youth bulges), which in sync with rapid urbanisation, has been a major contributor to political violence, especially in context of unemployment and poverty.

Many Muslim youth in India have found employment in Arab Gulf countries in recent decades. Although, their presence in these countries is often said to have increased the threat of radicalization, it is possible that the economic prosperity of Indian Muslim expatriates in the Gulf may have mitigated their inclination towards extremism. With Gulf States increasingly nationalizing their jobs, the return of the Indian expats to the country might accentuate the problem of radicalization and violent extremism in the future.

On a positive note, a large number of national role models coming from all communities and every section of the society serve as beacons for the youth to follow and emulate—national and societal icons and role models. Their success stories in a strong and secular India have helped citizens to remain committed to nation building and in keeping themselves away from the divisive messages emanating mainly from foreign sources.

Conclusion

In conclusion, the big debate is raging among Indian counter-radicalization experts on whether to continue following a diffuse, region-sensitive, low-key approach that has until now provided fairly acceptable results or should a more centralised, standardised, upgraded and coordinated policy be implemented across the country given the prospect of bigger challenges rising from the neighbourhood and witnessed in the state of Jammu and Kashmir. The jury is out and it is difficult to side with any of the arguments completely.

NOTES

1. Uditha Jayasinghe, 'Death Toll of Sri Lanka Bombings Lowered to About 250 From 359', *The Wall Street Journal*, 25 April 2019, https://www.wsj.com/articles/death-toll-of-sri-lanka-bombings-lowered-to-about-250-from-359-11556217671
2. Fayaz Bukhari and Alasdair Pal, 'Islamic State claims 'province' in India for first time after clash in Kashmir', *Reuters*, 11 May 2019, https://in.reuters.com/article/india-kashmir-islamic-state/islamic-state-claims-province-in-india-for-first-time-after-clash-in-kashmir-idINKCN1SH07Z
3. Raj Shekhar, 'IS names new emir in 'Bengal', issues threat to carry out attacks', 1 May 2019, https://timesofindia.indiatimes.com/india/is-names-new-emir-in-bengal-issues-threat-to-carry-out-attacks-in-india-and-bangladesh/articleshow/69122283.cms
4. Brynjar Lia, 'Abu Mus`ab al-Suri's Critique of Hard Line Salafists in the Jihadist Current', December 2007, Vol. I, No. I, CTC Sentinel, https://ctc.usma.edu/abu-musab-al-suris-critique-of-hard-line-salafists-in-the-jihadist-current/
5. Daud Khattak, 'Does Islamic State Have a Future in the AfPak Region?', *The Diplomat*, 20 December 2016, https://thediplomat.com/2016/12/does-islamic-state-have-a-future-in-the-afpak-region/
6. Vicky Nanjappa, 'ISIS' rise gives a boost to Wahhabism in India', *rediff.com news*, 7 July 2014, https://www.rediff.com/news/report/isiss-rise-gives-a-boost-to-wahhabism-in-india/20140707.htm
7. Adam Taylor and Rick Noack, 'Christianity under attack? Sri Lanka church bombings stoke far-right anger in the West', *The Washington Post*, 22 April 2019, https://www.washingtonpost.com/world/2019/04/22/christianity-under-attack-sri-lanka-church-bombings-stoke-far-right-anger-west/?utm_term=.7bb3b027d3de
8. Bhanuj Kappal, 'Decoding the ISIS phenomenon', *Livemint*, 7 September 2018, https://www.livemint.com/Leisure/jnXnDpCu0qpdw6Mx0p3tyH/Decoding-the-ISIS-phenomenon.html
9. The Economic System of Islam Taqiuddin an-Nabhani Hizb ut-Tahrir Fourth edition 1410/1418 A.H. (1990/1997 CE)Al-Khilafah Publications Suite 298 56 Gloucester Road London SW7 4UB e-mail: info@khilafah.comwebsite: http://www.khilafah.com
10. Syed Qutb, *Milestones*, Kazi Publications, Cairo 1964.
11. Abu Bakr Naji, *Management of Savagery: The Most Critical Stage Through Which the Islamic Nation Will Pass*, 2004 (published on the Internet).
12. Mustafa bin Abd al-Qadir Setmariam Nasar (aka Abu Musab Al Suri), *Call to Global Islamic Resistance* (2004), published on Internet
13. Adil Rasheed. 'Countering the Threat of Radicalisation: Theories, Programmes and Challenges', Journal of Defence Studies, Vol. 10, No. 2 April-June 2016, pp. 39-76, 2016
14. GS Bajpai and A. Kaushik, 'Thwarting Radicalization in India: Lacunae in Policy Initiatives', Social Crimonol 5: 166. doi: 10.4172/2375-4435.1000166
15. Adil Rasheed. 'Countering the Threat of Radicalisation: Theories, Programmes and Challenges', Journal of Defence Studies, Vol. 10, No. 2 April-June 2016, pp. 39-76, 2016
16. Ibid.

PART III

NIGERIA'S EXPERIENCE IN DEALING WITH VIOLENT EXTREMISM

8

Boko Haram Threats and Challenges of Nigeria's Counter Insurgency Strategy

Professor Kyari Mohammed

ABSTRACT

The Boko Haram insurgency is unprecedented and a different type of conflict from all previous internal security challenges that the security agencies have faced. Boko Haram has unleashed direct threat to lives, livelihoods and property in North-eastern parts of Nigeria. Religion inspired protest movement is now targeting culture and wants to impose Sharia on people by denouncing democratic values and equality among the people of all faiths. Nigeria is dealing with this challenge legally and through hard and soft options. Military alone does not have the answer to such complex conflicts thus non kinetic approach assume significance. It is imperative that Nigeria develop self-sufficiency in developing military capabilities to deal with Boko Haram. At the same time it is also imperative to avoid collateral damages and abuse of human rights. Counterinsurgency and counterterrorism must have human face and empathy. Out terrorizing people is a bad idea to pursue.

Introduction

Nigeria is Africa's most populous country with an estimated 198 million people, a military power in the sub region and continent with a history of quelling internal security challenges and contributing to multilateral peace keeping operations since the 1960s. Nigerian troops have participated in at least forty UN peace keeping missions, in the process successfully commanding eleven of these operations (Sanda 2010). Within the West African sub region Nigeria had helped enforce the peace and stabilize Liberia and Sierra Leone in the 1990s. Yet the Boko Haram insurgency within its borders and the struggle to contain it has raised serious concerns, about the country's response to new forms of warfare and lack of a definitive national security strategy to address it.

The Boko Haram insurgency is unprecedented and a different type of conflict from all previous ones that the security agencies had contained. Initially localized to the north east, it spread to some Nigerian urban centres and crossed the borders into neighbouring Niger, Chad and Cameroon republics. The insurgency has led to thousands of deaths, estimated at between 32,000 and 100,000 (Tukur 2017), displacement of more than two million persons, and caused the economic devastation of an otherwise food rich region of the country, now facing monstrous humanitarian disaster. The Boko Haram is reckoned to be one of Nigeria's deadliest and violent groups ever whose adherents are fanatically committed to their beliefs, and the group continuously changes its strategies and tactics including a resort to asymmetrical warfare to survive Nigeria's military onslaught.

Boko Haram is a threat to Nigeria at multiple levels with wide ranging consequences. First, it is a direct threat to lives, livelihoods and property in North-eastern parts of Nigeria. Localized around Maiduguri the Borno state capital, Boko Haram was most active and caused the most damage to lives and property in Borno, Yobe, Bauchi, and Adamawa states in its formative years. The group's violence appeared to be in concentric circles with Borno as its centre. Second, Boko Haram expanded its operations to the rest of northern Nigeria. By 2011 the group had launched attacks on Kano, Kaduna, Abuja, and as far south as Kogi state. In Abuja, the federal capital territory, Boko Haram had hit the national police headquarters and the United Nations Office complex in quick succession in July and August 2011. This act traumatized the international community and deeply embarrassed the government of Nigeria. Third, Boko Haram had become a real threat to Nigeria's neighbours Niger, Chad and Cameroon republics, which had until 2014 viewed the insurgency as a local Nigerian problem in which they were not eager to get involved. Attacks on their soils had squarely brought them into the conflict. These cross-border incursions by the insurgents led to the resuscitation of the regional military coalition, the Multi National Joint Task Force (MNJTF) which became a useful instrument in fighting the insurgency. Fourth, Boko Haram is not yet a threat to global peace and security but the potentials exist.

By 2014 Boko Haram had laid claims to large swathes of territory in parts of Borno, Yobe and Adamawa states. To cap it all, Boko Haram leader, Abubakar Shekau, declared a "caliphate" from Gwoza and offered allegiance and subordination to the Islamic State of Syria and Levant (ISIS/ ISIL). These symbolic acts and the abduction of 276 female students in their school in Chibok in April 2014, the cold-blooded killing of 42 school children at Mamudo and 59 at Buni Yadi in 2013 and 2014 respectively, the escalating violence on combatants and non-combatants alike, and wholesale ravaging of communities, had seriously called to question the capacity of the Nigerian state. The state had responded to the insurgent's violence with violence of its own, thus eliciting accusations of human rights abuse (Amnesty International 2012, 2015; Human Rights Watch 2012).

Fighting an insurgency based on religious belief is difficult. Though Nigeria has battled foes much bigger than Boko Haram, the group's unflinching belief in its cause as divinely inspired, its suicidal inclinations, its belief in salvation through martyrdom and its resort to asymmetric warfare makes it a difficult enemy for a conventional national military force. Thus, the Nigerian military has succeeded in substantially degrading the military capacity of Boko Haram, compelled it to abandon territories it occupied, and pushed it into operating in small bands. The aim of this chapter is to account for the threats and challenges posed by the Boko Haram insurgency to Nigeria and beyond and assess the strategies adopted to contain it.

Evolution of Boko Haram

Boko Haram began as a religion inspired protest movement of young person desirous of living a pious life in contradistinction to the sleaze and corruption of the larger society. They set up a commune in rural Kanama in the Yobe state of Nigeria in 2002. Their rejection of secularism, democracy, Western education, modernity and all its associated values defined Boko Haram. These messages remained constant except for change in emphasis. Mohammed Yusuf a fiery but not well learned Maiduguri based preacher became the ideologue and the arrow head of this group. Mohammed Yusuf developed his distinctly violent and extremist ideology that excommunicated all Muslims who did not share their views. By 2009 Boko Haram's ideology and religious views as a fringe Islamic group had become developed. The collision with the state as well as other Islamic groups had started by 2008. Boko Haram was defeated in an open confrontation with the military on the streets of Maiduguri between 28 and 31 July 2009. Mohammed Yusuf and several alleged members of the group were killed extra judicially thus sowing the seed of martyrdom and adding new grievances to existing ones. Following its defeat, the group went underground, regrouped and resurfaced in September 2010 with a prison break at Bauchi. This post 2009 phase of the conflict developed into an insurgency with intent to destabilize parts of the federation.

It was under leadership of the mercurial Abubakar Shekau that Boko Haram became increasingly violent and gravitated towards terrorism. As from 2010 through to 2013, the group engaged in urban warfare while embedded among civilians thus making it difficult for the military to apprehend them. Their expulsion from urban to rural areas in June 2013 made the group even more violent. In the ungoverned spaces they waxed stronger and occupied territories. Therefore the military's attempt to dislodge the insurgents from their urban recesses came with collateral damage that continued to be an albatross around the military's necks.

The Development of a National Security Framework

Nigeria had no laws specifically dealing with terrorism until the enactment of the Terrorism Prevention Act in 2011. The early response to the Boko Haram insurgency was primarily the use of military force which turned out to be insufficient and counterproductive quite early in the counter insurgency operations. Without a legal framework, and the police too indolent to engage in diligent prosecution of large number of cases before the courts, state officials resorted to extra judicial measures. This tarnished the image of the nation abroad and caused it heavily in reputation.

The Boko Haram insurgency confronted Nigeria with limited options in dealing with the aftermath: coercion, persuasion or a combination of both. The military was deployed in internal security operations to quell the Boko Haram uprising following inability of the police to cope in July 2009. Considering the group's very hostile preaching and demonization of government officials and especially security personnel there was little or no room left for diplomacy or any non-military resolution of the conflict. Besides

Nigeria's counter insurgency strategy was primarily coercion with half-hearted attempts at soft options following intractability of the conflict. It took five years of unceasing conflict with enormous cost to lives and property, and projecting the government in bad light both domestically and internationally, for the Federal Government to come up with its first attempt at soft options in 2014. Nigeria launched the Nigerian National Security Strategy (NNSS) and its main objective is to "apply all elements of national power to ensure physical security, build individual and collective prosperity, cause national development and promote Nigeria's influence in regional, continental and global affairs" (NNSS 2014). The strategy identified the country's core national security interests as the peoples' security and welfare, defence of its territorial integrity and sovereignty, and promotion of peace, democracy and economic growth and social justice. The most potent threats to the country, according to the strategy document include terrorism, insurgency, transnational organized crime, porous borders, and climate change, amongst others.

The Terrorism Prevention Act 2011 as amended in 2013 is Nigeria's first attempt at domesticating international anti-terrorism conventions and providing a comprehensive legal regime for combating terrorism. This Act defines what amounts to terrorism and prescribes the death penalty for the offence. The National Counter Terrorism Strategy was developed by the Centre for Counter Terrorism in the Office of the National Security Adviser in order to counter terrorism and prevent violent extremism. Its main objective was to ensure public safety using a whole of government approach (Bala and Ouedraogo, 2108:4).

The Policy Framework and National Plan of Action for Preventing and Countering Violent Extremism (P-CVE) is Nigeria's policy road map for preventing and countering violent extremism. This plan rests on four key objectives of: (1) strengthening institutions and coordination in countering and preventing violent extremism; (2) bolstering the rule of law and access to justice; (3) building community resilience through participation; and (4) integrating strategic communication into preventing and countering violent extremism (Musa 2018).

All aspects of the National Strategy were developed in the course of the conflict and are currently being implemented. This means that any gaps or shortcomings or positive lessons learnt can only be applied to future operations. Without a functional and well tested national security strategy Nigeria continues to rely on the military option in the counter insurgency operations with a sprinkling of the soft options.

The Hard Option

The fight against insurgency took on a distinctly military form from inception. The Joint Task Force (JTF) model involving a plethora of security agencies was cobbled together to respond. This surfeit of agencies also threw up its own challenges, especially as the military found it difficult to deploy and synergize with non-military personnel. This in part informed the disbandment of the JTF to be replaced by the Seventh Division of the Nigerian Army in 2013.

Another challenge of the war against Boko Haram was how to fight urban warfare in a heavily populated city like Maiduguri with little collateral damage. This is more so as Boko Haram will deliberately provoke reprisals by attacking military patrol vehicles or posts, knowing full well that the military will retaliate, often with maximum force. This military brutality against civilians as well as mutual suspicion between the local population and the military created a serious communication gap. The local populace piqued by cases of human rights abuses by security forces, through the Borno Elders and Leaders of Thought (BELT) called for its withdrawal (Olugbode 2011; Idris and Ibrahim 2012).

For all practical purposes Nigeria still prosecutes its counter insurgency operations without the much anticipated support of its Western allies. Limited cooperation in intelligence sharing, technical support and training has not made the desired impact. Robust support from Nigeria's allies will obviously have shortened the duration of the war. The activities of some international NGOs whose operations were opaque also created distrust between them and the military and some government agencies. Nigeria's coercive counter insurgency operations has succeeded in degrading the capacity of Boko Haram to take and hold territory, to take the fight to far off parts of the country such as Kano, Kaduna and Abuja with ease, and to threaten Nigeria's corporate existence. However the group still has enough capacity to sufficiently irritate the military at home while denting the country's image abroad.

Limitations of the Hard Option

The military option as adopted by Nigeria had obvious limitations which prolonged the conflict and pushed it towards intractability. First, military force has limited utility in counter insurgency operations. This was the first, and for many years, the only option available to the Nigerian state. The use of excessive force added fodder to the fuel and escalated the conflict, radicalized and mobilized passive members of the group and threw up new grievances that sustained the conflict. It was believed Boko Haram will wither away like Maitatsine. This victory turned out to be pyrrhic as the movement regrouped and resurfaced with even more violence in 2010. Military counter insurgency has succeeded in substantially degrading the capacity of Boko Haram to launch the mega attacks of 2011 to 2014 when it took the fight to the military including sacking their barracks in Monguno, Baga, Gwoza and Maiduguri or chasing troops across the border into Cameroon and Niger. They have also succeeded in reclaiming territory earlier lost to the insurgents; however, the insurgents have not been completely defeated as claimed. A complete cessation of conflict leading to return of normalcy will require more than brute force.

Second, the use of force as mentioned earlier led to human rights abuses and loss of hearts and minds by the military. As a reaction to the unceasing criticism of its excesses and non-compliance with its rules of engagement, the military established a Human Rights Desk aimed at addressing these concerns in conflict areas (NA 2016, Reliefweb, 2016). Third, the human rights abuses created a serious diplomatic problem for the country. Nigeria's attempt to procure arms and ammunition in the international market made brick wall even from its allies.

The Soft Option

By March 2014, Nigeria had reached the conclusion that it required more than brute force to defeat the Boko Haram insurgency. Thus, the Office of the National Security Adviser rolled out what it termed the soft options in countering violent extremism leading to terrorism. The first of these programmes was aimed at Boko Haram detainees in prison and breaching the divide between government and communities. This programme included de-radicalization, counter radicalization and strategic communication. This initiative, though promising, was adversely slowed down by the defeat of Goodluck Jonathan in 2015 and the allegations of theft and grand larceny levelled against the former National Security Adviser for diverting funds meant for prosecution of the counter insurgency operations to fund the presidential campaign of the former president. However, the state did not completely jettison the idea. This programme later formed the nucleus of the NNSS.

The Programme on Preventing and Countering Violent Extremism (P-CVE) is a component of the NNSS aimed at rehabilitating and reintegrating repentant Boko Haram militants back into their communities after twelve weeks of de-radicalisation and vocational training in a secure facility in Gombe. The OSC has since graduated its first batch of 95 out of 254 graduates including 20 minors (Leman 2018). However, the programme has had limited success and drawn a lot of criticisms. First, the emphasis on ex-insurgents to the detriment of victims does not seem to go down well with the communities that are expected to receive the deracialised. The communities' perception that ex-insurgents were favoured over and above victims and survivors needs to be handled with utmost caution. Second, stakeholders believe it is too early to start reintegrating ex-insurgents as the conflict is still on going. They, therefore, suggested a "ten-year window before defecting members can be reintegrated into local communities" (CDD 2016, 2). Reintegration is a very important component of DDR, however, for this to succeed; the communities must be carried along.

The Failure of Dialogue

The Nigerian state has not decided on whether to engage Boko Haram in talks or not. This may not be unconnected with the state's belief that it could militarily crush the insurgency, and in part to the perceived political coloration of the movement. Dialogue was an option that was not foreclosed but was not seriously pursued. Lines of communication between the state and Boko Haram were maintained but all efforts were clandestine.

There were various attempts at dialoguing with Boko Haram at both state and national levels. The late Ambassador Usman Gaji Galtimari chaired two of these committees set up by the government of Borno state and the Federal Government in 2009 and 2012 respectively. The Turaki Committee was charged with the responsibility of developing a framework for the granting of amnesty, disarmament of combatants, development of a "Victim Support Programme", and suggesting mechanisms for addressing the root causes of the insurgency (Abdullahi 2018, 178). The Turaki Committee led to the establishment of another committee on continuous dialogue with the insurgents. All efforts at dialogue were thwarted by the seeming unwillingness of Shekau to negotiate, bogus claims of impostors hoping to fleece the government posing as Boko Haram representatives, the fractious splintering of the insurgents, and the change of government in Nigeria. Incidentally Boko Haram did not show any eagerness to embrace the government's dialogue or amnesty carrot either. An indecisive government and a truculent insurgent leader ensured the continuity of military conflict in spite of attempts at mediation.

While both sides seemed bent on holding onto their hardened positions, the abduction of over 276 school girls at a secondary school in Chibok in April 2014 was to bring the two sides to engage a little more seriously. The Chibok incident brought global notoriety and dishonour to Boko Haram but also put tremendous pressure on the government to rescue the girls. A similar school girls' abduction in Dapchi in February 2018 also led to a negotiated settlement. Clearly the state and Boko Haram had been dialoguing with the assistance of some intermediaries but this has not led to a more comprehensive peace.

Conclusion

Nigeria has fought the Boko Haram insurgency continuously for ten years now. This has cost the country heavily in human lives and limbs, economic losses, infrastructural damage, and loss of social cohesion. The threat of the insurgents to national security has been diminished but not obliterated. Insurgency is a different kind of warfare for which Nigeria was not adequately prepared as a country, therefore, it responded with military force only for the first five years. There are several lessons to be learnt from the insurgency and the counter insurgency operations.

The Boko Haram insurgency is a potent threat to Nigeria and its neighbours, and if not handled with caution, it could threaten regional, continental and global peace by linking up with international jihadi movements. Second, Nigeria's COIN has shown that military force, though critical to defeating an insurgency, is not enough to end an insurgency or build peace. This will require soft options. Since 2014 Nigeria had used a combination of both hard and soft options, with the former dominating.

Another important lesson is that Nigeria should prepare for all forms of conflicts by developing a national strategy before the onset of war. Lack of a defined national security strategy was responsible for some of the gaps in the COIN operations. Policy, legal and operational frameworks should be developed, revised and modified from time to time. This will guarantee operational efficiency and effectiveness.

The issue of human rights abuses and war crimes will continue to be an albatross around the neck of the military. The best guarantee is to train troops to comply with the Geneva Convention and operate by their rules of engagement, and desist from human rights abuses in all situations. If this is not done, the reputation of the armed forces and image of the country will be dented.

National security is too serious an issue for narrow political bickering and scoring cheap political points. Political leaders and politicians, whether in government or opposition should not politicise national security issues. There must be a national consensus on state threatening security issues such that no political group should take advantage of national adversity. This way the country can easily and quickly end the insurgency.

This war has shown the futility of depending on foreign countries for basic military equipment. Nigeria should develop the capacity to produce basic arms and armaments by rejuvenating its Defence Industries Corporation and investing in research and development for military purposes. There is no alternative to self-sufficiency if Nigeria is to take its pride of place as a military power in the African continent.

REFERENCES

1. Abdul, Olayemi (2013), "Jonathan Shocks Borno Elders, Says FG Won't Withdraw JTF". May 8. www.newsdiaryonline.com/jonathan-shocks-borno-elderssays-fg-wont-withdraw. Accessed January 2016.
2. Abdulhamid, Y.H. (2018), "Before Operation Lafiya Dole: The Nigerian Army in the Counter Insurgency Operations in the Nigerian North East", in A.M. Ashafa and H. Jibrin, eds., The Nigerian Army in a Democracy: Essays in Honour of Lt Gen TY Buratai. Kaduna, Pyla Mak, pp. 295-308.
3. Abdullahi, Bolaji (2018), *On a Platter of Gold: How Jonathan Won and Lost Nigeria*. Lagos: Kachifo.
4. Abubakar, Rabe (2016), "DHQ Establishes Camp for Repentant Boko Haram Members", Press Release Nigeria, April 5, https://prnigeria.com/2016/04/05/dhq-establishes-camp-repentant-boko-haram-members/ Accessed 13 April 2018.
5. Adeniyi, Olusegun (2011), *Power, Politics and Death: A Front Row Account of Nigeria under the Late President Yar'Adua*. Lagos: Kachifo.
6. Adesomoju, Ade (2018), "AGF seeks stiffer sanctions against terrorists, financiers in new bill", *Punch newspaper*, Lagos. 10 April. http://punchng.com/agf-seeks-stiffer-sanctions-against-terrorists-financiers-in-new-bill/ Accessed 13 April 2018.
7. Adewumi, A.A. (2014), "The Battle for the Minds: The Insurgency and Counter—Insurgency in Northern Nigeria", *West Africa Insight*, Vol. 4 No. 2, 3—11.
8. Amnesty International [AI] (2012), Nigeria: Trapped in a Cycle of Violence. London: AI. https://www.amnesty.org/en/documents/AFR44/043/2012/en/ Accessed September 2017.
9. Amnesty International (2015), "Stars on Their Shoulders, Blood on Their Hands": War Crimes Committed by the Nigerian Military. London: Amnesty International. http://www.amnesty.org/download/ Accessed 10 April 2018.
10. Anwar, Kabiru (2017), "Boko Haram vs Hunters: Inside Adamawa's Other War", *Daily Trust*, 9 August, https://www.dailytrust.com.ng/news/general/boko-haram-vs-hunters-inside-adamawa-s-other-war/210667.html. Accessed 5 May 2018.
11. Bala S. and Emile Ouedraogo (2018), National Security Strategy Development: Nigeria Case Study, Working Paper Preliminary Draft. Dakar: Africa center for Strategic Studies. https://africacenter.org/wp-content/uploads/2018/07/Session-3-Bala-ENGLISH-1.pdf. Accessed 21 June 2019.
12. Barlow, Eeben (2017), "The Rise, Fall, and Rise Again of Boko Haram", February 1. http://africahornnow.com/2017/02/17/rise-fall-rise-boko-haram/. Accessed 21 June 2019.
13. BBC (2014), "Boko Haram Crisis: Nigeria Fury Over US Arms Refusal", 11 November. www.bbc.com/news/world-africa-30006066. Accessed June 2019.
14. Campbell, John (2014), U.S. Policy to Counter Nigeria's Boko Haram, Special Report No. 70. New Council on Foreign Relations. https://www.cfr.org/report/us-policy-counter-nigerias-boko-haram. Accessed 21 June 2019.
15. Care (2018), "Humanitarian Crisis in Nigeria and the Lake Chad Basin".
16. https://www.care.org/emergencies/global-hunger-crisis/humanitarian-crisis-nigeria-and-lake-chad-basin. Accessed 14 April 2018.
17. CDD (2016), "Policy Brief: Stakeholders' Dialogue on Government Approaches to Managing Defecting Violent Extremists", Abuja: Centre for Democracy and Development, nd. C. 2016.

18. Collyer, Rosie (2017), "Meet Aisha, A Former Antelope Hunter Who Now Tracks Boko Haram", *The Guardian*, 8 February. https://www.theguardian.com/world/2017/feb/08/antelope-hunter-boko-haram-nigeria. Accessed 5 May 2018.
19. Dakas, C.J. Dakas (2014), "Interrogating Nigeria's Counter Terrorism Strategy Through the Prism of Law and Human Rights", *West Africa Insight*, Vol. 4, No. 2, pp. 20-24.
20. Dasuki, Sambo (2014), "Sambo Dasuki: Nigeria's soft Approach to Countering Terrorism": Being a Presentation by Sambo Dasuki, National security Adviser on 18th March 2014 on the Roll out of Nigeria's soft Approach to Countering Terrorism held at Abuja, Nigeria. http://dailypost.ng/2014/03/19/sambo-dasuki-nigerias-soft-approach-countering-terrorism/ Accessed 14 April 2018.
21. FGN (1999), *Constitution of the Federal Republic of Nigeria*. http://www.wipo.int/edocs/lexdocs/laws/en/ng/ng014en.pdf. Accessed 26 April 2018.
22. Freeman, C. (2015), "South African Mercenaries secret war on Boko Haram". *The Telegraph*, www.telegraph.co.uk/news/worldnews/africaandindianocean/nigeria/11596210/South-African-mercenaries-secret-war-on-Boko-Haram.html. Accessed September 2017.
23. Higazi, A., B. Kendhammer, K. Mohammed, MA de Montclos and A. Thurston (2018), "A Response to Jacob Zenn on Boko Haram and al-Qa'ida", *Perspectives on Terrorism*, 12 (2). http://www.terrorismanalysts.com/pt/index.php/pot/article/view/703/1374. Accessed 28 June 2019.
24. Human Rights Watch (2012), *Spiraling Violence: Boko Haram Attacks and Security Force Abuses in Nigeria*. Chicago: Human Rights Watch. https://www.hrw.org/report/2012/10/11/spiraling-violence/boko-haram-attacks-and-security-force-abuses-nigeria. Accessed 13 April 2018.
25. Ibekwe, Nicholas (2017), "Nigerian Military Accuses Amnesty International of Fabricating Report of Extra Judicial Killings, Torture", *Premium Times*, 22 February, https://www.premiumtimesng.com/news/headlines/224261-nigerian-military-accuses-amnesty-international-fabricating-report-extrajudicial-killings-torture.html. Accessed 11 April 2018.
26. Idris, Hamza and Yahaya Ibrahim (2012), "Nigeria's Borno Elders Cry Out ...Genocide Going On in Borno, Yobe", *Daily Trust*, 12 August. https://allafrica.com/stories/201208170640.html. Accessed 28 June 2019.
27. Idris, Hamza and Ibrahim Sawab (2013), "Hopes Turn to Despair over 'Civilian JTF'", *Weekly Trust*, 29 June. https://www.dailytrust.com.ng/weekly/index.php/new-news/13113-hopes-turn-to-fears-over-civilian-jtf. Accessed 13 April 2018.
28. Leman, Hajara (2018), "Operation Safe Corridor Graduates 95 Ex-insurgents in Gombe State", *The Herald*, http://www.herald.ng/operation-safe-corridor-graduates-95-ex-insurgents-in-gombe-state/ Accessed 26 April 2018.
29. Mantzikos, Ioannis (2014), "Boko Haram Attacks in Nigeria and Neighbouring Countries: A Chronology", *Perspectives on Terrorism*, 8(6). http://www.terrorism analysts.com/pt/index.php/pot/article/view/391/html. Accessed 28 June 2019.
30. Mohammed, K. (2014), "The Message and Methods of Boko Haram", Marc Antoine Perouse de Montclos, ed., Boko Haram: Islamism, Politics, Security and the State in Nigeria. Leiden: IFRA—Nigeria, pp. 9-32. https://openaccess.leidenuniv.nl/bitstream/handle/1887/23853/ASC-075287668-3441-01.pdf. Accessed June 2019.
31. Mohammed, K. (2018), "The Origins of Boko Haram", Carl Levan and Patrick Ukata, eds., *Oxford Handbook of Nigerian Politics*. Oxford: Oxford University Press. Pp. 583-604.
32. Musa, Yaminu (2018), "Statement by Head of Nigeria Delegation to United Nations

High Level Conference on Counter Terrorism", New York. 28-29 June. https://www.un.org/counterterrorism/ctitf/sites/www.un.org.counterterrorism.ctitf/files/S3-Nigeria.pdf. Accessed 21 June 2019.

33. Musa, Yaminu (2018b), "Nigeria's Counter Insurgency Strategy: Boko Haram in Perspective", http://ctc.gov.ng/nigerias-counter-insurgency-strategy-boko-haram-in-perspective/. Accessed 21 June 2019.
34. Mustapha, A.R. (2014), ed., *Sects and Social Disorder: Muslim Identities and Conflict in Northern Nigeria*. New York: James Currey.
35. Nairaland (2011), "JTF Accuses Borno Elders of Backing Boko Haram—Politics". 15 July. www.nairaland.com/713753/jtf-acuses-borno-elders-backing. Accessed June 2013.
36. NNSS (2014), Nigeria National Security Strategy. http://ctc.gov.ng/wp-content/uploads/2017/08/NIGERIAN-NATIONAL-SECURITY-STRATEGY-2014.pdf. Accessed 12 January 2019.
37. Olugbode, Michael (2011), "Nigeria: JTF Accuses Borno Elders of Backing Boko Haram", This Day, 15 July. https://allafrica.com/stories/201107150485.html. Accessed 28 June 2019.
38. Punch (2019), "Boko Haram resurgence: Buratai retracts, commends soldier", Punch 21 June. https://punchng.com/boko-haram-resurgence-buratai-retracts-commends-soldier/. Accessed 22 June 2019.
39. Reliefweb (2016), "Nigeria Creates a Military Human Rights Desk", see https://reliefweb.int/report/nigeria/nigeria-creates-military-human-rights-desk. Accessed 13 April 2018.
40. Reliefweb (2017), "Nigeria Situation: UNHCR Regional Update 01-31 January. https://reliefweb.int/report/nigeria/nigeria-situation-unhcr-regional-update-01-31-january-2017. Accessed 5 May 2018.
41. Reliefweb (2018), "Nigeria: Humanitarian Response Plan (January-December 2018)", February 7. https://reliefweb.int/report/nigeria/nigeria-humanitarian-response-plan-january-december-2018. Accessed 5 May 2018.
42. Sanda, J.G. (2010), "Nigeria's Global Role in Peacekeeping: From the Congo through Lebanon to Bosnia Herzegovina", A.M. Jega and J.W. Farris, eds., *Nigeria at Fifty: Contributions to Peace, Democracy and Development*. Abuja: Shehu Musa Yar'Adua Foundation.
43. Tar, Usman (2018), "The Ecology of Insurgency and Counter Insurgency: The Impact of Armed Conflict on Environmental Security in North Eastern Nigeria", Paper Read at the First Zonal Annual Conference of the Nigeria Political Science Association, at Federal University Kashere, 24-27 April.
44. Tukur, S. (2017), "Shocking Revelation: 100,000 Killed, Two Million Displaced by Boko Haram Insurgency, Borno Governor Says" in www.premiumtimes.com, February 13, 2017. Accessed 11 June 2017.
45. US Homeland Security, (2012), Guide to the Analysis of Insurgency. https://www.hsdl.org/?abstract&did=713599. Accessed 22 June 2019.
46. Ward A. (2018), "How Do You Define Terrorism?", *The Rand Blog*. June 4. https://www.rand.org/blog/2018/06/how-do-you-define-terrorism.html. Accessed 21 June 2019.
47. Interviews: Gaji Galtimari and Gambo Gubio, 2014, Maiduguri. Mallam Ibrahim Isa, 2015, Abuja.

9

Cross Border Linkages between Violent Extremist Groups Operating in Sahel Corridor, Chad Basin and North African States

Usman A. Tar and Samuel Baba Ayegba

ABSTRACT

Violent extremist groups are increasingly becoming transnational, deeply networked, and seem to defy geopolitical and legal boundaries. This portends a great danger for national and international forces that seek to counter them. This chapter examines the linkage between violent extremist groups in the Sahel region, Lake Chad Basin and North African States and argues that the transformation of the world into a global village through the use of internet may well explain the escalation of violent extremism in the Sahel region. The chapter relies on secondary data and adopted the Social Movement Theory as a framework of analysis. It revealed that, the strategic location of the Sahel corridor and its vast ungoverned spaces has provided a "centre of gravity" for violent extremist groups to operate unchallenged, and therefore, suggests that since the Counter-Terrorism approach of using military approaches for Countering Violent Extremism (CVE) the Sahel has not yielded the desired results, governments and international partners should shift ground, by following non-coercive CVE means, that are targeted at countering violent extremist recruitment and ideology.

Introduction

In recent times, violent extremism as a global threat has continued to evolve. This has occasioned the increasing destabilization of the international security environment. Thus, the world has witnessed the proliferation of violent extremist groups such as Al-Qaeda, ISIS, Al-Shabaab, Boko Haram among others. The Sahel corridor, Chad Basin and North African States, have been categorized as the most conflict-ridden sub-regions in the world (N'Diaye, 2011). The increasing interconnectedness of global societies, paves way for international movement of people and illegal weapons from one country to another. Consequently, the Sahel region has become the epicenter of Jihadism in Africa, as Islamist groups such as Boko Haram have continued to use the vast and relatively empty area to hide, recruit and organize Jihad (Pujol-Mazzini, 2018).

Consequently, this paper examines the linkage between violent extremist groups operating in the Sahel corridor, Chad Basin and North African states. The paper is divided into seven connected sections. Following the introduction, we examine the key concepts that scaffold this paper, and dovetail into the theoretical framework of analysis. The third section contains the background of violent extremism in the Sahel region. The fourth section maps the dynamics of violent extremism. The fifth section traces the linkage between violent extremist groups in the study area. In the sixth section, we identify the various strategies and trajectories for countering violent extremism in the sub-region. In the seventh and final section is the conclusion.

Conceptual and Theoretical Framing

In this section, we describe the key concepts related to this chapter.

Globalization—is viewed as a process whereby social relations attain distance-less and borderless qualities, so that human lives are progressively played out in the world as a single place. The overall notion of globalization is that, technological advancement has created a milieu in which the global marketplace, rather than separate national markets is the important arena for economic competitiveness; this change has transformed the political balance among states, alliances and other interest groups (Scholte, 1997). In this chapter, Scholte's (1997), definition of globalization is adopted as the working definition in this chapter.

Violent Extremism—like it is with many concepts in the social sciences and humanities, there is no universal consensus regarding what exactly constitutes violent extremism. Thus, violent extremism is rarely defined. Violent extremism is usually believed to be a more comprehensive concept than 'terrorism', though they are largely identical in use. However, Glazzard and Zeuthen, (2016), argued that, though USAID's description is extensive, violent extremism is perhaps applied much more narrowly i.e. to Islamist violence alone, disregarding the many other forms of ideologically motivated or justified violence that affect countries. They further argued that, most of this work is on terrorism in or threatening the West. USAID's definition which views violent extremism as supporting, engaging in, formulating or otherwise supporting ideologically motivated or justified violence to further social, economic or political aims, is adopted as the working definition in this chapter.

Countering Violent Extremism (CVE)—There is no common agreement concerning what precisely is countering violent extremism, nor what form it should take. Introduced as part of an Obama administration counterterrorism strategy, the axiom "Countering Violent Extremism" (CVE) refers to a wide-ranging spread of ideas and strategies, aimed at deterring and understanding radicalisation According to the US Department of Homeland Security (2016), CVE denotes to proactive actions to counter efforts by extremists to recruit, radicalize, and mobilize followers to violence. Fundamentally, CVE actions intend to address the conditions and reduce the factors that most likely contribute to recruitment and radicalization by violent extremists. Where possible, CVE is to be fused into existing programs related to public safety, resilience, inclusion, and violence prevention (United Nations Office for Drugs and Crimes, 2018). In this chapter CVE is defined as non-coercive resources and strategies put in place by national governments and international organizations, to counter the threat of violent extremism.

Theoretical Framing—There are many possible theoretical frameworks that might be applied to understanding violent extremism. However, we shall dwell on Social Movement Theory (SMT). One of the foremost theoretical frameworks applied to radicalization processes and violent extremism is SMT. The Theory was propounded in the 1940s with the idea that, the movements arose from irrational processes of collective behaviour occurring under strained environmental conditions (what sociologists would call "Strain Theory"), producing a mass sentiment of discontent. Individuals would "join" a movement because they passively succumbed to these overwhelming social forces (Zald and McCarthy, 1987; Klandermans and Oegema, 1987). The SMT is considered appropriate in this paper, as perceptions generally from the theory create an attractive framework for systematically studying the processes of radicalization and influence within militant extremist movements.

The Sahel: Sub-Saharan Africa's Centre of Gravity

The Sahel region of Africa is a 3,860-kilometre arc-like land mass lying to the direct south of the Sahara Desert and extending east-west across the breadth of the African continent. A largely semi-arid belt of barren, sandy and rock-strewn land, the Sahel marks the physical and cultural evolution between the continent's more fertile tropical regions to the south, and its desert in the north. The vast size of the Sahel, no doubt, makes it a strategic location in Sub-Saharan Africa. Concerns abound over the region's vast spaces, often beyond the reach of the state, in an era of violent criminal and political movements operating across borders. The Sahel also suffers from ethno-religious tensions, political instability, poverty and natural disasters (Integrated Regional Information Networks, 2008).

Map 1: Geographical Map of the Sahel Region

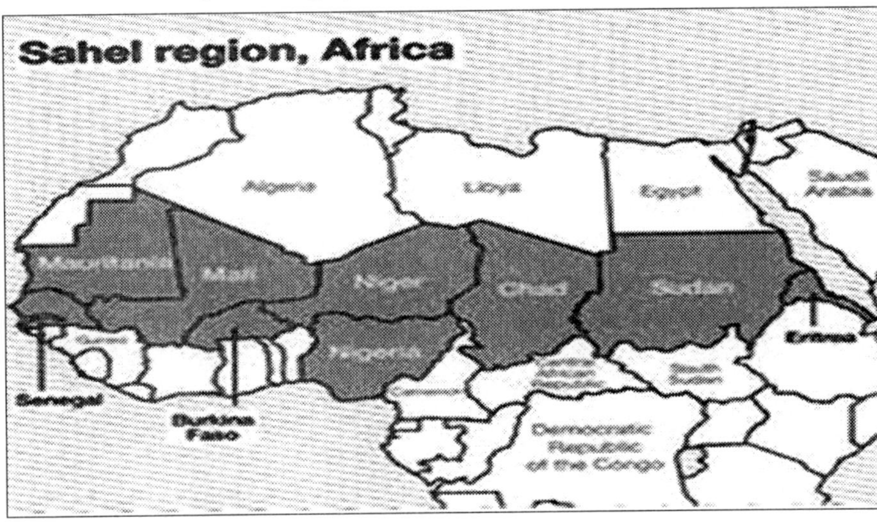

Source: The Conversation.

In recent years, the Sahel has been in the global spotlight due to famines, religious terrorism, anti-state rebellions, and arms, drugs and human trafficking. The pace of high-profile terrorist attacks in Sub-Saharan Africa has deepened in recent years, and the death toll now competes with that of other regions, where violent extremist groups are active. Several emerging trends in violent extremist movement on the continent are impacting how governments in the region, local communities, and international actors react. Since the rebranding from (The National Counterterrorism Center, 2014).

Though groups operating in the Sahel have exclusive backgrounds and dynamics, it is generally documented that, they have at the very least, communicated with one another. Yet, what is not clear, is the degree of inter-group alliance (US Department of State, 2012). More so, because the Sahel region by virtue of its strategic location and vast ungoverned space, acts as a ***'Centre of Gravity'*** in the current conflict between violent extremist groups and States in the region.

Mapping Violent Extremist Groups in the Sahel Region

Armed Islamist groups have proliferated in North and West Africa since 2011, amid political upheaval in the Arab world, governance and security crises in Libya and Mali, and an Islamist insurgency in northern Nigeria. Political institutions in Algeria and Morocco have remained comparatively stable, but both countries have claimed to have broken up domestic and transnational terrorist cells and regularly express concern about spillover. Libya and Algeria are home to groups whose pledges of allegiance to the Islamic State have been publicly accepted by IS leadership (Botha and Abdile, 2014; Caliphate Global Workforce, 2016).

Map 2: Conflict Map of the Sahel Region

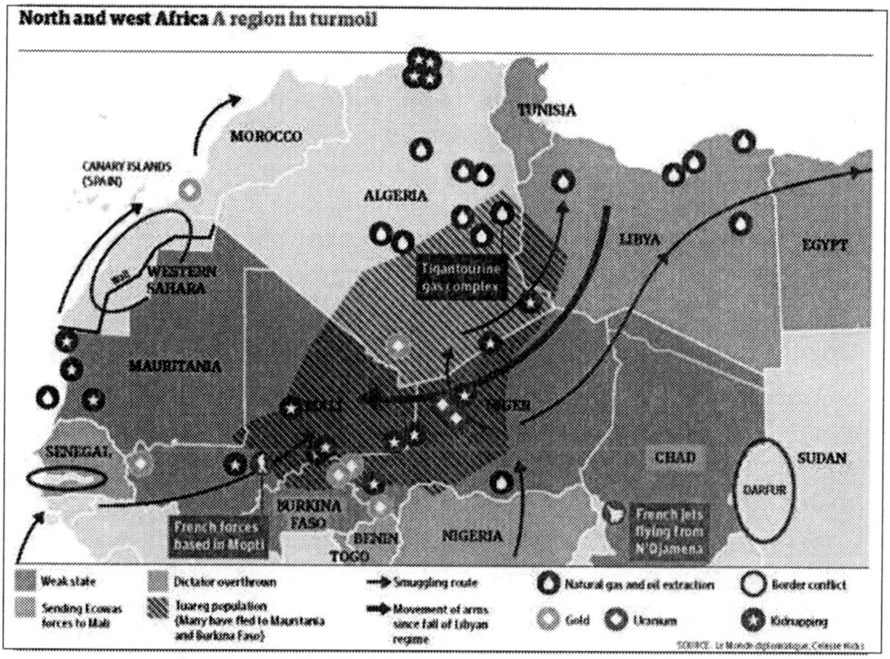

Source: nesastrategist.wordpress.com

The oldest continuously active transnational Islamist terrorist group in the Sahel is AQIM, which grew out of Algeria's 1990s civil conflict and began to carry out attacks in West Africa's Sahel region in the early 2000s. Recently, it has sought ties with extremist groups in Tunisia and Libya. The group, which has long displayed internal tensions, has reproduced a number of offshoots and splinter movements. These include Al Murabitoun, among others (Williams, 2016).

Al Shabaab held significant territory in south-central Somalia, including the capital Mogadishu, in the late 2000s, until a U.S.-backed African Union (AU) military force gained momentum against the insurgency in 2011-2012. Additional troop contributions have since allowed troops from the AU Mission in Somalia, and the nascent Somali government to reclaim further territory. Al Shabaab continues to wage a violent campaign against the Somali government, the AU mission, and international targets in Somalia; it has taken advantage of security gaps to re-infiltrate rural areas that AMISOM has been unable to hold (Cilliers, 2015).

Boko Haram's ideology encompasses a worldview that combines an exclusivist interpretation of Sunni Islam, one that rejects not only Western influence but also democracy, constitutionalism, and more moderate forms of Islam, with "politics of victimhood" that resonate in parts of Nigeria's underdeveloped north. Some of Boko Haram's fighters have reportedly been drawn into the group by financial incentive or under threat. Particular conditions in northeast Nigeria gave rise to Boko Haram, which is responsible for a far higher level of deadly violence than any other violent Islamist group in Africa (Comolli, 2015). Also, the shrinking of Lake Chad, once one of Africa's largest lakes and now described by the U.N. Food and Agriculture Organization as an "ecological catastrophe," has exacerbated tensions among communities in the area that Boko Haram has reportedly sought to exploit (Mercy Corps, 2015).

From the foregoing trends and as shown in Map 2, the conflict arising from violent extremism in individual states are not happening in vacuums, rather, it's an indication of an entire region embroiled in conflict. However, these developments in the Sahel region are the products of both local and global dynamics; these dynamics are discussed below:

The Explosion of African-Led Groups—Al Qaeda's first acknowledged African affiliate, Algerian-led Al Qaeda in the Islamic Maghreb (AQIM), was long presumed to have limited appeal among West African Muslims, and its interest in criminal activities often appeared to conceal its ideological commitment. Nevertheless, the rise of moderately powerful, locally led violent Islamist groups in Somalia, Nigeria, and Mali over the past decade questions past assumptions about the limited prospects for Islamist terrorism on the continent. Thus, Africa seems to have become a ground for competition between Al Qaeda affiliates and the Islamic State over recruits, affiliates, and perceived legitimacy.

State Collapse in North Africa—Furthermore, state collapse in Libya, forced political transitions in Tunisia and Egypt have provided new vistas of opportunities for armed groups, to create safe havens for training, increase their geographic spread, recruit followers, and equip themselves. Thus, contrary to some hopes, increased political openness has not protected Tunisia against domestic radicalization and recruitment. Conflict in Libya has spilled over its borders, engendering new flows of arms and combatants into Tunisia and West Africa's Sahel region. Similarly, political instability in North Africa has also drawn African recruits seeking to join groups based in Libya, or seeking to transit through North Africa en route to other global hotspots. This dynamic is further reinvigorated by the mutual distrust among North and Sub-Saharan African governments, which has regrettably subdued counterterrorism cooperation.

A shift in Tactics from Regular to Irregular Warfare—Years before the "Islamic State" announced its caliphate in Iraq and Syria in 2014, Islamist extremist groups in Africa sought to hold, and in some cases govern, territory. For instance, Al Shabaab began to assert territorial control in Somalia in the mid-2000s, as did AQIM and two local affiliates in Mali in 2012, followed by Boko Haram in Nigeria and Islamic State-linked groups in Libya in 2014.

Violent Extremism in the Sahel Region: A Linkage Analysis

Globalization has aided the funding and coordination of violent extremist groups around the world. Williams (2008) submits that, with the globalization, the global flow of arms is no longer the exclusive control of nation-states, who find it difficult to track violent extremist activities, since they have become decentralized and de-territorialized, having cells in different parts of the globe. Thus, violent extremist groups have acquired the capability to challenge national forces (Hassan and Mukhtar, 2016). Clearly, the existence of global interdependence chain, and interconnections has made possible the instant broadcast of terrorists' messages to global audience (Steger, 2013). Also, in order to spread their messages, recruit new adherents, and launch attacks, violent extremist groups utilize tools provided by globalization. In addition, given the globalization of organized crime in the last two decades, most weapons being used by terrorists' groups are obtained through illicit arms deals hatched, facilitated, and executed by the process of globalization. Besides, globalization facilitates funding and coordination of terrorist groups around the world. Accordingly, globalization is largely at the root of international collaborations and linkages between violent extremist groups in the world and the Sahel region in particular. The manifestations of these linkages are mapped in this section.

In Nigeria for instance, Boko Haram has expanded its operations beyond Nigeria's borders in recent years, in part due to increased military pressure from within Nigeria. Lake Chad's islands and waterways, Nigeria's vast Sambisa Forest, and the remote Mandara Mountains along the Nigeria-Cameroon border have proven effective safe havens for Boko Haram fighters. The group has drawn some of its membership from neighbouring countries, though there are no reliable public estimates of the number of non-Nigerian nationals in the group. Boko Haram has operated in northern Cameroon since at least 2013, and it began a series of cross-border attacks into Chad and Niger in early 2015 when those countries deployed troops into Nigeria in an effort to roll back its territorial gains. The group has links with other Islamic groups within and outside Africa. Its activities and operations are coordinated from Mali with funding and training from a number of sources including a United Kingdom-based Al-Muntada Trust Fund, while its membership has spread to other West African countries such as Benin, Niger, Mauritania and up to Cameroon and Chad which also provide sanctuary for the group members.

The linkages between Boko Haram, its splinter Ansaru and AQIM are less clear. When Boko Haram first transitioned into a jihadist group after 2009, most scholars and policymakers dismissed its affiliation with AQIM and al-Qa'ida core as only rhetoric. The idea that an inexperienced domestic insurgency from northeast Nigeria would be embraced by the broader transnational jihadist community was rebuked as aspirational at best. Yet, by the summer of 2009, evidence suggested that Boko Haram members were training with AQIM (Meleagrou-Hitchens, 2015). In 2010, AQIM leader Droukdel declared that AQIM would provide Boko Haram with weapons, support, and training (Allison, 2016). This collaboration between Boko Haram and AQIM is supported by public statements from both groups, as well as clear indications that Boko Haram's suicide attack on the United Nations office in Abuja, Nigeria, in 2011 employed tactics that were strikingly similar to bombings by AQIM (Institute for Economics and Peace, 2015).

Reports suggest that Sub-Saharan Africans are among IS-Libya's fighters. Some have allegedly been lured by financial incentives, while others may be driven by ideological or personal motives (Blanchard, 2016; Wehrey and Alrababa'h, 2015). In February 2016, CIA Director John Brennan told the Select Senate Committee on Intelligence that Libya was "the most important theatre for ISIL outside of the Syria-Iraq theatre, they have several thousand members there, they have absorbed some of the groups inside of Libya, including Ansar al Sharia that was very active prior to ISIL's rise (Brennan, 2016). Military operations against the Islamic State by Libyan militia forces had succeeded in reversing some of the group's gains as of mid-2016. Nevertheless, unresolved political disputes among Libyans and some Libyans' hostility to foreign military intervention limit options available to the United States and other concerned outsiders (*The Telegraph*, 2016).

Al Qaeda operatives and other violent Islamist extremist groups have had a presence in East Africa for two decades, although the extent of their operations has varied over time. Al Shabaab emerged in predominately Sunni Muslim Somalia in the early 2000s, amid a proliferation of Islamist and clan-based militias that flourished in the absence of central government authority. Al Shabaab drew support across clans, promoting a vision of uniting ethnic Somali-inhabited areas of Kenya, Ethiopia, Djibouti, and Somalia under an Islamic caliphate. Some of its founding members reportedly trained and fought with Al Qaeda in Afghanistan, and known Al Qaeda operatives in the region were associated with the group in its formative years.

According to Meleagrou-Hitchens (2015), Al Shabaab's ability to recruit abroad and the presence in Somalia of foreign fighters, among them U.S. citizens, have been of significant concern to U.S. policymakers. Its ties with other terrorist groups, most notably Al Qaeda and its Yemen-based affiliate, and its threats against international targets also elevate its profile among extremist groups on the continent and have made it a target of direct counterterrorism operations by the United States and other Western countries (Allison, 2016).

Although collaboration was once questioned, it is now widely indicated that AQIM has linkages to al-Murabitun, MUJAO, and the Nigerian terrorist groups Boko Haram and Ansaru. The linkage between AQIM and other groups is better appreciated from a historical setting. AQIM was formed in January 2007, formally rebranding from its previous name, the Salafist Group for Preaching and Combat (GSPC). The official affiliation with al-Qa'ida, beginning several months prior, was largely seen as an effort to maintain relevancy as an extremist group on the global stage, but the group's interest was still strictly regional in nature. The GSPC, formed in 1998, was itself a derivative of the Armed Islamic Group (GIA) (US Department of State, 2012). While much of the overarching ideology, a leading tenet of which is a Salafist Qur'anic interpretation, remains unchanged, smaller philosophical and personal disagreements eventually led to numerous spinoffs and splinter cells (Cruickshank, 2013). In the wake of a personality clash with AQIM leader Abdelmalek Droukdel and other junior leaders in northern Mali, Belmokhtar split from the group and formed the Katibat al-Mulathamin (The Veiled Ones). Belmokhtar's group merged with MUJAO in August 2013 to create al-Murabitun. Notwithstanding whether any of these groups continue to work with AQIM and its leader Droukdel, it is widely understood that the various units under Belmokhtar's control claim allegiance to al-Qa'ida core, led by Ayman al-Zawahiri (Ouellet, 2014).

Looking at the linkages amongst violent terrorist groups in the Sahel region revealed a major feature that has given impetus to the partnerships—their ***adaptive capacity***. Differences in ideology are not mutually exclusive in group membership, funding, and coordination. On the contrary, splinters of AQIM, such as al-Murabitun and the AQIM ally in northern Mali, Ansar al-Din, collaborate at least marginally. There is even some evidence that Boko Haram and its splinter group Ansaru have both trained and coordinated with AQIM, al-Qa'ida core, and even Somalia's al-Shabab (US Department of State, 2013). Sahelian violent extremist groups seem prepared to change their names and sacrifice personal and ideological variances. The merger of al-Mulathamin and MUJAO in August 2013 (themselves splinters of AQIM) created a larger and better coordinated group, al-Murabitun, which is asserting its prominence in the region (Jones, 2014; Rodriquez, 2014; Scott and Daly; 2006).

Strategies for Countering Violent Extremism (CVE)

In this section, we look at some of the strategies for Countering Violent Extremist (CVE), which we outlined briefly:

The Kinetic Approach: Counter-Terrorism and Counter-Insurgency (CT-COIN) Operations

According to the US Department of Treasury (2012), the lack of any real enforcement mechanism impedes the incentive for governments, and even private sector organizations, to stop paying ransoms, leading to off-the-record deals with kidnappers and hefty payments to AQIM and its affiliates, averaging $5.4 million per ransom in 2011, an increase of nearly $1 million from the year prior. Furthermore, multinational kidnap-for-ransom insurance, consulting, and negotiating firms charge premiums to lone businessmen and large corporations alike, creating an insurance and consulting market worth roughly $500 million in 2011. The primary advice given by most kidnap consulting and negotiation firms is to not contact the U.S. or host-country governments, but rather communicate solely with the firm (*The Economist*, 2013).

Furthermore, African-led responses to violent extremist threats remain constrained by limited resources, institutional weaknesses, conflicting political agendas, corruption, sensitivities over domestic sovereignty, regional rivalries, and uneven engagement among affected states. These challenges have undermined various continental efforts. According to the Africa-based Institute for Security Studies, only roughly one-third of African countries have counterterrorism legislation that comports with the AU recommendations, however, raising questions about the extent to which some governments rank the threat a high priority (Allison, 2016).

The Non-Kinetic Approach—Countering Violent Extremism (CVE)

It is the position of this chapter that, since the CT approach of using military or policing resources to counter violent extremism, in the Sahel has not yielded the desired results, governments and international partners should shift ground by pursuing CVE preventative approaches using mostly non-coercive means, that are targeted at countering violent extremist recruitment and ideology as advocated the Social Movement Theory (SMT). Consequently, the following actionable strategies are recommended to address areas of education, media, training of youths, and the creation and distribution of accessible literature about preventing extremism:

Internet Censorship: Leveraging the Power of Information Technology. CVE strategies and radicalisation models have increasingly used the internet as a mechanism to realize their aims, justified by their assertion of the internet as a source of inspiration for violent extremists. Strategies to combat the "terrorist use of the internet" have been around for many years but it is ISIS' prolific use of social media, including the live-streaming of attacks, which has seen irresistible pressure brought to bear on technology companies who had earlier maintained their distance from government efforts in this area.

Fostering Partnership for CVE. According to the most recent European Commission Communication on CVE, the absolute priority must be to prevent more people from being radicalized, and ensure that those who already are, enter de-radicalization programs and are prevented from spreading terrorist propaganda and hate speech. The implementation of such policies is devolved to the Member States which are on the "front line" through their "security and judiciary bodies, teachers, social workers and civil society.

Curricula Drive for Preventing and Countering Violent Extremism. There is the need for the development of a credible, well-accepted holistic and comprehensive curriculum for preventing and countering violent extremism with the collaboration of all stakeholders, and especially those who understand them best. This will in turn guide the development of messaging material—literature, audio and multimedia.

Media Regulation: Managing Narratives in the Public and Private Domains. The media at all levels, electronic, print and social media, serve as conduit for the dissemination of extremist narratives and counter-narratives. The saying that "half of the battlefield is the media field" is apt. The media provides near equal opportunities for both state and non-state actors in disseminating their stories. Thus, both the armed forces and enemy combatants enjoy some access to the media space. However, the state reserves the right and capacity to regulate, control and censor media content and therefore, relevant state agencies are duty bound to deny disseminatory access to violent extremists.

Development and Nurturing of Effective Change Agents. In the management of violent extremism and terrorism, change agents are necessary to provide a bunker against extremism and violence. Change makers are pivotal individuals who are visible in society, enjoy access to citizens, and have the capacity to influence public opinion. There is a need to support the training and development of more credible and charismatic resource persons (especially among youth) in critical skills for content production and presentations on preventing and countering violent extremism.

Train-the-Trainers Course: There is a need to support *Train-the-Trainers Courses* which are managed by credible grassroots NGOs or Educational Institutions with courses for especially young Imams, religious leaders and activists. Course content should cover the use of relevant CIT and the media, the principles and objectives of Islamic jurisprudence, responding to common Muslim and non-Muslim misconceptions about Islam and Islamophobia, improving interfaith relations and gender equity, strategies for social reform, conflict management and the etiquettes of disagreement, preventing and countering violent extremism and other forms of religious extremism that are of concern to peaceful coexistence, and presenting a values-oriented paradigm of Islam.

Conclusion

The Sahel region has been branded as the most conflict-ridden sub-regions in the world. In the past, there was well-ordered distinction between national and international extremism. Today, this incongruity is no longer substantial, as the activities of supposedly indigenous violent extremist groups exceed national borders. This is marked by a complex network of private sponsorship, financial and mutual commitment that links dispersed groups together. Accordingly, linkage between terrorist organizations epitomizes one of the essential fundamentals of contemporary extremism.

Consequently, this chapter problematized the linkage between violent extremist groups in the Sahel region, Lake Chad Basin and North African States. The Sahel region is still a critical area to monitor during the coming years. The combination of weak central governments, porous borders, and vast open land allows terrorist groups such as AQIM, Boko Haram, Mokhtar Belmokhtar's al-Murabitun, among others to operate with few restraints. These groups have continued to collaborate amongst themselves, highlighting the linkages between the various actors, even those with marginally different ideologies and objectives, and the adaptivity of violent extremism in the Sahel region.

NOTES

1. Allison, S. (2016). "Côte d'Ivoire Attack: Resurgent al-Qaeda in the Islamic Maghreb flexes its muscles," *Daily Maverick*, March 14, 2016.
2. Asafa, J. (2010). "Conceptualizing and Theorizing Terrorism in the Historical and Global Context", *Humanity and Society*. Vol. 34(4), pp. 317-338.
3. Backes, U. (2010). *Political Extremes: A Conceptual History from Antiquity*. London: Routledge.
4. Blanchard, C. (2016). CRS Report RL33142, *Libya: Transition and U.S. Policy*, by [author name scrubbed]. CRS analyst Christopher Blanchard contributed to this section.
5. Botha, A., and Abdile, M. (2014). *Radicalisation and al-Shabaab recruitment in Somalia*, Institute for Security Studies Paper 266, September 2014.
6. Brennan, J. (2016). Senate Select Committee on Intelligence, Worldwide Threat Assessment of the U.S. Intelligence Community, hearing, February 9, 2016.
7. Brady, H. Schlozman, K., and Verba, S. (1999). "Prospecting for participants: Rational expectations and the recruitment of political activists," *American Political Science Review*. Vol. 93. Pp. 53–168.
8. Cilliers, J. (2015). "Conflict trends in Africa: a turn for the better in 2015?" ISS, November 2015.
9. Comolli, V. (2015). *Boko Haram: Nigeria's Islamist Insurgency*. London: Hurst.
10. Cruickshank, P. (2013). "Algeria Gas Facility Attack Fuels Jihadist Rivalry," *CNN*, January 30, 2013.
11. Federal Bureau of Investigation (FBI). (n.d.) What is Violent Extremism? Retrieved: https://cve.fbi.gov/whatis/. (Accessed on 10th May, 2019).
12. Fwa, K.L. (2016). "Globalization and Africa's Security Challenges for the Twenty-First Century". In Tar, U.A., Mijah, E.B., and Tedheke, E.U. (Eds.). *Globalization in Africa: Perspectives on Development, Security, and the Environment*. Lanham: Lexington Books. Pp. 219-238.
13. Glazzard, A., and Zeuthen, M. (2016). Iolent Extremism. GSDRC Applied Knowledge Services. Retrieved: https://gsdrc.org/professional-dev/violent-extremism/. (Accessed on 9th May, 2019).
14. Harvey, D. (1989). The Condition of Post-modernity, Oxford: Basil Blackwell.
15. Hassan, M.B., and Mukhtar, J.I. (2016). "Globalization and Transnational Terrorism: Linkage between Global Terrorist Organizations". In Tar, U.A., Mijah, E.B., and Tedheke, E.U. (Eds.). *Globalization in Africa: Perspectives on Development, Security, and the Environment*. Lanham: Lexington Books. Pp. 239-256.
16. Institute for Economics and Peace (2015). *Global Terrorism Index 2015*, November 2015.
17. Jones, S.G. (2014). "The Extremist Threat to the U.S. Homeland," House Committee on Homeland Security, January, 15, 2014.
18. Klandermans, B., and Oegema, D. (1987). "Potentials, Networks, Motivations and Barriers: Steps Towards Participation in Social Movements," *American Sociological Review*, Vol. 52, pp. 519–531.
19. Kimball, C. (2002). *When Religion Becomes Evil: Five Warning Signs*. New York: Harper.
20. Lofland J., and Stark, R. (1965) "Becoming a world saver: A theory of conversion to a deviant perspective," *American Sociological Review*, Vol. 30, pp. 862–874.
21. Meleagrou-Hitchens, A. (2015). "Terrorist Tug-of-War", *Foreign Affairs*, October, 2015.
22. Mercy Corps (2015). "Motivations and Empty Promises", Voices of Former Boko Haram Combatants and Nigerian Youth, February, 2015.

23. N'Diaye, B. (2011). Conflicts and Crises in West Africa: Internal and International Dimensions. In Jaye, T., Garuba, D., and Amadi, S. (Eds.). *ECOWAS and the Dynamics of Conflict and Peace Building* Dakar: CODESRIA, pp. 27-44.
24. Neuman, P. (2010). "Prisons and Terrorism Radicalisation and De-radicalisation in 15 Countries," A policy report published by the International Centre for the Study of Radicalisation and Political Violence (ICSR): 12.
25. Ouellet, E. (2014). "The Institutionalization of al-Qaeda in the Islamic Maghreb (AQIM)," Terrorism and Political Violence, 2014; personal interview, anonymous, U.S. Embassy, Niamey, Niger, January 21, 2014.
26. Rodriguez, D.M. (2014). "Posture Hearing," Senate Armed Services Committee, March 6, 2014.
27. Pujol-Mazzini, A. (2018). "Islamist groups turn their attention to West Africa", *The Washington Post,* July 3, 2018.
28. Scholte, J.A. (1997). 'The Globalisation of World Politics'. In Smith, S and Baylis, J. (Eds.), The Globalisation of World Politics: An Introduction, Oxford: Oxford University Press.
29. Scott, G., and Daly, S.A. (2006). Al-Qaida: terrorist selection and recruitment. Santa Monica, California, RAND Corporation.
30. Steger, M. (2013). *Globalization: A Very Short Introduction* (3rd Edition). Oxford: Oxford University Press.
31. *The Caliphate's Global Workforce* (2016). Combating Terrorism Center (CTC) at West Point, April 2016.
32. *The Economist* (2013). "Kidnap and Ransom Insurance. I'm a Client...Get me Out of Here," *Economist*, June 27, 2013.
33. *The Telegraph* (2016). ISIL recruiting migrant 'army of the poor' with $1,000 sign-up bonuses,", February 1, 2016.
34. *The Washington Post (2013).* "U.S. Chose Not to Kill Mali Terror Leader in 2003," February 4, 2013.
35. United Nations Office for Drugs and Crimes (UNODC) (2018). "Preventing and countering violent extremism (PVE/CVE)". Retrieved: https://www.unodc.org/e4j/en/terrorism/module-2/key-issues/preventing-and-countering-violent-extremism.html. (Accessed on 10th May, 2019).
36. U.S. Department of Homeland Security (2016). What is Countering Violent Extremism? Retrieved: https://www.dhs.gov/cve/what-is-cve. (Accessed on 10th May, 2019).
37. U.S. Department of the Treasury (2012). Remarks of Under Secretary David Cohen at Chatham House on 'Kidnapping for Ransom: The Growing Terrorist Financing Challenge', October 5, 2012.
38. U.S. Department of States (2016). Country Reports on Terrorism 2015, June 2, 2016.
39. U.S. Department of State (2013). Foreign Terrorist Organization Designation, March 21, 2013. Retrieved: www.state.gov/r/pa/prs/ps/2013/03/206493.htm. (Accessed on 12th May, 2019).
40. Tar, U.A. (2016). "Terrorism, Violent Conflict and Democratic Governance in Nigeria". Lead Paper presented at the National Conference on *The Dynamics of Democratic Practice in Nigeria 1999-2015,* held at the Aminu Kano Centre for Democratic Research and Training, Mumbayya House, Bayero University, Kano, 9-10 November.
41. Wehrey, F., and Alrababa'h, A. (2015). "Rising Out of Chaos: The Islamic State in Libya," Carnegie Endowment, March 5, 2015.

42. Wiktorowicz, Q. (2015). *Radical Islam Rising: Muslim Extremism in the West*. Lanham, MD: Rowman and Littlefield Publishers.
43. Williams, P.D. (2016). *War & Conflict in Africa (2nd Edition)*. Cambridge: Polity.
44. Williams, P.D. (2008). Violent Non-State Actors and National and International Security. International Relations and Security Network Series, Zurich: Swiss Institute of Technology.
45. Zald, M., and McCarthy, J. (1987). *Social Movements in an Organizational Society*. New Brunswick, NJ: Transaction Books.

10

Multi-National Joint Task Force and Counter Insurgency Operations in the Lake Chad Basin

Lt Gen Lamidi Oyebayo Adeosun

ABSTRACT

In recent times, terrorism and insurgency have emerged to occupy the front burner of national defence and security of most countries of the world. The scourges of terrorism and insurgency have serious implications for governance, law and order. On their parts, states have devised both municipal and transnational mechanisms for countering violent extremism and insurgency. In Africa's Lake Chad Basin (LCB), contingent states have developed a regional mechanism for counter-insurgency through security regionalization which has enabled for a more robust regional platform for security cooperation. This chapter examines the role of Multi-national Joint Task Force (MNJTF) in counter-insurgency operations in the Lake Chad Basin region of Africa. The chapter reveals that the establishment of the Force has played an important role in the countering the insurgent activities. It led to the recapture of many towns hitherto captured by the Boko Haram insurgents, regained the freedom of hundreds of kidnapped persons, assisted in the return of peace and economic activities amongst others. The strategy and concept of operations of the MNJTF has led to mission success and paradigm shift on regional security in the region. The chapter recalls my personal experience as a former Commander of the MNJTF.

Introduction

The Lake Chad Basin is gradually emerging as Africa's latest Regional Security Complex (RSC). What Kelly (2007) calls "new regionalism"—which privileges regional security—is very much in evidence in the LCB (see also Buzan, 1986, 1991). Following a rise of violent insurgencies and terrorism in the region, member countries of the Lake Chad Basin Commission (LCBC) have transformed a pre-existing regional initiative for countering cross-border banditry into a larger and more robust regional counter-terrorism and counter-insurgency outfit known as the Multi-National Joint Task Force (MNTF) (Tar and Mustapha, 2016). The establishment of the MNJTF is an excellent initiative for the return of peace in many deserted communities along the waters of the Lake Chad. The importance of the Lake Chad to the lives of people and animals around the region cannot be overemphasized. Hence, every effort needs to be made to ensure the security of the Lake Chad Basin Area. The LCB has been one of the main hubs of economic activities for the people in the North, West and Central parts of Africa. The area is governed and managed by a commission known as the LCBC which was established on 22nd May 1964 with its headquarters at N'Djamena, Chad Republic following the signing of Fort Lamy Convention by the four countries bordering the Lake; Cameroon, Chad, Niger and Nigeria. Subsequently, other countries such as Central African Republic (CAR) and Libya joined commission in 1996 and 2008 respectively. Sudan was admitted in July 2000 but has observer status because it has not ratified the founding convention. Other countries with observer status include Algeria, Egypt, Republic of Congo and Democratic Republic of Congo (DRC). The aim of the commission is to regulate and control the use of water and other natural resources in the basin as well as initiate, promote and coordinate natural resources development projects and research (Waziri, 2017).

The Lake Chad Basin has a total landmass of 1,350 sq km and lies between Latitude 13°0′ North and Longitude 14°10′ East. It has an estimated population of over 12 million people and it is worthy to note that over 68 million people cutting across the LCBC Member countries get their water needs from the Lake (Agbiboa, 2017). The area is endowed with various natural resources and the major occupation of the populace has been cattle rearing, fishing and farming. The economy of the area started deteriorating following the end of the Chadian conflicts which pushed some of the unrepentant militias to the Islands of Lake Chad. The militias continued to cause mayhem on the populace of the area by collecting their hard earnings, food stuffs and cattle at will without any iota of provocation. (Fah, 2007; Waziri, 2017).

Map 3: Map of Lake Chad Basin Showing Areas Affected by Boko Haram Insurgency

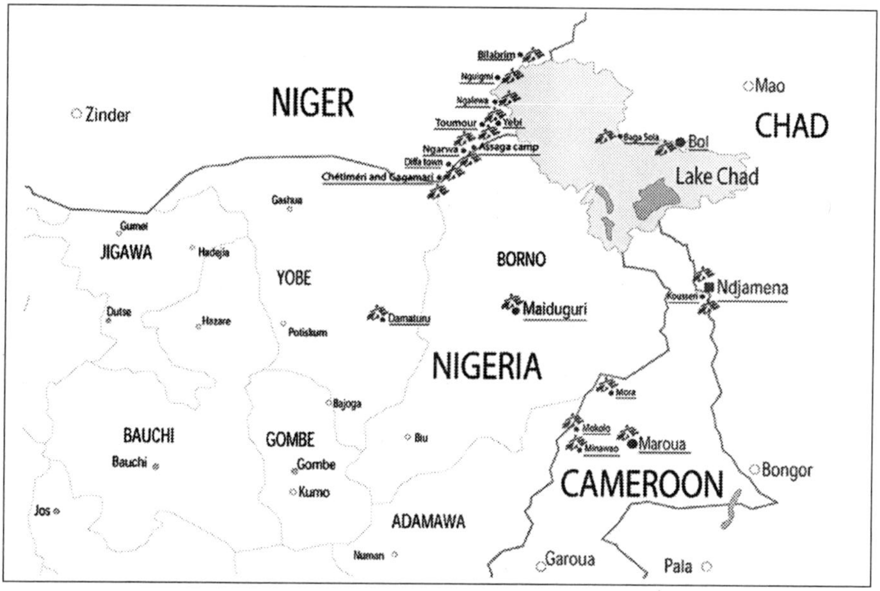

Source: www.msf.org.uk (2019)

Additionally, the armed bandits hindered free flow of goods and services among the LCBC member countries and carryout other heinous activities along the major roads linking the countries. Their continuous dastardly activities which threatened the safety of lives and property of inhabitants of the Basin led to the establishment of the MNJTF. With the emergence of the Boko Haram Terrorists (BHTs) group, the mandate of the MNJTF was changed from checkmating the activities of anti-banditry in the LCB to the fight against BHTs group (Tar and Mustapha 2016; Osakwe 2017; Nkwi, 2017).

Background to the Multi-National Joint Task Force

The history of MNJTF could be traced to 1994 when it was established by Nigeria with Headquarters at Baga to checkmate trans-border armed banditry around the general area of Lake Chad Basin and to facilitate free movement along Nigeria's northeast border. During these periods, the island of Lake Chad was a safe haven for most rebels expelled from Chad during the conflicts in the country. The rate of poverty in the LCBC member countries further increased the rate of the atrocities in the area and the major roads linking the neighboring countries. Initially, the Force only liaised with the military and security agencies of the LCBC member countries until 1998 when it received a boost and the Force was made fully multinational following the joining of the coalition by Chadian and Nigerien Forces with the purpose of dealing with common cross—border security challenges within the Lake Chad Region. The establishment of the MNJTF in 1994 completely changed the tide of events in the area. The MNJTF was able to douse the situation until 2009 when the BHT group surfaced within the general area. This made the mandate of the MNJTF to be expanded to include the fight against the BHT group in addition to checkmating anti-banditry activities in the region (Yoroms, 2016).

In the last quarter of 2014 and the first quarter of 2015, BHT heightened their activities leading to the dislodging military locations including the erstwhile MNJTF headquarters in Baga. The activities of the BHT group further stalled, crippled and halted all socio-economic life in the region. This necessitated the remodeling and re-operationalization of the MNJTF to commence new operations on 30th July 2015 with Cameroon, Chad, Niger and Nigeria as Troops Contributing Countries (TCCs). The Republic of Benin also pledged to contribute troops, assist in preventing the crisis from escalating and completely eliminating the threat they posed with a view to restoring economic activities and enhancing the lives of the people. Furthermore, the MNJF headquarters was relocated from Baga in Nigeria to Ndjamena, the capital of Chad Republic. The MNJTF is currently operating in concert with the African Union—Peace and Security Commission (AU-PSC) mandate which approved the deployment of 8,700 personnel for MNJTF. The AU later amended the strength and approved personnel strength of 10,000.

The LCBC member countries held various meetings known as Extraordinary Summit of Heads of State and Government hosted in Abuja, Nigeria on 11th June 2015. This was the final strategic level meeting that authorized the immediate operationalisation of the MNJTF and the Adoption of Emergency Development Plan. At the end of their deliberations, they took the following decisions:

- Approved the Concept of Operations (CONOPS) as well as other Strategic, Operational and related documents of the MNJTF for the fight against BHT group.
- Approved the immediate deployment of the MNJTF Headquarters at N'djamena by implementing its human, logistics and financial requirements;
- Approved the deployment of the national contingents to the MNJTF under the operational command of the MNJTF Commander

assisted by his Joint Headquarters by 30th July 2015.

- Approved the funding of the sum of 30 Million Dollars USD for the installation and equipping of the MNJTF Headquarters.
- Approved the establishment of the Executive Secretariat at the Headquarters of the Mission and its Executive Secretary.
- Approved the nomination of the 3 key post of responsibility of the MNJTF Headquarters as follows: (a) Force Commander who shall be a Nigerian General (Until the end of the mission). (b) Deputy Force Commander to be rotational every 12 months between Cameroon, Niger and Chad, and (c) Chief of Staff to be rotational every 12 months between Cameroon, Niger and Chad.
- Requests the African Union's support to the MNJTF in its operations, logistics and general mission support by mobilizing financial support.
- Resolved to seek the support of strategic partners, notably European Union, France, United Kingdom and United States of America in favour of the MNJTF.
- Requests the President of the UN Security Council to make a declarative statement in support of MNJTF Operations against the BHT group.
- Adopted the Emergency Plan for Development in the Lake Chad Basin. (UNO Report, 2015).

From the foregoing, it is apparent that the MNJFT is designed as a regional outfit with troop contribution from member states of the LCBC. In addition, the command and control of the force is designed to be led by Nigeria—being the preponderant regional hegemon, but other key staff responsibilities were to be contributed, on rotational basis, by other member-states of Cameroon, Chad and Niger. The ability of the member-states of LCBC to pull off this agreed formula for mission command and control of the MNJTF seems to defy the usual politics that defines regional security brokering in Africa.

Mandate of the MNJTF

Consequent to the above decisions by the LCBC member states and Benin and at their request, the African Union (AU) PSC authorized the MNJTF, within its Area of Operations (AO), to achieve the following mandates:

- Create a safe and secure environment in the areas affected by the activities of Boko Haram and other terrorist groups, in order to significantly reduce violence against civilians and other abuses. These include sexual and gender-based violence in full compliance with international law, including international humanitarian law and the UN Human Rights Due Diligence Policy (HRDDP).

- Facilitate the implementation of overall stabilization programmes by the LCBC Member States and Benin in the affected areas, including full restoration of states' authority and the return of IDPs and refugees.
- Facilitate, within the limit of its capabilities, humanitarian operations and the delivery of assistance to the affected populations.

Political Objective

The MNJTF seeks to enhance cooperation and information sharing between the LCBC Member States and also support the national authorities in meeting their four obligations on regional security issues related to the Boko Haram and other terrorists groups. In particular, it contributes to the following:

- Assist in the full restoration of state authority in the affected areas as well as support national authorities of the affected LCBC Member States in their primary responsibilities to put an end to impunity, ensure the protection of civilians, restore security and public order through the implementation of appropriate measures;
- Support to the development and implementation of overall stabilization programmes and post-conflict reconstruction strategy by the LCBC Member States and Benin in the affected areas.

Mission, Strategic Posture and End State

In line with the decisions by the LCBC Member States, the MNJTF's mission is to operate with the AU PSC authority to eliminate Boko Haram Terrorists in order to create a safe and secure environment and facilitate the stabilisation in the areas by using all the necessary means with its capacity. In order to create a safe-secure environment and contribute to stabilizing the situation in the affected areas, and using all necessary conventional means within its capacity and with the support of relevant bilateral partners as well as regional and international organisations, the MNJTF:

- Carries on and execute security operations to regain full control of the areas under Boko Haram threat and occupation.
- Support the member countries of the LCBC to effectively exercise and maintain State Authority in the areas affected by the activities

of Boko Haram and other bandit groups and provides protection to the civilian population under immediate threat. (Agbor, 2017)

On the other hand, the strategic end state of the MNJTF is to ensure the presence and influence of Boko Haram Terrorists is completely eliminated. The security conditions are to be re-established for the states exercising full authority over the areas affected by the activities and assuming their responsibilities for the protection of the population, properties and livelihood means as well as for addressing regional security and human rights challenges. Operational cooperation is adequately enhanced in the region and the LCBC Member States can implement the overall stabilization programmes in the affected areas.

Tasks and Responsibilities of the MNJTF

Within the framework of its mandate and in its Area of Operation (AO), the MNJTF is to carry out the following tasks:

- Conduct security operations to prevent the expansion of Boko Haram and other terrorists' group activities and eliminate their presence.
- Facilitate operational coordination amongst the TCCs, LCBC member states, Benin and other stakeholders in the fight against Boko Haram and other terrorist groups, based on the intelligence collected from relevant African structures and/or availed by partners.
- Conduct patrols and other types of operations in the AO.
- Conduct operations to disrupt the supply lines of Boko Haram Terrorists and other terrorist groups, preventing the transfer of arms and ammunition and other type of support.
- Ensure, upon request and within the means and capabilities of the MNJTF, the protection of civilians under immediate threat, IDP and refugee camps, humanitarian workers and other civilian personnel.
- Actively search for, and free all abductees, including the young girls abducted in Chibok town of Nigeria in April 2014.
- Undertake effective psychological operations to encourage defections from Boko Haram and other terrorist groups.
- Provide, upon request, escorts to humanitarian convoys.
- Support regional efforts to arrest and bring to justice all those responsible for war crimes and crimes against humanity as well as the protection of witnesses and vulnerable groups.

- Ensure the protection of the MNJTF personnel's facilities and equipment.
- Coordinate with other agencies such as the Regional Intelligence Fusion Unit (RIFU), to obtain intelligence on Boko Haram and other terrorist groups.
- Liaise with the International Agencies on the observance of human rights.
- Liaise with relevant law enforcement agencies within the AO.
- Support the implementation of international standards with regard to human rights.
- Support national authorities to restore and maintain law and order situation within the AO.
- Liaise with relevant local administrative authorities within the AO.
- Support the relevant local administrative authorities in restoring the civilian administration.

The MNJTF Command and Control Structure

Like other conventional military commands, the MNJTF command structure is organized into 3 levels; Strategic, Operational and Tactical levels. At the strategic level, the LCBC in close coordination with the AU Commission, serves as the strategic Headquarters for the MNJTF, while at the operational level, the Operational Headquarters of the MNJTF is established in N'djamena, Chad and is staffed by personnel from LCBC Member States and Benin Republic. It also comprises relevant bilateral and international partners, particularly from the P3 (USA, UK and France) through the Centre for Coordination and Liaison (CCL). The MNJTF HQ and its military and civilian staff operate under the authority of the MNJTF Commander. Finally, at the tactical level, the MNJTF ground forces comprise of national contingents pledged from the countries affected by Boko Haram and other terrorist groups. The Forces comprise tactical combat units and other units deemed necessary. The MNJTF HQ facilitates the conduct of joint, simultaneous and coordinated patrols and other types of operations. The three levels structure of the MNJTF ensures that each level provides the relevant support to ensure mission success.

Facing the Enemy: Countering Boko Haram Insurgency

The MNJTF is acutely aware of the dynamics, structure, and *Modus Operandi* of the Boko Haram Insurgents. The actual name of Boko Haram is *Jama'atul Ahlis Sunna Lidda'awati Wal Jihad which means "Sunni Group for Preaching and jihad*. It is a radical Islamic religious group created in 1997 and became popular under the Late Mohamed Yusuf, an extremist preacher, in 2002 at the city of Maiduguri, the capital city of Borno State, Nigeria. The group moved to the political side and attracted young students at odds with authority at universities. Since the killing of its leader in 2009, the group under its new leader Abubakar Shekau has continued to carry out numerous attacks, targeting security agencies, civilians, police, churches, mosques, and public facilities, including schools (Osakwe, 2017). More recently, the Boko Haram terrorist group has suffered several defeats, and has been restricted to the border areas of the Lake Chad Basin Countries. Consequently, they have resorted more to the use of IEDs, suicide bombings, and occasional attacks on isolated villages. Some highlights on BHT activities are as follows:

- Boko Haram is organised in cells with several factions operating independently. The command and control is decentralized. It recruits usually by force or using finance to attract youth in the local settlements. The financing of Boko Haram is mainly coming from robbery, illegal trade, cattle rustling as well as links with other terrorist groups within and outside the region; couple with ransom fees from kidnapped persons.
- The objective of Boko Haram is to establish a caliphate in the North-East Nigeria and to extend its territories to neighbouring countries of Niger, Chad, and Cameroon. To achieve this objective, the group tries to undermine the state's authority within the area under its control and enhance its influence on local population through terrorism.
- The centre of gravity of Boko Haram is the freedom of manoeuvre of its different factions. Its major strengths are: decentralised command and control system, strong motivation (ideology), capacity to conduct coordinated symmetric and asymmetric actions, conceal itself within the population and the knowledge of the field. Its main weaknesses are: its systematic use of violent actions, the decimation of its cells, and the unanimous condemnation of the group by the international community and its conscription method of recruitment. Currently, the funding and logistics have been drastically reduced and the split in its leadership is a weakness that is being exploited by MNJT forces.

Profiling Boko Haram Capability and Courses of Actions

The MNJTF regularly conducts and reviews terror threats in the LCB. It was established that the most probable Course of Action (COA) of Boko Haram is simultaneous conduct of combined actions with asymmetric attacks against Nigerian forces. The most dangerous COA is suicide attacks by infiltrated elements against the back positions of the government forces, attacks against key infrastructures and strategic cities instilling fear among the population and propaganda. They also indulge in the use of the Road Side Improvised Explosive Devices (RSIED) (Agbor, 2017).

The Boko Haram fought in bands of 50-300 usually using pick-up vehicles mounted with high caliber weapons. They are noted for rampage and arson on villages as well as kidnapping people especially women and girls. They also abduct young men and boys, turning the boys as foot soldiers and the girls as forced wives. In the alternative, they use kidnapped persons to seek for ransom as was the case with the school girls kidnapped from Dapchi town in Yobe State of Nigeria. However, their capability has been drastically degraded especially by troops of the MNJTF in conjunction with troops of national and bilateral operations.

Boko Haram's Allegiance to Islamic State in Iraq and Syria

The Boko Haram terrorist group pledged their allegiance to Islamic State in Iraq and Syria (ISIS) on 7th March 2015 which was subsequently accepted by the leadership of the ISIS on 13th March 2015. They claimed to have established an Islamic State in West Africa (ISWA) comprising of the 4th Region of Cameroon and 4th region of Chad in Central Africa as well as 5th region of Niger and North-eastern parts of Nigeria in West Africa. These areas form the major parts of the MNJTF area of operational responsibility.

MNJTF Disposition and Combat Readiness

To counter the Boko Haram insurgency, the MNJTF adopted the CT-COIN approach which is a kinetic measure that involves coordinated land and aerial attacks on insurgents' locations, hot pursuit of the enemy, and targeted mop up operations to clear areas that are recaptured from the insurgents. To do this, the MNJTF is organized into four Sectors and a headquarters. All the sectors have their headquarters in their respective countries, while the coordinating headquarters remain in Chad. The sectors can be moved and relocated from time to time based on operational exigencies. The first Sector has its headquarters deployed in Mora, Cameroon and its sub-sectors are in Maltam, Maroua and Mora (co-located with the HQ). The second Sector has its headquarters located at Baga Sola in Chad Republic. Its sub-sectors are in Ngouboua, Kangalam and Bagasola (co-located with the HQs).

The third Sector has its headquarters in Baga, Nigeria. The Sector has 3 battalions at Baga town, Cross Kauwa and Garin Giwa respectively. The fourth Sector has its headquarters in Diffa, Niger Republic. The Sector has deployments at Diffa, Bosso, Baroua and Toumour. The approved manpower of the MNJTF as contained in the CONOPs is 8,700 all ranks. However, a further assessment of the situation on the ground showed that, the approved strength would not effectively cover the entire MNJTF AO. Hence, the LCBC countries agreed to increase the strength to 10,000. This was approved by the AU in December 2016. Funding is provided by member states of the LCBC through the Secretariat of the LCBC. Equipment is mainly provided by troop-contributing countries; however, special procurement is also conducted to augment the operational and tactical capability of the forces.

Phases of the MNJTF Operations

The MNJTF operations are premised on the various compositions of troops pledged by the TCCs. These include motorized and mechanized battalions, gendarmerie, engineers, amphibious elements, artillery and other support elements. The entire operation is conducted in five phases.

- *Common to all Phases:* this is the generic phase under which the MNJTF forces maintain a reserve capability (up to a battalion size); secure the logistical LOCs; ensure permanent Force security measures; collect intelligence throughout the AO; establish liaison with all actors and at all levels (including national Security and Defense Forces—SDF, partner NGOs, IOs and UN Agencies); and maintain the MNJTF its headquarters at N'Djamena.
- *Planning for Deployment:* this encompasses conduct of planning activities (CONOPS Development); force generation; reconnaissance missions to potential future deployment sites; force preparation of units on standby to be ready for deployment; deployment of the Sector HQs; integration of forces deployed and operating in the AO; build-up of the logistical support arrangements; commencement of a public information and communication campaign; and mapping of refugees camps and IDP sites
- *Deployment:* Under this phase, troops are deployed on combat missions to the various targets in the AO. Specifically, this phase involves control by each force component of its dedicated AO; seizure and control of key areas in the AO; secure mobility corridors

and main locations with significant population density; consolidation of strongholds; support to CIMIC and other psychological operations; and preparation of operations.

- *Conduct Offensive Operations:* this phase involves the conduct of specific, target offensive missions with emphasis on the following: isolate and neutralize BH factions; disorganize C2 and communications systems; disrupt supply lines; disorganize smuggling networks; reduce military capability; clear hideouts and training centers; protect most vulnerable populations; facilitate, upon request, the delivery of humanitarian assistance even under fire; neutralize logistical support bases; conduct stop and search operations to capture key Boko Haram leaders; search for and free all persons abducted and provide security to refugee camps, as feasible
- *Stabilisation*: This phase involves the provisions of stablilisation operations and services to civil population. It involves the following: reduce isolated resistance elements; search BH hideouts; facilitate the return of IDPs and refugees; support the re-establishment of state authority in areas freed from BH occupation; support the implementation of actions towards the enhancement of public order in the concerned areas; promote delivery of the social fabric; and contribute to the initial steps of a Demobilization, Disarmament and Reintegration (DDR) process.
- *Force Drawdown:* this is a forecast phase that involves preparedness for ending the mission. This involves the following: reassessment of the security situation in the AO; readjust the deployment of units on the ground; redeployment as necessary; rotation if necessary; dismantling of logistical support arrangements; etc.

Conduct of Operation GAMA AIKI

Operation GAMA AIKI was the first major offensive operation conducted by the MNJTF after its full formation. This operation commenced on the 13th June 2016 with the objective of clearing Boko Haram terrorists from the wide corridors of Damasak, Gashigar, Abadam, Malam Fatori and other Islands of Lake Chad. This in turn was to facilitate the seamless operations of Sectors 2, 3 and 4 of Chad, Nigeria and Niger respectively, along Komadougou River and Islands of Lake Chad.

While the MNJTF was finalising the plans and sourcing for logistics for the operation, BHTs pre-empted the operation by attacking Bosso on

3 and 6 June 2016, which during some logistics items, arms and ammunition were carted away. The civil work ongoing in the construction of Bailey bridge from Bosso across the Komadougou River which was aimed at improving operational efficiency was also destroyed during the attack. This development led to re-adjustment of the initial plan, in line with principle of flexibility, which saw the introduction of a bilateral operation between Chad and Niger to stabilize Bosso area. Thereafter, the operation was launched from 3 different axes:

- Sector 1 advanced northwards to form a blocking position at the Cameroonian boundaries with Chad and Nigeria around the Lake Chad area as against the initial plan of concentrating the forces, first at Diffa for the clearance.
- Sector 2 advanced to clear Kaiga Ngouboua—Litiri—Madayi—Kangarwa.
- Sector 3 advanced to clear Baga—Alagarno—Doro Naira—Kangarwa
- Sector 4 was to secure Diffa and surrounding villages while preparing to join up in the next phase of the operation (Waziri, 2017)

Operation GAMA AIKI which was adjudged successful was concluded on the 8th October, 2016. During the conduct of the operation, a high level of cooperation, synergy and effectiveness in the conduct of joint and combined operations were recorded. First, there were precision air strikes from Chadian, Nigerien and Nigerian fighter jets, leading to effective coordination of air operations. Secondly, there were extensive use of combined Intelligence, Surveillance and Reconnaissance (ISR) provided by ISR assets of Nigeria, Niger and the Center for Liaison and Coordination (CCL) to positively influence tactical operations of the ground troops. Thirdly, the capture of Madayi by Sector 2 resulted in the killing of a large number of Boko Haram terrorists and recovery of armaments. Fourthly, the capture of Alargano, Doron Naira, Kangarwa, Metele, Dogon Chuku, Abadam which led to the recovery of vehicles, armament and other logistics by Sector 3 of the MNJTF. Fifth, the successful clearance of 6 villages by Sector 1 MNJTF in the northern border areas of Cameroon and Nigeria which include the Cameroonian village of Gore Mahamat and Nigerian villages of Saguir, Kirta-Wulgo, Gore Blankafe, Damure and Chaugry and which usurped the Boko Haram of land and operatives. This resulted in the arrest of 24 Boko Haram terrorist accomplices, including a woman and some logistics facilities. Sixth, the rescue of over 3,800 captives or abductees at Damure village and adjoining areas by Sector 1 which were subsequently handed over to Operation LAFIYA DOLE at Gambarou IDP Camp in Nigeria resulted in providing succour to the civilian population. Seventh, the successful rescue of 88 captives or abductees (a man, 43 women and 44 children) from Garere and Dogon Chuku by Sector 3 resulted in boosting public confidence in the operations. Eight, the liberation of Damasak by Sector 4 MNJTF and the successful defence of Diffa and its Airport which is the Airbase and Tactical HQ for the Operation GAMA AIKI denied the BH of their long-held claim to the area. Finally, the seizure of Malam Fatori by the combined troops of Sectors 3 and 4 from Nigeria and Niger respectively supported by air assets from TCCs. The pressure on the Boko Haram terrorists also led to the surrender of 96 terrorists to Sector 2 Chad and 16 Boko Haram terrorists and some accomplices to Sector 4 Niger.

Achievements, Challenges and Prospects

There is no doubt that the MNJTF has recorded significant strategic and operational successes. At the strategic level, among its mission successes include (a) coordination and facilitating the speedy signing of MoU and SIA between MNJTF/LCBC, the African Union and TCCs; (b) coordination the reception and prompt operational deployment of the AU-assisted CODAN Radio and Motorala communication equipment as well as training of the TCCs personnel on the equipment; (c) improved cooperation and synergy between the MNJTF forces and national/bilateral forces within and around MNJTF AO; and continuous handling of IDPs/refugees through provision of foodstuff and other essential needs within the MNJTF AO.

On the other hand, the MNJTF has also recorded some operational achievements: (i) effective coordination of air operations within MNJTF AO leading to precision of air strikes by Chadian, Nigerien and Nigerian fighter jets in support of ground operations; (ii) extensive use of combined ISR provided by assets of Nigeria, Niger and the Center for Liaison and Coordination (CCL) complemented by Human Intelligence (HUMINT) to positively influence tactical operations of the ground troops. Degrading the BHTs capability through coordinated offensive operations thereby reducing frequent attacks on own troops and main supply route within the MNJTF AO and building the confidence of the populace. Other successes recorded include: (iii) the Capture of Madayi, Alargano, Doron Naira, Kangarwa, Metele, Dogon Chuku, Abadam by the Force which led to the recovery of vehicles, armament and other logistics; and (iv) the successful clearance of Nigerian and Cameroonian villages in Southern and Eastern Borno in conjunction with troops of Operation LAFIYA DOLE; (v) the rescue of over 8,570 captives/abductees most of which were handed over to Operation LAFIYA DOLE troops for transportation to IDP Camps (Total of 4,690 handed over at the Banki Axis, 3,800 at Gambarou Axis while 88 were rescued from Garere and Dogon Chuku of Baga Axis). Furthermore, the force achieved the liberation of Damasak and seizure of Malam Fatori by the combined troops of MNJTF and Operation LAFIYA DOLE supported by air assets of TCCs. Similarly, about 1,077 Boko Haram terrorists members were neutralized while a total of 643 BHT members were arrested with their logistics. About 32 terrorists' camps and IED making factories were destroyed and several equipment/weapons which include motorcycles, vehicles, AK-47 rifles, boats and other logistics were captured. The pressure on the Boko Haram terrorists subsequently led to the surrender of 1,032 Boko Haram terrorists to MNJTF troops in Chad and Niger.

In spite of the modest achievements highlighted above, there are some challenges that are still being faced by the MNJTF. The most critical challenges include inadequate lift capability, difficulty in sustaining troops, inadequate engineers and amphibious capability as well as lack of dedicated intelligence surveillance and reconnaissance assets.

Inadequate Lift Capability: The lack of adequate lift capability has limited the offensive capability of the forces due to extensive AO and the widely dispersed nature as well as tactics of the BH terrorists. In order to ensure that MNJTF is highly mobile, effort is being made by the leadership to provide fighting vehicles and TCVs, POL and 15 other critical logistics items. It is indeed vital for the MNJTF lift capability to be enhanced in order to make it an even more mobile and effective force.

Lack of Dedicated Airlift Capability: Air lift capability remains the backbone of any successfully operation. MNJTF presently has no air capability. Lack of aircraft (fixed wing and helicopter) remains a problem in the MNJTF operations. The headquarters relies on the TCCs to assist in this regard. Additionally, the provision of ground to air communication is vital for the successful conduct of air operations. The headquarters is however making effort to ensure MNJTF is provided with fixed wing aircraft, helicopter and its associated ground to air communication gadgets. This will assist in ensuring effective coordination of operations as well as command and control of the entire MNJTF area of responsibility.

- ***Difficulty in Sustaining Troops:*** The CONOPs stated that the TCCs were to provide all logistics requirements for its Force. It is striking to note that after the Commander's initial operational visit to the Sectors, it was apparently clear that the LCBC member countries may need additional resources to sustain the troops operationally.

- ***Inadequate Engineer, Amphibious and IED Detonation Capability:*** The nature of MNJTF AO, especially along the Lake Chad Basin Area requires the employment of specialized engineer and amphibious equipment. However, it is worthy of note that Sectors 1, 2 and 3 have amphibious elements though without the required platforms to ensure robust amphibious operations within the MNJTF AO. Furthermore, there is an increase in the employment of IEDs along major and minor roads within the MNJTF AO by the BHTs leading to varying degrees of human and equipment casualty. Unfortunately, the MNJTF IED detonation capability is hampered by lack of adequate equipment to easily identify and detonate the IEDs. Additionally, the skilled manpower to tackle this challenge is also limited. As such, the HQ is working out modalities to ensure the MNJTF is equipped with the necessary platforms and equipment to tackle this challenge. (UNO Report, 2015).
- ***Lack of Dedicated Intelligence Surveillance and Reconnaissance Assets:*** Adequate intelligence gathering within the AO is lacking due to the absence of dedicated ISR assets. In the conduct of their operations, various sectors lack ISR assets which would have provided them with current BH disposition and probable real time imagery on the ground. Presently, the sectors rely heavily on HUMINT and other sources which may not be instantly available at time of need. In addition, the Centre for Coordination and Liaison (CCL) at N'Djamena provides some air reconnaissance assistance to HQ MNJTF. It is however observed that these assets do not have the MNJTF as priority since the same machinery supports the BARKHANE operations in the Sahel region. However, during the conduct of Operation GAMA AIKI, more real time ISR support was provided by ISR from the TCCS and CCL which was crucial to the successes achieved (Agbor, 2017).

Conclusion

The use of regional mechanism for countering insurgency in the LCB fits into the strategy of pursuing regional security through kinetic model (Agbiboa, 2017; Agbor 2017). As a result of the transnational efflorescence of the Boko Haram insurgency in the LCB, the MNJTF was remodelled and re-energized from its initial form of an anti-banditry fighting force to a counter-terrorism fighting force. This was due to the mayhem of the BHT whose activities climaxed around December 2014 to January 2015. This Chapter has attempted to give a brief background to the MNJTF and highlighted the Command and Control Structure. Thereafter, the adversary and MNJTF disposition was highlighted. Afterwards, an assessment of current and future operations, especially the conduct of the highly successful Operation GAMA AIKI was highlighted. Finally, some of the modest achievements and challenges facing the MNJTF were highlighted. The MNJTF as a counter-terrorism force has made significant strides but there is room for improvement and this would be achieved as the force metamorphoses and with increased logistics support and vital operational enablers.

NOTES

1. Agbor T.I. Abdullahi L.F. (2017), 'Taming the Monster: Boko Haram' in Mohammed M. and Abdullahi L.F. (eds), *Global Terrorism: The Nigerian Experience in Taming Boko Haram*, Lagos, Nigeria
2. African Union (2004), Protocol to the OAU Convention on the Prevention and Combating of Terrorism, Addis Ababa: African Union.
3. Agbiboa, Daniel E. (2017), "Borders that Continue to Bother Us: The Politics of Cross-Border Security Cooperation in Africa's Lake Chad Basin," *Commonwealth & Comparative Politics*, Vol. 55, No. 4, pp. 403-425.
4. Assanvo, William; Abatan, Jeannine Ella A and Sawadogo, Wendyam Aristide "Assessing the Multinational Joint Task Force against Boko Haram," West Africa Report, Institute of Security Studies, No. 19, September 2016 Online: https://issafrica.s3.amazonaws.com/site/uploads/war19.pdf
5. Athie, Aïssata (2018), "Coordinated Response Key to G5 Sahel Joint Force Success," https://reliefweb.int/report/mali/coordinated-response-key-g5-sahel-joint-force-success.
6. Bassey, Celestine O. (1996), "Alternative Models for Peace-Keeping in Africa: A Sub-Regional Model," in Vogt, M. A. and Aminu, S. (eds.), *Peace-Keeping as a Security Strategy in Africa: Chad and Liberia as Case Studies*, (Vol. 2), Enugu: Fourth Dimension Publishing Co., Ltd.
7. Boulding, Kenneth (1962), *Conflict and Defense*, New York: Harper & Row.
8. Buhaug, Halvard (2006), "Relative Capability and Rebel Objective in Civil War," *Journal of Peace Research*, Vol. 43, No. 6, pp. 691–708.
9. Buhaug, Halvard (2010), "Dude, Where is My Conflict? LSG, Relative Strength, and the Location of Civil War," *Conflict Management and Peace Science*, Vol. 27, No. 2, pp. 107-128.
10. Buzan, Barry (1986), "A Framework for Region Security Analysis," in Buzan, Barry and Rizvi, Gowher (eds.), *South Asian Insecurity and the Great Power*, London: Macmillan.
11. Buzan, Barry (1991), *Peoples, States and Fear: An Agenda for International Security Studies in the Post-Cold War Era* (2nd Ed.), Boulder: Lynn Rienner Publishers.
12. Buzan, Barry (2000), "The Logic of International Security in the Post-Cold War World," in Hettne, BjÖrn; Inotai, András and Sunkel, Osvaldo (eds.), *The New Regionalism and the Future of Security and Development*, New York: St. Martin's Press.
13. Buzan, Barry and Wæver, Ole (2003), *Regions and Powers: : The Structure of International Security*, New York: Cambridge University Press.
14. Connor, Gregory (2017), "Understanding the Drivers of the Boko Haram Insurgency 'Violent Extremism' in the Lake Chad Basin," Norwegian Institute of International Affairs.
15. Desgrais, Nicolas (2017), "Jihadi Threat in the Sahara-Sahel Region and New Ad Hoc Regional Security Mechanisms," Nordic Africa Institute, Uppsala, 22-24 November.
16. ECCAS to Join the Fight Against Boko Haram, https://www.prc.cm/en/news/audiences/1127-eccas-to-join-fight-against-boko-haram
17. ECOWAS Donates Food to People in the North East of Nigeria to Fight Against Food Insecurity, http://www.ecowas.int/ecowas-donates-food-to-people-in-the-north-east-of-nigeria-to-fight-aganst-food-insecurity/
18. ECOWAS, Protocol A/SP.3/5/81 Relating to Mutual Assistance on Defence.

19. Ejiga, G.O. (1996), "Analysis of the Operational Aspects of the OAU Peace-Keeping in Chad," in Vogt, M. A. and Aminu, S. (eds.), *Peace-Keeping as a Security Strategy in Africa: Chad and Liberia as Case Studies* (Vol. 2) Enugu: Fourth Dimension Publishing Co., Ltd., pp. 367-386.
20. Fah, Gilbert L. Taguem (2007), "The War on Terror, The Chad-Cameroon Pipeline, and the New Identity of the Lake Chad Basin," *Journal of Contemporary African Studies*, Vol. 25, No. 1, pp. 101-117.
21. Kelly, Robert E. (2007), "Security Theory in the 'New Regionalism,'" *International Studies Review*, Vol. 9, No. 2, 2007, pp. 197-229.
22. Kupolati, R. (1996), "The Nigerian Contingent in the OAU Peace-Keeping Operation in Chad," in Vogt, M. A. and Aminu, S. (eds.), *Peace-Keeping as a Security Strategy in Africa: Chad and Liberia as Case Studies*, (Vol. 2), Enugu: Fourth Dimension Publishing Co., Ltd., pp. 387-398.
23. Médecins Sans Frontières / Doctors Without Borders (MSF) (2016), Lake Chad: Trapped in deadly violence. https://www.msf.org.uk/article/lake-chad-trapped-in-deadly-violence. Accessed 20/07/2019 5:50pm
24. Nkwi, Walter Gam (2015), "Terrorism in West African History: A 21st Century Appraisal," *Austral: Brazilian Journal of Strategy & International Relations*, Vol. 4, No. 8, pp. 78-99.
25. Nolan, Cathal J. (ed.), *Power and Responsibility in World affairs: Reformation Versus Transformation*, Westport: Praeger, 2004.
26. Obamamoye, Babatunde F. (2017), "Counter-terrorism, Multinational Joint Task Force and the Missing Components," *African Identities*, Vol. 15, No. 4, pp. 428-440.
27. Osakwe, CCC, (2017) 'Counter Boko Haram Terrorism: Initial Response' in Mohammed M. and Abdullahi L.F. (eds), *Global Terrorism: The Nigerian Experience in Taming Boko Haram*, Lagos, Nigeria
28. Patrick, Stewart, "Multilateralism and the US National Interest," in Nolan, Cathal J. (ed.), *Power and Responsibility in World affairs: Reformation Versus Transformation*, Westport: Praeger, 2004, pp. 165-213.
29. Pérouse de Montclos, Marc-Antoine (2014), "Nigeria's Interminable Insurgency? Addressing the Boko Haram Crisis," Research Paper, Chatham House, London.
30. Pérouse de Montclos, Marc-Antoine (2017), "Boko Haram: A Jihadist Enigma in Nigeria," in Hentz, J. and Solomon, H. (eds.), *Understanding Boko Haram: Terrorism and Insurgency in Africa*, Routledge, London.
31. Pérouse de Montclos, Marc-Antoine (ed.) (2015), *Boko Haram: Islamism, Politics, Security, and the State in Nigeria*, Tsehai, Los Angeles.
32. Pérouse de Montclos, Marc-Antoine; Magrin, Géraud; Chauvin, Emmanuel and Rangé, Charline (2018), "Development and Governance: A Fragile Space," in Pérouse de Montclos, Marc-Antoine and Magrin, Géraud (eds.), *Crisis and Development: The Lake Chad Region and Boko Haram*, Paris: Agence Francaise De Developpement (AFD).
33. Radio France Internationale, "Fighting against Boko Haram: Completion of the Multinational Joint Task Force," 23 August 2015, www.rfi.fr/ afrique/20150823-fin-reunion-lutte-contre-boko-haram-tchad.
34. Statehouse, Office of the President, Federal Republic of Nigeria, Speech of President Muhammadu Buhari during the second Regional Security Summit on 14 May 2016, www.statehouse.gov.ng/index.php/news/2221- president-buhari-s-speech-at-the-2nd-regional-security-summit.

35. Tar, Usman A., and Mustapha, Mala (2017), "The Emerging Architecture of a Regional Security Complex in the Lake Chad Basin," *Africa Development*, Vol. XLII, No. 3, pp. 99-118.
36. Thompson, William (1973), "The regional Subsystem: A Conceptual Explication and Propositional Inventory," *International Studies Quarterly*, Vol. 17, No. 2, pp. 89-117.
37. Umoh, Ubong Essien (2015), "Cameroon, Nigeria and the Bakassi Conflict: Building Blocks for a Non-Democratic Peace Theory," *Journal of International Relations and Development*, Vol. 18, No. 2, pp. 227-247.
38. United Nations Security Council, Report of the Secretary General on the Situation in Central Africa and the Activities of United Nations Regional Office for Central Africa, May 2015.
39. Waziri I.M. (2017), "International Involvement in the fight against Boko Haram" in Mohammed M and Abdullahi LF, (eds), *Global Terrorism: The Nigerian Experience in Taming Boko Haram*, Lagos, Nigeria.
40. Yoroms, G.J. (2016), 'Counterterrorism Measures in West Africa' in Wofula O and Annedi B (eds), *Understanding Terrorism in Africa: Building Bridges and Overcoming the Gaps*, Institute of Security Studies, Pretoria.

11

Amnesty, Disarmament, Demobilisation, Reintegration and Security Stabilisation in the Niger Delta: A Critical Impact Assessment

Colonel S Inuwa

ABSTRACT

This chapter presents a qualitative critical impact assessment of the amnesty disarmament, demobilisation and reintegration (DDR) programme launched by the Nigerian state in the Niger Delta region in 2009 with the aim of stabilising the security situation in the Region. The assessment examined the contributions of each phase of the ADDR programme towards achieving security stabilisation. The study posits that while the grant of amnesty and the subsequent disarmament that follows contributed to security stabilisation by restoring relative safety and confidence on the part of the citizens, demobilisation and reintegration failed short of any meaningful contribution to security stabilisation. The chapter concludes that there is a high potential that the Region may relapse to violence. However, this depends on the Nigerian state ability to assert its monopoly of violence as well as address the grievances that gave rise to the conflict.

Introduction

Historically, violent agitation by the people of the Niger Delta region over oil started with the abortive Isaac Adaka Boro's secessionist revolt in the 1960s (Adetoun, 2005: 47). However, the conflict reached a turning point with the emergence of the Movement for the Emancipation of the Niger Delta (MEND). It is apparent that MEND represented the most organised and ferocious phase of the Niger Delta conflict and succeeded in escalating the Niger Delta conflict to a new dimension by crippling oil production and revenue to the state (Ikelegbe, 2010: 40). However, in 2009 the Federal Government granted amnesty to the militants that paved way for a disarmament, demobilisation and reintegration programme in the Region. The first phase took place from 6 August – 4 October 2009 during which 20,192.00 militants were disarmed (Federal Government of Nigeria Niger Delta Amnesty Programme, 2011: 32). Similarly, 2, 909 weapons were surrendered, and 295,153 ammunitions recovered as well as 1, 853 and 3, 454 unexploded ordinances, D-caps, dynamite and magazines respectively (Ibid). The second leg of disarmament took place in 2010, during which 6,166 militants were disarmed.[1] In the third round that took place in late 2012, a total of 3,642 militants surrendered their weapons bringing the total number of militants that disarmed in the entire programme to 30,000.00.[2] These disarmed militants subsequently went through the process of demobilisation and reintegration.

Against this background, this chapter presents the outcome of a critical qualitative impact assessment study undertaken between August 2013 - January 2014 to interrogate the efficacy of the ADDR programme in achieving security stabilisation in the Niger Delta. The data used in this analysis were generated through semi-structured in-depth interviews during which 53 respondents were interviewed in Abuja, Edo, Bayelsa, Delta and Rivers states and 1 in London. Similarly, 2 Focus Group Discussions were held, one with residents of a local oil producing community and another with ex-militants. Each of the Focus Group has 7 and five participants respectively.

Concepts are highly contested in social science (Ramsbotham, et al 2005: 30), it is therefore pertinent to define and clarify the key concepts to be used in this chapter. The concepts of disarmament, demobilisation and reintegration are key to understanding of the chapter and they are used as defined in the United Nations Disarmament, Demobilisation and Reintegration Standards (UNIDDRS, 2006).

Amnesty and Security Stabilisation in the Niger Delta

Varied mechanisms can be adopted by societies undergoing violent conflicts to end violence and stabilise the security situation. Often amnesty is resorted to when DDR is contemplated in the absence of military defeat between the warring parties. For instance, Walter (1997: 335-364 and 2002: 3-43) posits that the primary concern of warring parties, when asked to disarm, is not the question of how to reach a consensus over land, power sharing or the underlying grievances that led to the war but instead the fear of whether their personal security will be guaranteed during and after demobilisation. Walter's assertion was further supported by Scharf contention that:

> *Leaders of the various parties to a conflict must cooperate to put an end to the fighting and violations of international Humanitarian Law. Yet, it is unrealistic to expect such leaders to agree to a peace settlement if, directly following the agreement, they would find themselves or their close associate facing life imprisonment...the offer of amnesty may be a necessary bargaining chip to induce human rights violators to agree to peace and relinquish power (Scharf, 1999: 508-509).*

In a similar vein, Freeman (2009: 37) posits that 'amnesties are usually seen as one of the key incentives or preconditions for a successful DDR program.' Accordingly, evidence from this study suggests that without the offer of amnesty the Niger Delta militants would not have agreed to disarm. A top MEND commander expressed the opinion that without being offered amnesty they would not have agreed to go through the DDR process because of the significant risk to their lives. According to him:

> *...at some point, we got fed up that we could not even continue again. But another point too [was that] even though we are bored and tired of the struggle there is no way we can just keep the arms or throw them away and...walk in the communities or come to Warri and walk ... as free men ... [For] somebody like Tompolo...any day... [the government] get him, they won't even be going to court they have to kill him the way they killed Yusuf that Boko Haram guy...so how can such a person leave the struggle and come [out from the creeks]. It was just to continue until one day when God have something good for us...*[3]

What all these responses illustrate is that even though the Niger Delta militants were war fatigued they were not willing to go through the ADDR process without the safety of their lives guaranteed. Furthermore, evidence from this study suggests that in the context of negotiated settlement, amnesty may be a necessary evil needed to navigate the war to peace transition in war-torn societies. This is because the immunity from prosecution that the amnesty offered the militants addressed the security dilemma that pervades their minds thereby serving as a powerful inducement for them to disarm and demobilise.

Disarmament and Security Stabilisation in the Niger Delta

Essentially, 'disarmament should achieve the removal of the means by which civil wars have been executed and lead to the creation of a stable environment, thus strengthening confidence and security building among combatants, the government and the population' (Alden, *et al*, 2011: 14), a point also reiterated by Meek and Malan (2004: 23). However, to what extent disarmament contributed to security stabilisation in the Region, a military respondent that served with the Joint Task Force (JTF) deployed in the Niger Delta observed that judging from the manner it was conducted and the quantity of weapons recovered, the disarmament phase fell far below the minimum standards provided in the UN IDDRS (2006). He described the disarmament process in this way:

> *What... took place was that prior to the amnesty programme, leaders of each camp...were identified, they were now told to compile names of people that were under their supervision. So, it is possible that a lot of sharp practices might have taken place...they were just at liberty to submit whatever names they wanted.... The veracity of the names they submitted as their boys would be in dispute because no one knew, whatever I tell you was the size of my camp is [what] you take because you weren't there. So that also might have affected the quantity of arms that were recovered. Even after the amnesty, there were still insinuations that look what they recovered in terms of arms wasn't even up to half of what the holdings of these boys were.... So when it comes to the issue of knowing how many militants each person had, how many arms were collected I want to say that government may not have had any say over it because it was a matter of what they brought.... So I think it was just a matter of good faith, bring your arms and they brought it...*[4]

Corroborating the above, another retired military general that participated in the disarmament and demobilisation processes argues that due to Nigeria's porous maritime boundary which the Niger Delta region occupies, even as disarmament was going on, small arms and light weapons were continually smuggled into Nigeria.[5] Therefore, this study contends that the security stabilisation achieved in the Niger Delta was a consequence of the symbolic significance of the amnesty granted and disarmament ritual that took place than the quantity of weapons recovered. This explains why even though the Niger Delta region was still characterised with hidden arms caches, the security situation tremendously improved in the immediate aftermath of the disarmament programme. Additionally, the fact that the granting of amnesty emboldened the militants who hitherto were in the creeks to come out as freemen strengthened the symbolic significance of the programme and its contribution to security stabilisation in the Region. Therefore, in the case of the Niger Delta ADDR programme, irrespective of the manner the disarmament phase was conducted, its confidence building impacts and significance in terms of contributing to security stabilisation in the short-term cannot be underestimated.

Demobilisation and Security Stabilisation in the Niger Delta

Demobilisation is the formal and controlled discharge of combatants from active service whether from the armed forces or any armed group, and its main objective is to reduce or totally break up the armed forces or armed group. Likewise, Alden *et al* (2011: 14) and Vries & Wiegink, (2011: 40) argue that demobilisation is aimed at breaking the command and control (C2) structures under which combatants operate thereby making it difficult for them to return to armed rebellion. This suggests that for demobilisation to contribute to security stabilisation in the Niger Delta it must lead to the dismantlement of the command and control (C2) structures as well as personal loyalties that exist between the top generals, middle-level commanders and foot soldiers. Similarly, it must also destroy the relations between foot soldiers as peers so that the capacity to re-unite will be significantly neutralised. Breaking the C2 structures of the Niger Delta militants was a critical prerequisite for achieving security stabilisation because they represent Second Generation militias which Francis (2005: 1-3) theorize as Africa's intractable security menace. However, despite this necessity, opinions expressed by several respondents in this study suggest that demobilisation has not successfully achieved this primary objective. Respondents in this study observed that this was mainly because of the initial miscalculation of paying the foot soldiers through their former commanders. For instance, a Niger Delta specialist notes that as far as the C2 structures are concerned:

> *It is intact, nothing has changed; the structures are intact. By design... you pay the followers through their leaders so if I am a leader and I have three hundred boys you pay the boys through me. What does that mean; those boys are still loyal to me. So, the structures are intact it is just that now they are dormant they can be activated if they decide to.*[6]

In a similar vein, another member of the Disarmament and Demobilisation Committee corroborated the above assertion by noting that:

> *In a demobilisation programme, the whole idea is to return the individual...to his individuality; go back to the way you were...[But] you see right now what we are doing is dangerous, and I fear because down the*

> *road the government is...paying the boys through their leaders...So if you keep paying them through their leaders it means you did not demobilise them...*[7]

The above respondent went further to elaborate on the logical consequence of paying the ex-militants through their former commanders by contending that:

> *...the so-called militants that they had demobilised still form a body of militants under command of their former leaders. So you have not demobilised them; so tomorrow now, all they will need; it's just...get a few arms now, say, 'boys let's start again', you know...those leaders are still in control and if you [want to] see them, all you have to do is go to social occasions that these militants' leaders attend and see the kind of crowd that follows them.*[8]

Thus, the failure to successfully achieve the goal of demobilisation means that the mutually reinforcing connection between disarmament and demobilisation critical for long-term security stabilisation was missed in the Niger Delta ADDR process. Furthermore, another reason why demobilisation could not achieve its supposed goal centres on the manner *inducement* was applied. Generally, incentive is meant to encourage and sustain the commitment of combatants to the DDR process and the overall peace process to the extent of not contemplating a return to violence. However, in the context of the Niger Delta ADDR programme, inducement was applied in such a crude way that it became counterproductive to the goal of effective demobilisation. This was because the Nigerian government identified and concentrated on key commanders with the largest followers of foot soldiers and high capacity to threaten oil production and offer them huge monetary compensation through contract awards[9] which empowered them economically. A key member of the Presidential Amnesty Planning Committee described the doctrine of inducement used by the Nigerian government as a policy of *patronage and exclusion.*[10] She posited that the government limited its sharing of payoffs to selected powerful militant commanders while those considered less powerful were completely excluded and alienated.

Patronage and exclusion were counterproductive to the goal of demobilisation and the entire Niger Delta ADDR programme in several ways. One of such consequences as noted by an expert on the region, was the likelihood that the relative stability achieved in the Niger Delta was not due to successful dismantling of the C2 structures of the militants groups, but of the patronage that was extended to the 'top generals'[11] a form of peace buy-off. The second implication was that it strengthened the economic dependence of the so-called demobilised foot soldiers on their former commanders in order to cope with economic realities of living off the business of rents seeking by the barrel of a gun. This was because the reinsertion allowance was too inadequate to sustain their previous standard of living that the war economy provided them. The only way for those excluded from the ADDR patronage to cope with the effect of a sudden fall in their standard of living was to continually depend on their commanders thereby preserving and strengthening the existing line of C2 structures. In the long-term, this portends serious threat to security stabilisation in the Niger Delta because it offers the selected 'top generals' a high capacity to remobilise. In a similar vein, a Niger Delta academic expert reiterated that the selective application of patronage ensures the existence of 'networks that can be reactivated at very short notice.... So when people say, oh if something doesn't happen in the Niger Delta, we will go back...they are not joking. They are not joking because they know that the networks are still intact.'[12] Additionally, the policy of patronage and exclusion was counter-productive to security stabilisation by leading to the emergence of peace spoilers in the Niger Delta. Stedman (1977: 8) posits that spoilers can be from inside or outside the peace process. He maintains that an insider spoiler usually signs a peace agreement indicating his/her willingness to comply with the terms of peace agreement only to later renege on the entire or key provisions of the agreement. However, insider spoilers are likely to comply with the terms of the settlement and remain committed to it so long as the peace process continues to benefit them. Alternatively, 'outside spoilers are parties who are excluded from a peace process or who exclude themselves and use violence to attack the peace process' (Ibid: 8). Evidence from this study shows that the exclusive nature of the Niger Delta ADDR patronage system gave rise to *insider-outsider spoilers*. These spoilers emerge mostly from middle-level commanders who originally were part of the peace process and signed the renunciation of militancy bond but because of being marginalised and alienated they reneged on their renunciation of militancy thereby becoming *insiders turned outsider spoilers*. Such peace spoilers re-mobilised to the creeks established new camps and recruited their own foot soldiers thereby re- igniting a new cycle of violence. A pertinent example was the case of John Togo a field commander under 'Government Ekpemupolo alias General Tompolo'. 'General Tompolo' was the overall MEND commander but John Togo was his field combat commander, nevertheless the ADDR patronage was exclusively given to Tompolo with John Togo completely side-lined. Meanwhile, all efforts by

John Togo to access some patronage from the state were blocked by 'General Tompolo' which prompted him to reneged on his renunciation of militancy and return to violence. A military officer serving with the JTF observes that:

> *...John Togo was...the so-called war commander of Tompolo...Tompolo...was more of a spiritual leader than of a fighter so Togo was his actual commander the head of the foot soldiers for the prosecution of the conflict but they gave recognition to Tompolo and he felt cheated because he asked for a share which from what I heard, Tompolo refused to give him. Even when he asked for a contract from Governor Oduaghan of Delta state, Tompolo will use some people to go and block him because he is very close to the government. So, John Togo now said if this is it and the whole thing started from the creeks, well I am going back to the creeks. I am going back to go and get my own share. I think in the process, he killed soldiers and he was of course taken out.*[13]

Clearly, the case of John Togo demonstrates a typical case of an insider who later became an outsider peace spoiler due to the grievance of exclusion and marginalisation.

The problem of peace spoilers was not limited to the rank of former middle-level commanders but even among the foot soldiers. For example, a key member of the TCND asserted that some of them that '...were not caught in the web of this distribution of patronage...'[14] felt cheated and undermined the relative peace in the Niger Delta by attacking their former bosses. A pertinent case was the report by Okhomina (2013) titled '*Gunmen kill 13 policemen in Bayelsa state*'. The reporter revealed that some disgruntled foot soldiers formerly under the command of ex-MEND South Wind commander, Kile Selky Torughedi alias General Young Shall Grow, attacked and killed 13 policemen deployed to provide security during the internment of the 'general's' late mother at Azuzuama Sothern Ijaw Local Government Area of Bayelsa state.[15] The boys were aggrieved because the General has abandoned them despite the government patronage he got.

Additionally, the ADDR patronage system also encouraged the emergence of *outright outsider peace spoilers*, a situation Greenhill and Major (2006: 10) describe as '...dogs that did not originally bark may later emerge, threatening...'. For example, the emergence of Kelvin Ibruvwe who in 2013 proclaimed himself as the leader of *Liberation Movement for the Urhobo People (LIMUP)* (an ethnic nationality in Delta state), attests to the veracity of these assertions. Kelvin Ibruvwe and his followers took up arms against the state and declared that:

> *We are giving this ultimatum because the cheating is too much, the federal and state governments had neglected us for so long and now we want them to hear us because for over 50 years now, they have been drilling oil from our community which is the second best oil in this country, yet we have nothing to show for it. There is hunger everywhere; graduates have no jobs. So, we want the government to listen to us and that is why we are giving them 60 days' ultimatum to listen to us or else we will shut down all the well heads in the area. If they like, they should bring soldiers. When we want to strike, no amount of security can stop us ...When the Ijaws and Itsekiris [were]... agitating with arms, we the Urhobo youths chose to be peaceful, but what did we get? We are rather left out completely in the amnesty programme [my emphasis]. Is it not the same oil that the Ijaws and Itsekiris produce that is also produced in Kokori, which has the second-best oil in Nigeria? So, what is our crime? (Orosevwotu, 2013: 2).*

It is apparent that Kelvin and his followers were angered by the patronage extended to Ijaw youth and want the same treatment extended to them. The emergence of Kelvin illustrates the fact that the use of patronage and exclusion if not carefully planned and implemented during DDR can generate further conflict and instability. Therefore, demobilisation failed to achieve the breakdown of existing vertical and horizontal C2 structures of the various militant groups in the Niger Delta. This suggests that the potential for the Niger Delta region to relapse into violence remains very high.

Reintegration and Security Stabilisation in the Niger Delta

Reintegration is the final phase in the DDR process as outlined in the UN IDDRS (2006). While according to Berdal (1996: 39) reintegration consists of '...medium-and long-term programmes, including 'cash compensation, training or income generation meant to increase the potential for the economic and social reintegration of ex-combatants and their families.' Reintegration is the critical phase of the DDR process because its success determines whether ex-combatants and society at large can return to the path of long-term peace (Shibuya, 2012: 85). Therefore, it is key to the restoration of security and stability in the aftermath of violent conflict and the benchmark of measuring the overall success of any DDR programme. Thus, the extent to which reintegration can contribute to security stabilisation in the Niger Delta depends on the degree to which the ex-militants are socially, politically and economically reintegrated into society. However, the assessment here will be limited to social and economic reintegration.

Social Reintegration and Reconciliation

After being demobilised, ex-combatants are confronted by several personal challenges such as their separation from and the destruction of the social network they relied on during war, which Hazen (n.d.: 1-11) refers to as the war family. Likewise, they are also confronted with stigma and rejection by family and community members (Operational Guide to the UN IDDRS, 2014: 172). This implies that 'an ex-combatant who has economic opportunities but who is socially isolated or excluded cannot be considered as successfully reintegrated' (Ibid.) All these underscore the importance of ex-combatants achieving social reintegration. Thus, if the ex-militants are to be socially accepted and reintegrated, a genuine process of social reconciliation must be pursued to change the negative community perception about them. Conversely, the ADDR programme lacked any social reintegration and reconciliation agenda. Corroborating this assertion, a female staff member of a nongovernmental organisation contends that:

> *There should have been a kind of sensitisation on the amnesty programme because... the amnesty programme is actually giving them pardon and if the Federal government has given them pardon it means that their communities also should forgive them for whatever they had done...and that was what...should have been done... there should have been some sessions of healing or some form of restorative justice...to prepare the community, to say that this person actually did all these things but he is a different person now and we should accept him. That was not done, that was not done.*[16]

Also, a Niger Delta development activist argues that 'it is obvious... everybody was not carried along. The community was not even thought [of,] it was not even remembered as a critical...[stakeholder]... [in] the entire amnesty that has a role to play.'[17] The obvious implication of neglecting social reintegration and reconciliation agenda in the programme is that many of the communities to which the ex-militants were expected to return to still harbour negative perceptions about them. This suggests why most of the ex-foot soldiers are settling in the capital cities of their states instead of their local rural communities.[18] Residing in cities makes it easier for them to conceal their identity as ex-militants and to escape negative perception from the society.

Economic Reintegration

As asserted by Kingma (2000: 28) economic reintegration is the process through which ex-fighters and their households build up new livelihoods by engaging in productive activities and gainful employment. Therefore, the failure to achieve economic reintegration '...can lead to considerable insecurity at the societal and individual levels, including rent-seeking behaviours through the barrel of a gun' (Colleta *et al*, 1996: 18). Supporting this position, Collier (1994: 343-351) argues that failure to adequately cater for ex-combatant's economic wellbeing will trigger an avalanche of micro and macro security challenges. In line with conventional practice in DDR, the economic reintegration of the Niger Delta ex-militants was prioritised. For instance, a documentary titled '*Presidential amnesty programme Niger Delta 2014*' provided insight on the achievements being recorded in economic reintegration of the ex-Niger Delta militants. The transcript of the documentary revealed that:

> *...out of ... 30,000 persons enlisted in the first, second and third phases of the Presidential Amnesty programme an appreciable number of them totalling 5,000 are currently undergoing training spread across... 104 universities and 22 skilled acquisition centres in 28 countries and 19 training institutions in 8 states of the country. About 1,000 of them in the oil and gas sector have graduated and currently in training (sic), 29 have graduated in...engineering in France. Over 13,000 delegates have graduated from local and foreign training centres in various skills acquisition programmes. At a ceremony in Lagos recently.... The Chief Host and President Goodluck Jonathan's Special Adviser on Amnesty Matters Honourable Kingsley Kuku introduced to the public 65 youths who trained and qualified as commercial pilots and 61 youths who trained and qualified as aircraft maintenance engineers. The training was carried out by world-class aviation companies like Boeing and Lufthansa.*[19]

Furthermore, the Head of the Reintegration Department at the Office of the Special Adviser to the President on Niger Delta revealed the successes being recorded in the area of human resource development of the ex-Niger Delta militants. According to him:

> *...some of them now are in Lufthansa, doing what we call type rating to move from one level of being a pilot to the topmost level of what we call the end level new generation level. Some of them, six amongst those people and the deprived communities, six of them are distinction holders from UK universities from a post-graduate programme, 14 of them are pursuing PhD, of course, you know that 19,000 more of them are currently in training... is the only DDR programme that is training somebody to be a PhD holder, is the only DDR programme in the world that is not targeted at training artisans... it is succeeding...because we have people who will fly planes, we have people who are already flying and earning money, we*

have instructors from the programme teaching in institutions including flying institutions...currently... we have over 16,000 graduates. And now we have taken it to a new level we are collaborating with Schneider in France to train people in power generation...[20]

However, it is pertinent to point out that for economic reintegration to contribute to security stabilisation in the context of DDR certain fundamentals about it must be right. First, it is necessary that the genuine ex-combatants are given priority in the training opportunities being offered. Conversely, evidence from this study suggests that many of the ex-militants have been short-changed. A female staff member of a non-governmental organisation observed that many of the ex-militants were frustrated because they had been abandoned with all the promises made to them not fulfilled.[21] Corroborating this, a former MEND commander testified that most of his boys have not attended any form of reintegration training whether at home or abroad yet they are the actual fighters.[22] He argues that these are the boys that are falling back to the creeks to do all these things because they don't have hope.[23] These revelations suggest that the possibility of economic reintegration to contribute to security stabilisation in the Niger Delta has been undermined because most of the genuine ex-militants have been short-changed. Furthermore, for economic reintegration to enhance security stabilisation the trained ex-combatants must also have access to gainful employment or financial capital to start up small scale business. However, judging from the response of a Niger Delta female respondent, a lot of those trained are yet to be gainfully employed.[24] In the same vein, a MEND commander contends that '... the rehabilitation process was very successful. But the other area that is yet to be successful even up to ... today is the creation of jobs.'[25] In a similar vein, the Special Coordinator of the Amnesty Programme revealed that 11,768 of the ex-militants are yet to be empowered.[26] However, the fact that so many are returning to unemployment may be storing up longer-term potentials for the resurgence of violence. Additionally, the failure to engage those trained portends serious risk for sustaining the current relative stability achieved in the Niger Delta region. This is because the training has triggered a revolution of rising expectations of job opportunities and better life (International Crisis Group African Report No 231, 2015: 3). But regrettably, such expectations were dashed due to lack of opportunities for gainful employment. Evidently, the above failure reinforces the conditions for further grievance, frustration and the potential to resort to rent-seeking behaviour through the barrel of a gun on the part of the ex-militants. Consequently, as in the case of demobilisation, economic reintegration has failed to consolidate the relative stability achieved via the grant of amnesty and disarmament.

Conclusion

This chapter attempted a qualitative critical impact assessment of the Niger Delta ADDR programme, this is in terms of to what extent the programme has achieved or contributed to security stabilisation in the Niger Delta. The chapter argues that the grant of amnesty to the Niger Delta militants has contributed to security stabilisation in the Region because it responded to the security dilemma that confronted the militants as regard to what would happen to their safety in the aftermath of demobilisation. Similarly, the chapter maintains that despite the manner disarmament was conducted, it succeeded in stabilising the security situation in the Niger Delta in the short-term. However, the relative stability achieved was not consolidated by successful demobilisation and reintegration. This was because instead of demobilisation to dismantle the existing vertical and horizontal C2 structures of the various militants' commanders; it further reinforced and strengthened them. Consequently, the obvious outcome of the demobilisation process is a legacy of high capacity to remobilise on the part of the former top commanders.

The high capacity to remobilise was further reinforced by the failure to achieve economic reintegration of the less powerful commanders, middle-level commanders and foot soldiers. Furthermore, the effectiveness and potential for economic reintegration to contribute to peace consolidation was undermined by the lack of access to reintegration training opportunities by many of the genuine ex-militants and the inability to secure jobs by those already trained due to a mismatch between types of training offered and existing market opportunities. Therefore, the current situation suggests that the Niger Delta region will continue to oscillate between peace and violence. However, whether the Region will experience lasting peace or gravitate towards violence depends on the ability of the Nigerian state to address the sources and drivers of the conflict as well as assert its monopoly of violence.

NOTES

1. Interview with respondent 001- member Disarmament and Demobilisation Implementation Committee, September 2013. Also, corroborated in a commentary written by Murphy Ganagana in a special report titled 'Three Years of Amnesty Implementation: The Facts, The Figures' contained in Quarterly Newsletter Published by the Presidential Amnesty Office Vol. 1 No. 3. Being an anniversary edition.
2. Ibid.
3. Respondent 038, November 2013.
4. Respondent 009, October 2013.
5. Respondent 002, October 2013.
6. Respondent 032, November 2013.
7. Respondent 042, December 2013.
8. Respondent 042, December 2013.
9. The mode of distributing the ADDR patronage was through the award of mulita-million-dollar security contracts for pipelines surveillance as pay-offs to the top militants' commanders. For instance, Joab-Peterside et al., (2012: 12), provided figures of the monetary patronage extended to some of the top commanders. According to them 'the breakdown showed that Government Ekpumopolo received the lion's share of $ 22.5 million yearly, while former warlord, Dokubo Asari, collects $9 million every year to keep his estimated 4000 soldiers at bay. Ateke Tom and Ebikabowei Boyloaf Victor Ben each collect $ 3.5 million apiece.'
10. Respondent 047, December 2013.
11. Respondent 032, November 2013.
12. Respondent 046, December 2013.
13. Respondent 012, October 2013.
14. Respondent 008, October 2013.
15. The report by Okhomina was also confirmed by the 'general' during the interview I had with him.
16. Respondent 020, November 2013.
17. Respondent 022, November 2013.
18. Personal observation during field work
19. This information was sourced from a transcription of the commentary of a documentary tilted 'Presidential amnesty programme Niger Delta 2014' available at https://www.youtube.com/watch?v=Ap8OJh-AlG8 and accessed ....
20. This information was sourced from a transcription of a live television interview held with Mr Lawrence Pepple, Head of the Reintegration Department at the Office of the Special Assistance to the President on Niger Delta Amnesty Programme. The live interview programme was titled 'Niger Delta Presidential Amnesty program assessment-The Journey So Far'. Available at https://www.youtube.com/watch?v=7BSWte1Oidg.
21. Respondent 020, November 2013.
22. Respondent 039, November 2013.
23. Ibid.
24. Respondent 025, November 2013.
25. Respondent 041, November 2013.
26. See story titled 'Amnesty Office yet to empower 11,768 ex-militants-Boroh'. Available

at: http://theeagleonline.com.ng/amanesty-office-yet-to-empower-11768-ex-militants-boroh/ (Accessed 26 July 2016).

REFERENCES

1. Adetoun, B. (2005). 'The role and functions of research in divided society: a case study of the Niger Delta region of Nigeria,' in Robinson, E. P. G., Schnabel, M. S. A. and Osaghae, E. (ed.) Researching conflict in Africa: insights and experiences. Tokyo: United Nations University Press, pp. 47-55.
2. Alden, C., Thakur, M. & Arnold, M. (2011). Militias and the challenges of post-conflict peace: silencing the guns. London Zed Books.
3. Berdal, M. R. (1996). Disarmament, demobilization after civil wars. New York: Oxford University Press.
4. Colleta, N., Kostner, M. & Wiederhofer, I. (1996). The transition from war to peace in Sub-Saharan Africa. Washington: World Bank.
5. Collier, P. (1994). 'Demobilization and insecurity: a study in the economics of transformation from war to peace', Journal of International Development, Vol. 6, No. 3. pp. 343-351.
6. Federal Government of Nigeria Niger Delta Amnesty Programme (2011). Assessing the dynamics of and sustainability of the Niger Delta Amnesty Programme: a presentation to the House Committee on Niger Delta. Abuja: Office of the Special Adviser to the President on Niger Delta.
7. Francis, D. J. (2005). 'Introduction', in Francis, D. J. (eds). Civil militia: Africa's intractable security menace? Aldershot Hants: Ashgate Publishing Company, pp. 1-29.
8. Freeman, M. (2009). 'Amnesties and DDR programs', in Patel, A. C., Greiff, P. D. and Waldorf, L. (ed.). Disarming the past: transitional justice and ex-combatants. New York: Social Science Research Council, pp. 36-85.
9. Greenhill, K. M., and Major, S. (2006/07). 'The perils of profiling: civil war spoilers and the collapse of intrastate peace accords.' International Security, Vol. 31, No. 3, pp. 7-40.
10. Hazen, J. M. (n.d.). Social integration of ex-combatants after civil war. Available at: www.un.org/esa/socdev/sib/egm/paper/Jennifer%20Hazen.pdf (Accessed 9th May 2013).
11. Ikelegbe, A. (2010). Oil, resource conflicts and the post conflict transition in the Niger Delta Region: beyond amnesty. Benin City Nigeria: Centre for Population and Environmental Development.
12. International Crisis Group (2015). Curbing violence in Nigeria (III): revisiting the Niger Delta Africa report No 231. [Online]. Brussels, Belgium. Available at: http://www.crisisgroup.org/~/media/Files/africa/west-africa/nigeria/231-curbing-violence-in-nigeria-iii-re-visiting-the-niger-delta.pdf (Accessed: 29 September 2015).
13. Joab-Peterside, S., Porter, D. and Watts, M. (2012). Niger Delta economies of violence working paper No. 26 rethinking conflict in the Niger Delta: understanding conflict dynamics, justice and security. Available at: http://siteresources.worldbank.org/INTJUSFORPOOR/Resources/Watts_26_Revised.pdf (Accessed: 14 June 2015).
14. Meek, S. Malan, M. (2004). 'Identifying lessons from DDR experiences in Africa' Workshop Report Kofi Annan International Peacekeeping Training Centre (Ghana) Accra, 10-12 August. Available at: http://www.iss.co.za/pubs/monographs/no106/

Contents.html (Accessed 13 November 2012).
15. Okhomina, O. (2013). 'Gunmen kill policemen in Bayelsa', 6 April, Leadership (Online) Available at: http://leadership.ng/nga/articles/51594/2013/04/06/gunmen_kill_13... (Accessed: 18 June 2013).
16. Orosewotu, P. (2013). 'Delta's most wanted kidnap suspects gives govt 60 days' ultimatum', The Nation, 19 September, pp. 2.
17. Ramsbotham, O., Woodhouse, T., & Miall, H. (2005). Contemporary Conflict Resolution (2nd ed.). Cambridge United Kingdom and Malden, USA: Polity Press.
18. Scharf, M. P. (1999). 'The amnesty exception to the jurisdiction of the International Criminal Court,' Cornell International Law Journal, Vol. 32, No. 3, Article 8, pp. 507-527.
19. Shibuya, E. R. (2012). Demobilizing irregular forces. Cambridge: Polity Press.
20. Stedman, S. J. (1977). 'Spoiler problem in peace processes', International Security Vol. 22, No. 2 (Fall). pp. 5-53. Greenhill, K. M., and Major, S. (2006/07). 'The perils of profiling: civil war spoilers and the collapse of intrastate peace accords.' International Security, Vol. 31, No. 3, pp. 7- 40.
21. United Nations (2006). Integrated disarmament, demobilization and reintegration standards—forward. New York: United Nations.
22. United Nations (2014). Operational guide to the integrated disarmament, demobilization and reintegration standards. New York: United Nations.
23. Vries, H. D. & Wiegink, N. (2011). 'Breaking up going home: contesting two assumptions in the demobilization and reintegration of former combatants', International Peacekeeping 18: 1. pp. 38-51.
24. Walter, B. F. (1997). 'The critical barrier to civil war settlement', International Organization, Vol. 51. No. 3, pp. 335-364.
25. Walter, B. F. (2002). Committing to peace: the successful settlement of civil wars. Princeton New Jersey: Princeton University Press.

12

Terrorism, Insurgency and the Quest for De-radicalization in Nigeria

Hussaini Jibrin and Zaharaddeen Sulaiman

ABSTRACT

Like many other nations in the world today, especially in Africa, Middle East and South America, Nigeria is increasingly challenged by radical youth conflicts in the form of terrorism and other related violent activities. Although many scholars are of the view that this kind of security threat is not new in the nation's history, the conventional approach of dealing with the radical groups causing havoc has, in very recent time, taken a new dimension diverting from the use of conventional military approach in Internal Security Operations (ISO) and focusing to more peaceful approach. This is done primarily in order to de-radicalise the violent insurgent members that are operating either individually or in groups, and make them useful and productive members of the wider civil society. The chapter adopts historical research methodology by using both primary (oral interviews) and secondary (published works on the related subject matter) sources for reconstruction of history. Finally, a meta-analysis is used to discuss the diversity of new peaceful methods of de-radicalisation adopted by the Nigerian State and their level of success or otherwise.

Introduction

Since independence on 1st October 1960, the Nigerian federation witnessed various forms of youth militancy and radicalised activities. These activities and violent behaviour were as a result of misguided beliefs embedded in some radical ideologies. Such ideologies are of different types ranging from political, ethnic, sectional, economic and religious. This has no doubt created a lot of setbacks in the implementation of development planning, consolidation of democracy, scientific and technological advancements as well as execution of other projects geared toward general development of the nation. In short, the rise of radical behaviour and the violence accompanying it has eaten deep into the fabric of nation building process in Nigeria causing serious damage to human and material capabilities. Security action by the military in Internal Security Operations mounted by the government against these insurgents and radical groups has taken a heavy toll on the national resources and personnel for so long. As such the Nigerian government revised its methods to include non-Military approach in identifying and subduing the threats of insurgents, radical groups and violent behaviours.

It is against this backdrop that this chapter explores the mechanisms and policies put in place by the Nigerian government in order to promote de-radicalisation of both active and non-active members of violent insurgent groups. Indeed, such radical behaviours seem to be among the most rampant security challenge characterised as militancy, terrorism or insurgency carried out across the country. Thus, the chapter is mainly divided into the following sub-sections; an Overview of Youth Radicalism in Nigeria, Theoretical Framework, Conventional Approach to De-radicalisation in Nigeria, the Search for another Option, Soft—Approach or Peaceful Methods and Conclusion.

An Overview of Youth Radicalism in Nigeria

Today, Nigeria can be classified among the top centres of radicalism in the world as a result of the widespread ideological violence and radical conflicts going on in different parts of the country. For us to properly understand the current de-radicalisation programs, it is important to turn briefly into the history of the radicalisation itself in the country and we need to be clear what radicalism is about. The word radicalism originated from a Latin word *radical is* which means political change from the root. In political studies, 'Radicalism' means a belief that society needs to be changed, and the changes can only be carried out through revolutionary means (Wikipedia). However, in strategic and military parlance, radicalism could be described as inspired, affiliated or grudge-based violence that could qualify as terrorism (Kamolnick, 2014: xi). On the other hand, radicalisation and violence almost always beget terrorism.

In an attempt to conduct a survey of youth radicalism and terrorism in the most populous blacks' country in the world, we will realise that the nature of the violence and uprisings vary in the two major different sections of the country: north and south. Whereas youth restiveness in the northern parts of the country is to a large extent associated with religion dictated by some misguided Muslim groups, on the other hand, violence is dictated by ethno-economic and political realities in the southern parts of the nation. But it is important to mention here that, both northern and southern radicalised groups operated against the Nigerian state in the interest of the leaders of the radical groups to the detriment of improved welfare of the masses which they mostly claimed to have been fighting for. The leaders of the groups encourage teaming number of illiterates and literate-without-job youth through good package of wages and salaries, training, sophisticated weapons, hard drugs and other intoxicated substances to fight, proclaiming freedom for the entire peoples in the various societies where such conflicts affect. Examples of these radical ideological groups operating in southern Nigeria include: Movement for Actualization of Sovereign State of Biafra (MASSOB), Movement for Emancipation of Niger Delta (MEND), Odudua People's Congress (OPC) to mention but a few. Today, the most pressing youth radical movements in this region are the MASSOB and the Niger Delta militants who operated in different groups in the region.

In northern Nigeria, the most active radical groups proclaim religious ideology and use it to push home their demands. On a number of instances, such radical religious ideology justifies operations of terror groups involving massive killings that qualify as terrorism. Thus, terrorism in the name of religion continues to bedevil northern parts of Nigeria. Religious terrorism take a form of inter and intra-religious upheavals (Isa, 2016). No doubt, the end result of this is to the benefit of only the group leaders, not the ordinary followers. Imparting radical ideologies in the minds of the young followers was always emphasised in place of simple and basic tenets of the two major religions in the region: Islam and Christianity. In Islam, for instance, which is the dominant, just like in any other revealed/Semitic religion in the world, there are divisions or denominations among the followers arising from differences in human reasoning, interpretations and historical factors guiding understanding of the Sacred Texts. This paved way for the emergence of radical groups that extremely went beyond the simple and basic missions of the religion. There was the radical Muslim group called the *Maitatsine* which caused uprisings in the 1980s and early 1990s. Members of this radical religious group were properly dealt with through military approach. There were the Shiite uprisings since 1990s to date being approached militarily, and the current Salafi/Wahabi/*Boko Haram* (BH) insurgency that is being dealt with since 2009 through the conventional military approach (Kabiru, 2012). Although the conventional military approach was used in all these instances, it did not stop the violence resulting from them to spill over to other areas of northern Nigeria. There is need here to examine the empirical evidences of the conventional approach used by the Nigerian government in its bid to neutralise the radical groups and their violent behaviour before proceeding to explore the extent to which it is effective or otherwise.

Theoretical Framework

In order to give this chapter more proper understanding or easy comprehension, there is the need to adopt a theoretical base upon which all subsequent analysis would be derived. This would aid researchers and interested academics not only to sufficiently relate their ideas in a subtle manner, but also to provide definite boundaries to the issues being analysed. In fact, researches that fail to be based on sound theoretical frameworks of analysis are susceptible to provide either fallacious information or feeble and weak analysis that could not be easily coordinated in searching solutions to a societal problem. However, each research has its own peculiar theoretical framework of analysis, depending on the nature, requirements and objectives that the research sets to achieve.

Against this backdrop, therefore, this chapter is basically historical in character. In other words, its theoretical framework reflects considerable historical methodology and analysis. An attempt is made to trace the gradual development of governmental and non-governmental initiatives aimed to combat radicalisation in Nigeria. However, this historical approach augmented by occasional detailed analysis of specific policies initiated and implemented over time. Therefore, a second method, the meta-analytical approach, is adopted in order to broaden the outlook of the chapter. This is done in order to not only to augment the historical approach and strengthen analysis, but also to buttress the argument. As a theoretical framework and method of research, meta-analysis emphasised the use of multifarious but relevant sources of information in order to deepen understanding of a particular research problem. As such, meta-analysis is specifically adopted here in order to pool different categories of information materials such as published books, periodicals, other documents, research papers and direct personal interviews with people involved in the government's de-radicalisation policies. This particular theoretical approach satisfies the historical ideal of "cumulation" (Stanford, 1994:17). According to Stanford, historical researches have to be cumulative; that is, they have to be based on the proper understanding and appreciation of previous researches on the same subject. However, such previous researches should provide insight into the subject they discussed. As a result, historical researches could be both analytical and comparative in such a way that they either support or falsify arguments.

So, the present chapter simply makes use of two different and ideologically different theoretical approaches, but mutually productive in resonating different salient voices on the same subject. While the historical approach is expected to provide long term experiences as published is extant literature from the past down to the present, the meta-analytical approach pools the various information together in order to find areas of convergence and divergence. Each of the two approaches would aid in the general analysis and sufficient understanding of problematic areas within the subject of radicalisation and de-radicalisation in Nigeria.

Conventional Military Approach to De-radicalisation in Nigeria

The above preliminary discussion suggests that issues concerning conflicts of radical ideologies are not new in Nigeria. Therefore, the Nigerian state has throughout the period of its existence responded positively in quelling the menace at different periods. For instance, in February 1966, the military was deployed in the Niger Delta to suppress Isaac Jasper Boro led insurgency. The 12-day counterinsurgency operation was a hurried combination of personnel of the Nigerian Army and Nigerian Navy. By 1992, Decree No. 23 appeared to have established the first Counter-insurgency Joint Operation that approximated a Joint Task Force setting in the Niger Delta. It was the Rivers State Internal Security Task Force (RSISTF). The task force was set up and deployed in response to the rising agitations by the Movement for the Survival of Ogoni People (MOSOP) in Ogonil and the failure of the Nigeria Police Force (NPF) to effectively manage the mutating crisis. Both the NN and NA were involved in the RSISTF operations. RSISTF was made up of one NA brigade (2nd Amphibious Brigade), Nigerian Navy Ship (NNS) PATHFINDER, supported by 97th Special Operations Wing of the Nigerian Air Force (NAF) and elements of the NPF (Ubong, 2017). RSISTF was also used to respond to the Ogoni crisis of May 1994 when the four Ogoni chiefs were murdered. Its mission was initially to suppress Ogoni protests and later to maintain peace, law and order in Rivers State (Ubong, 2017). It was this agitation led to the assassination of Ken Saro-Wiwa, radical activist in the area, and his collaborators during the early 1990s. However, with the return to democracy in Nigeria in 1999, under the pretence of fundamental human rights and freedom fighting many radicalised youth groups emerged fighting the

Nigerian state in the name of struggle for oil resource control. Their activities have been threatening peace among people and oil exploration in the Niger Delta region in the south till date.

With regards to the MASSOB youth radical ideology in South-eastern parts of Nigeria, its origin could be traced to the Nigerian Civil War, executed around 1967 and 1970. The Civil War was also conventionally crushed through the use of military approach. However, the political ideology which stirred up emotions leading to the Nigerian civil war continued to exist in the minds of the secessionists throughout the subsequent military regimes that followed in Nigeria. Similarly, under the pretence of freedom of self-expression under civilian rule, the same violent radical ideology resurfaced in full force indoctrinating thousands of youth. The same cases were handled or treated militarily largely with thorough expertise in professionalism of the Nigerian Army.[1]

Part of the conventional way of dealing with terrorism can also be seen in the manner in which the government quelled the *Maitatsinet* error as a religious group in Kano, northern Nigeria. In December 1980, the challenge of containing a religious crisis by a group of fanatic Muslims in the city of Kano, northern Nigeria confronted the Nigerian Army. The Nigeria Police Force's management of the crisis was a failure; hence the Military was summoned to take over. For instance, in the battle of Shahuci, on 18th December 1980, the Police deployed barely one hundred and fifty men against over three thousand religiously radicalised fanatics. The former was routed and their impoverished logistics and transport were depleted by the latter (Elaigwu, 2003). It was at this point that the Federal government decided to involve the military by sending a delegation of some Army officers from the office of the Quartermaster-General of the Nigerian Army, who was also the acting Chief of Army Staff, Major-General Dumuje. This delegation travelled to Kano and assessed the volatile situation. Its mandate was to decide whether or not the military should be involved. On the arrival of the delegation to the scene, they were welcomed by gun fire from the "Maitatsine" fanatics. (Zahradeen, 1988) On the 26th December, President Shehu Aliyu Shagari formally mandated the Army to take over from Police and quell the riots. (Elaigwu, 2003) The mandate was given to the Army on Friday evening, but no section of the general public knew what mode of operation would be taken against the radical group. Many people speculated that the frequency with which the Air force aircrafts flew over the area gave strong indications that nothing short of bombing would be undertaken (Zaharadeen, 1988).

Earlier than this period, by 24th December 1980, about one thousand people including police men, soldiers and members of the public were killed in Kano during an encounter with *Maitatsine* people. Therefore, with this grief and the mandate, on Sunday 28th December, at about 5.30 am soldiers from 146 Infantry Battalion, of Three Infantry Brigade aided by armoured vehicles from 202 Battalion Kaduna moved in to put down the revolt. The operation was commanded by the then Major Halilu Akilu. The operation which took the Police almost ten days without any meaningful progress took the soldiers only few hours. By the afternoon of the same day, the main enclave of the insurgents was demolished, all the buildings around were reduced to rubbles and most of the inhabitants of the area killed while the rest took to their heels (Zahradeen, 1988).

Another example of the conventional approach to dealing with radical religious ideologies in Nigeria can be seen in the series of clashes between the Nigerian Army and the members of Islamic Movement in Nigeria popularly known as Shi'ites (See, Yandaki: 2017).

Some Past Experiences and Challenges Encountered

During the long period when the Nigerian government and its population relied on the use of military force to quell insurgency and suppress radicalisation in its polity, there was considerable success. However, the success recorded upon the subsequent use of non-violent measures was tremendous. In comparative terms, the non-violent measures seem to record more success not only in avoiding the use of violence but also in winning over radicalised members of violent groups. Therefore, the multitude of non-violent methods employed seem valid and acceptable so much so that they not only augment, but are gradually beginning to supplant the conventional violent military approaches hitherto employed. It is noteworthy at this juncture that, the initial response to de-radicalisation in Nigeria entails efforts from both governmental and non-governmental agencies.

Government initiatives centred on the application of force and violence through its military and police. All these aimed to assert the superiority of the government over all its territories and the people who occupy such territories. Although the government has the power and legal authority to force loyalty and submission on its citizens and all other elements occupying its territories, civilian concerns over extra-judicial violence perpetrated and conducted by government security forces on innocent civilians has been identified as a major challenge that threatens violent de-radicalisation measures. Instead of helping security agents in the discharge of their duties of identifying, apprehending and/or subduing criminals violently, civilians have showed contempt towards these agents. This attitude from the civilian public had slowed down swift success in the military approach in the past (Aliyu, 2019). As a result, success was slow and significantly low. However, the slow success recorded by the military and other security agencies may also be as a result of poor government commitment in funding and the provision of modern equipment to its security personnel. Insurgents and radical groups, on the other hand, often use modern and more sophisticated weapons. In addition, other violent equipment were regularly improvised. One could only imagine the swift success of insurgents in ravaging hundreds of communities in North-eastern Nigeria during 2013 and 2014 (Harnischfeger, 2014). During the period media outlets in Nigeria have reported of complete sacking of Military base in Yobe State by armed radical groups. To such and other related problems, governments have bigger roles to play in the provision of funds, manpower and military equipment in order to show its full commitment in combating radicalisation and internal insurgency.

On the other hand, the civilian population in the areas affected by violent radical insurgencies have also improvised militia groups and other alternative violent means of dealing with radical groups. This could be termed as *Communal Approach to De-radicalization* (CAD). In Nigeria, with the formation of civilian militia known as Civilian Joint Task Force (or simply Civilian JTF) especially around 2013 by some youth at Hausari quarters, Monday Market and Babban Layi in Maiduguri (most affected areas by the radical group) armed themselves and patrolled their areas dealing with any member of the society known to be upholding radical ideologies. (Hussaini, 2018) This could be understood given the predilection that supply of military support by government is grossly inadequate. In addition, the military may have the difficulty of sufficient understanding of the local terrain where the radical groups operate. For example, in the Niger Delta region of Nigeria where violent and radical militancy takes place against the Nigerian government and the various concessionaire companies exploring oil, the numerous creeks and rivers render the area not only difficult to access but also hard to police. It was the same case in the terrain of North-eastern Nigeria where the sun baked arid land seems the same over hundreds of miles. To surmount such difficulties, local population decided to provide the required support needed to guarantee the security of their own communities through the formation of an armed militia which is called civilian JTF. Such a militia, or civilian JTF, comprised of volunteered locals and other concerned individuals about the security of the area. Their job was to augment government security efforts, especially in providing local information of the terrain and surveillance. The civilian JTF also undertakes overnight vigilante of local communities against attacks by violent radical groups.

One important element that characterised such armed militia or civilian JTF across Nigeria was their lack of formal training in combating insurgency and urban violence. This factor is a serious handicap on the part of their operations. For one, most members of the civilian JTF were not familiar with the rules of engagement. Hence, a concept known as 'Jungle Justice' is often associated with their activities. In its literal sense, jungle justice is used to denote a situation where civilian JTF felt obliged to subdue any possible threat using violence. Therefore, whatever measures taken by the civilian JTF against radical groups and insurgents seems justified. This included execution of suspects. As a result, not all civilian JTF groups formed received blessings from the government. Their activities were constantly checked and halted in order to forestall extra-judicial executions and unlawful behaviour. Despite these challenges, our submission here is this, the role played by the civilian JTF in de-radicalization exercise of the BH insurgents cannot be overemphasized.

The Search for another Option

As a result of the catastrophic impact of the Boko Haram insurgents and their activities on thousands innocent citizens in northern Nigeria and the nation at large, the Nigerian security policy makers saw the need for a paradigm shift from the conventional military approach of ending radicalism to some alternative ways. Perhaps, this has to do with the increasing occurrences of some fresh related crisis in other parts of the country despite the prevalent military in Internal Security Operations (ISO) against insurgents. Such other related crises included cattle rustling and armed banditry that also has elements of youth radicalism against both the state and ordinary people. This is what led to the decision to resort to other more professional ways of ending radicalism among the Nigerian youth. These can be appreciated in the following sub-headings:

Soft–Approach (or Peaceful Method)

Nigeria was not the first nation to develop alternative methods of dealing with insurgents, radicalised groups and terrorists operating within its boundaries. The United States has for long formulated sound strategies of dealing with insurgents and radical groups. In fact, its policies include monographs suggesting non-violent measures of de-radicalisation in other countries like Nigeria (Hill, 2010). Since 2014, the Nigerian government has come up with a broad outline of dealing with both active and non-active insurgents and members of radical groups fighting within and across its national boundaries (English, 2018: 13). However, the most active plans were especially designed for the insurgents fighting in the Lake Chad region (Bukarti and Bryson, 2019: 6). The first comprehensive and active plan was the formation, empowerment and intensified operations of the Multinational Joint Task Force (MNJTF) under the Office of the National Security Advisor (ONSA). The MNJTF's primary plan involved violent methods employed through military action. Such actions were taken not only to pacify fighters, but also to secure occupied areas and promote peace and peaceful coexistence among the local people. However, the plan under MNJTF later involved non-violent measures aimed to cater for non-active members of radicalised groups under a plan known as Operation Safe Corridor (OPSC).

Through a number of organised processes, this operation engaged different professionals to provide different services in order to neutralise and reform former fighters termed as 'clients' according to the programme (Barkindo and Bryans, 2016). Therefore, OPSC's outreach could be conveniently studied depending on the nature and attitude of ex-fighters that were targeted by the specific programmes. Such ex-fighters and their attitudes fall into two broad categories:

- *Captured (or Non–active) fighters*: as observed by Bukarti and Bryson, these are those members of radicalised groups who were captured in active fighting, disarmed and taken into government custody (Bukarti and Bryson, 2019).
- *Surrendered clients*: these are those who willingly give up their membership of radicalised groups and opt to make peace with government. Such willing desire by the clients to lay down arms may arise from misunderstandings generated within the ranks of the radicalised groups, or a perceived hopelessness of continued fighting by members of radicalised groups.

Therefore, in line with the global need to effectively devise viable processes of tackling former fighters and make them fit for reintegration back into the civil society, the OPSC came up with some 'soft methods' or peaceful processes aimed at, not only countering the threat of ex-fighters to the government and military personnel, but also to sufficiently ensure the security of ordinary citizens living in the civil society. These processes could be analysed in the following components, as follows:

Engagement

One of the most portent methods aimed at de-radicalisation of ex-fighters is direct engagement or involvement with the clients. This method entails confidential one on one interaction or conversation between the clients and selected professionals such as psychiatrists, sociologists, therapists, psychologists and clerics. Such interactions could be in the form of interrogations or simple friendly discussions with particular clients. However, the aim of such a verbal engagement or discussion with the client is both to downplay tensions and political grievances on the part of the client, and to create a serene platform of understanding to pump the client for information. Basically, this method is devised as an assessment strategy, and it has proven vital in understanding the radical ideologies that influenced fighters not only in Nigeria, but across the globe as well. The method also assisted in providing assessment for actions to be taken by officials as well as evaluation for the clients.

Depending on the nature of involvement of the client in the radicalised behaviour and violent fighting either individually or in groups, one or more of these professionals comes close to the client either to interrogate or in a confidential conversation and mutual interaction. One characteristic of engagement with the client is the absence of physical force or any form of coercion. This is done in order to build not only the confidence of the client but also to enable them develop considerable trust of the professionals interrogating them. The main objective of such professionals was to extract information from the clients and to monitor their general behaviour. On the other hand, information extracted from clients is assessed and used to develop comprehensive methods of dealing with individual clients. For example, the level of commitment to radical ideologies of clients was assessed and weighed against their repentance or otherwise. This invaluable information helps tremendously to determine the next course of action to be taken on the client. Similarly, such pieces of information gathered on different individuals are often collated and used to develop a sound theoretical analysis of radical behaviour among clients operating within similar or the same ideology.

Therefore, such a method of de-radicalisation often takes precedence before official conviction of clients to prison sentences. However, it should be noted that almost all the programmes of de-radicalisation in Nigeria were prison based. As such, even when clients were not officially convicted, such clients remain in the custody of prisons. All programmes and plans aimed at de-radicalisation seem to begin from such a 'waiting' period. On another note, engagement as a plan aimed at de-radicalisation is a continuous process that could take years. In other words, it rarely ends in a short time. Officials assigned to the ex-fighters continue to make contact with their clients and even after the clients have been reintegrated back into the civil society. This is done in order to ascertain progress or otherwise for the radicalised behaviour in the clients. In short, engagement method in de-radicalisation is a relevant process that continues to manifest at different stages of the entire process of de-radicalisation, even in other processes such as intervention (Kangiwa, 2019).

Intervention

As a method, intervention does not signify the violent approach provided by the military. It is a plan that comes either independently or immediately following the result and analysis of long conversations with clients. As an independent plan (Zamani 2018: 4), it comprises structured processes designed to assist both the clients and the official personnel responsible for the de-radicalisation of the clients. On the other hand, intervention as a process comes into effect based on the information gathered from the clients through engagement and conversations. The main purpose of intervention plan is to devise viable and appropriate means of de-radicalising clients and prepare them to be fully integrated into the civil society based on the information gathered through engagement. So far, intervention has functioned for both captured and surrendered clients (Interview: Peter, 2019). However, relatively few clients failed to make it into the next stage of the de-radicalisation process.

As a peaceful plan to counter radical ideologies and neutralise national threats, the purpose of intervention in the process of de-radicalisation of clients involves moral support provided by therapists and/or business experts or entrepreneurs. The therapists begin the process by concentrating on the provision of moral and psychological support to the clients' state of mind and reform their behaviour. Depending on the attitude of the clients, therapies are usually arranged either on a daily or weekly basis to be conducted on the client. Sometimes, psychologists and psychiatrics are also involved in the therapy of clients. Reports are passed based on the analysis of clients' psychological and emotional behaviour. Such analysis is meant to determine the suitability or otherwise of the clients to the next step of the de-radicalisation process such as training, counselling and education.

At a certain stage, when clients begin to show significant changes and improved behaviour, the entrepreneurial experts begin to pay them visits in order to train them (the clients) on certain business skills such as shoe mending, sewing/tailoring, soap making, carpentry, etc. The idea of training the clients in entrepreneurial skills evolved out of the conviction among experts that, most of the radicalised fighters were previously recruited due to their poor economic condition, lack of business skills or both. Training the clients in entrepreneurial skills is therefore important at all stages of the de-radicalisation process, as this would make them well—equipped with the required skills to lead independent and productive lives by the time they were deemed fit to be reintegrated back into the civil society. Similarly, it is believed that developing their skills over a long period of time would make them appreciate themselves and endear them to the prospects of building a more befitting and productive career. As a prison-based programme, most of the modern prisons in Nigeria provide such opportunity for clients. However, other prisoners who were not clients share the same privilege of training in entrepreneurial skills (Interview, Joseph: 2019).

Neutralisation

After identifying the exact factors and radical ideology in play that led to violent behaviour of clients in terror groups, the next stage to deal with radicalised behaviour is through neutralisation. This is usually achieved through education. However, the education process of clients is basically commensurate with the type of radical ideology that influenced their radical behaviour. For example, if the radical ideology that dictated clients' previous violent behaviour emanated from political grievances, therefore, structured political education is required to counter the radical ideology. Similarly, if radical religious beliefs were the prime motive of radical behaviour and violence among clients, clerics were assigned to de-radicalise the clients through religious education (Interview: Aliyu, 2019).

Educating the clients to abandon their previously held radical ideology and behaviour is a delicate process. It requires a comprehensive background, analysis and clear understanding of the client's behavioural history, including their responses to other processes of de-radicalisation such as engagement and intervention. In most Nigerian prisons religious clerics were the major educators of clients. Religious instructions were structured and moderated in order to provide a sound basis aimed at de-radicalisation of clients. Such religious instructions usually take place on a weekly basis with a view to enhance mutual coexistence among different clients with different ideological and doctrinal inclinations. In the same vein, this mutuality would enhance their prompt reintegration in the larger society upon release. According to some prison wardens involved in the prison based de-radicalisation programmes, religious instructions seem to be extremely efficient in the neutralisation of clients. Such religious instructions seem to transform clients into peace loving and humane inmates. Apart from their violent backgrounds, clients who received weekly religious instructions seemed to be the best behaved-inmates in Nigerian prisons.

In addition to moderate religious instructions, clients were exposed to rigorous counselling from professional counsellors and sociologists. The clients were made to attend counselling sessions both individually and in groups. Individual counselling for the clients inculcates the desire to concentrate on their internal moral and psychological developments. While on the other hand, group counselling reiterates social behaviours and peaceful coexistence among all people. However, the general idea behind the introduction of counselling to the clients is to emphasise peace and security as necessary ingredients of development in the society. Similarly, clerics could also act as counsellors to clients in prison. The structured religious instructions that clerics organise to clients were meant not only to reform the moral and social behaviours of clients through choices, but also to serve to stir up the emotions of clients and challenge them on the need to promote social peace and harmony.

Rehabilitation

Sometimes the best way to effect the transition of clients from ex-fighters to ordinary law abiding people who fit into the civil society is attained through incarceration in prison. A number of ex-fighters from radical groups in Nigeria were serving prison sentences. However, long term prison sentences hardly make a lasting impression of de-radicalisation on ex-fighters. On the contrary, English believes that prisons are "incubators of radicalisation" and perhaps extremists ideologies matured in prisons (English, 2018). Therefore, for the sake of de-radicalisation Nigerian prisons opted to be broader in their outlook and service delivery in order to enable the successful implementation of de-radicalisation processes. In this way, clients or ex-fighters were often isolated from the rest of the criminals in the prisons. In fact, contacts between the two categories of criminals were reduced to a minimal.

The main aim is to adequately and sufficiently transform clients' behaviours and make them fit and productive members of the larger society without any formal or informal interference. This is just the beginning of the process of rehabilitation of clients in Nigerian prisons. The process takes precedence immediately following official verdict to serve prison sentence. In essence, the programme of rehabilitation is officially meant for clients serving prison sentences. Those clients on probationary stay were kept separate from those serving sentences. Therefore, their treatments vary accordingly. For those clients serving prison sentences, there are laws and modalities of de-radicalisation as stipulated by both international laws and national operational directives (Azimazi, 2018). Interestingly, the national operational directives have been active and expanded considerably to cater for those clients not yet convicted. Therefore, the above three (3) modalities discussed earlier were officially structured, implemented and maintained in order to provide the clients with the clear mind-set attainable while serving their prison sentences.

Recommendations

Careful study of the political economy of the people in the insurgency affected areas in Nigeria reveal that there is clear manifestation of failure of good governance in both northern and southern regions over time. Apart from acute unemployment, at many levels government fail to provide social amenities such as sound education, employment, potable drinking water and health facilities at the local level for the benefit of the ordinary people. These grievances and discrepancy that emerged out of the wide gap created between haves and haves-not as well as the influence of many factors easily paved way for unemployed youth to be brainwashed and recruited to any kind of insurgency. The pressing poverty caused by unemployment and lack of opportunity often compelled youth into unacceptable activities capable of providing stable incomes. In a nut shell, the radicalised youth who join the groups, do so mostly in order to get means for human survival as pointed above. In this consideration, we recommend the following as part of the strategies for de-radicalisation of insurgents in Nigeria.

- Creation of more job opportunities and provision of social amenities at all levels (cities, towns and villages).
- Private wealthy individuals (Nigerians) who invested huge amount of wealth in other parts of the world should be encouraged to invest at home for more job opportunities because government alone cannot provide jobs to its teaming population.
- Foreign investors from different parts of the world should also be encouraged to invest in different parts of our country in order to supplement government and private individual efforts in job creation for peace to be achieved.
- Government should control religious activities through religious bodies in order to check-mate the activities of radical clerics.

- Governments (States and Federal) should engage moderate religious leaders intensively in the various de-radicalisation programmes.
- Parents should be more up and doing in the upbringing of their children (know who they interact with and their ideologies) and the provision of their (children's) needs.
- Governments should discourage politicians from politicizing religious ideas and religious differences in their political struggles.
- Government should encourage teaching of history as a subject in our schools at all levels for educating children our lost value systems that upheld our peaceful coexistence in the past.

Conclusion

The chapter examined the background of the Nigeria's conventional approach to de-radicalisation and the current efforts being made to do away with the menace completely. All the above points are part of a structured process of de-radicalisation. The processes could either be effected in the outlined sequence or in random order. It all depends on the personal needs of the clients involved. Generally, therefore, the processes were expected to expose the clients as stake holders in maintaining peace, harmony and security of the general polity.

NOTES

1 The group under their current leader, Nnamdi Kanu threatened to stop the 2019 general elections by not allowing people to come out and vote but they were contained peacefully by the Army.

REFERENCES

1. Azimazi, S. (2018), "Policy and Legal Framework for Deradicalisation of Violent Extremist Offenders," Working Paper for SUPPORT TO THE NIGERIAN PRISONS SERVICE'S DE-RADICALISATION PROGRAMME.
2. Bulama, A.B. and Bryson, R. (2019), *Dealing with Boko Haram Defectors in the Lake Chad Basin: Lessons from Nigeria*, Tony Blair Institute for Global Change, p. 6. Available at:
3. Barkindo, A. and Bryans, S. (2016) "De-Radicalizing Prisoners in Nigeria: Developing a Prison Based De-Radicalisation Programme," in *Journal for Deradicalization*, no. 7.
4. Dogarawa,B. "Understanding Ideology—Based Extremism," Working Paper for SUPPORT TO THE NIGERIAN PRISONS SERVICE'S DE-RADICALISATION PROGRAMME.
5. Elaigwu, V.A. (2003), *The Military and the Management of Civil Crises in Nigeria, 1960-1993*, Nigerian Defence Academy Press, Kaduna
6. Harnischfeger, J. (2014), "Boko Haram and its Muslim Critics: Observations from Yobe State," in Montclos, M. P. (ed.), *Boko Haram: Islamism, Politics, Security and the State in Nigeria*, (Leiden: African Studies Centre
7. Hill, J. N. C. (2010), *Sufism in Northern Nigeria: A Force for Counter Radicalization?*, (Carlisle: Strategic Studies Institute).
8. http://en.m.wikipedia.org-political-radicalismWikipedia, accessed on 5th /04/2017
9. History of the Zealots form Wikipedia free Encyclopedia
10. https://institute.global/insight/co-existence/dealing-boko-haram-defectors-lake-chad-basin-lessons-nigeria Accessed on 30th April, 2019.
11. Hussaini, J. 'Civilians in the Frontline of Counter-Insurgency Operations: The Civilian Joint
12. Task Force in the War against the *Boko Haram* in the Northeast, Nigeria' by Department of History and War Studies, Nigerian Defence Academy, Kaduna, Nigeria, *forthcoming*.
13. Isa, K. H. (2016) 'Religion and Society in Kano Metropolis: A Historical Study of Muslim Intra-faith Relations, 1978-2015', Ph.D Thesis, Department of History, Usmanu Danfodiyo University, Sokoto, Nigeria
14. Kamolnick, P. (2014), *Countering Radicalization and Recruitment to Al-Qaeda: Fighting the War of Deed*, Carlisle: strategic Studies Institute, US Army War College
15. Palmer R.R. and Others, (2007), *A History of the Modern World to 1815*, (10th Edition) M.C. Graw-Hill Companies, New York
16. Pettinger, T. (2016), "De–radicalization and Counter—radicalization: Valuable Tools for Combating Violent Extremism, or Harmful Methods of Subjugation?," in *Journal for Deradicalization*, no. 12,2017.
17. Stanford, M. (1994), *A Companion to the Study of History*, (Oxford, U.K: Blackwell Publishers).
18. Ubong, E.U, 'Joint Task Operations in the Niger-Delta, 2003-2017', in (ed), Ashafa, A.M. and Hussaini, J. *The Nigeria Army in a Democracy Since 1999: A Professional Demonstration to of Military Subordination to Civil Authority: Essays in Honor of Lt Gen TY Buratai*, Pyla-Mak, Kaduna, Nigeria

19. United Nations Office on Drugs and Crime, (2016), *Handbook on the Management of Violent Extremist Prisoners and the Prevention of Radicalization to Violence in Prisons*, (New York: United Nations).
20. Yandaki, A.I. (2017), 'The Nigerian Army in a Democracy: Towards the Taming the Shi'ite Menace', in (ed), Ashafa, A.M. and Hussaini, J. *The Nigeria Army in a Democracy Since 1999: A Professional Demonstration to of Military Subordination to Civil Authority: Essays in Honor of Lt Gen TY Buratai*, Pyla-Mak, Kaduna, Nigeria
21. Zahradeen, N.S. (1988), *The Maitatsine Saga*, Huda-huda Publishing Company, Zaria
22. Zamani, A. (2018), "Programming Based on Assessment," Working Paper for SUPPORT TO THE NIGERIAN PRISONS SERVICE'S DE-RADICALISATION PROGRAMME.
23. __________, (2018), "Assessment," Working Paper for SUPPORT TO THE NIGERIAN PRISONS SERVICE'S DE-RADICALISATION PROGRAMME.
24. **Interviews**

SN	*Name*	*Age*	*Occupation*	*Place of Interview*	*Date of Interview*
1	Lawal Aliyu	40	Prison Officer	Katsina Central Prison	March, 2019
2	Ayuba Peter	59	Prison Officer	Katsina Central Prison	March, 2019
3	Lawal A. Kangiwa	60	Prison Officer	Katsina Central Prison	March, 2019
4	Martins Joseph	48	Prison Officer	Katsina Central Prison	April, 2019

PART IV

LESSONS LEARNT AND WAY AHEAD

13

Lessons Learnt and Way Forward for India to Deal with Violent Extremism

*Maj Gen BK Sharma, AVSM, SM** (Retd) and*
Brig Narender Kumar, SM, VSM (Retd)

ABSTRACT

Polarisation, dysfunctional institutions, perceived marginalisation of communities based on their identity and geographic and historical specificities are the main factors conducive to the rise of violent extremism.[1] External and internal actors do play important role, however, deliverance of governance and redressal of grievances is cornerstone to conflict resolution. Engagement with the disaffected section of society is a stepping stone for reintegration of rebels and insurgents. It would require co-designing of new strategies and strengthening existing strategies. India has focused on winning hearts and minds, people friendly operations, employment of just force and political intervention to kick start the process of reconstruction, reconciliation and reintegration of disaffected population with the state.

Idea of India

The people of India gave themselves a republic that is sovereign, socialist, secular and democratic and a constitutional system that guarantees every citizen justice, liberty and equality. John Rawl had said that, 'justice is the first virtue of social institutions' and that in 'a just society the liberties of equal citizenship are taken as settled and the rights secured by justice and are not subject to political bargaining or to the calculus of social interest.'[2] The responsibility of the state is to ensure that the values enshrined in the Constitution of India are upheld and instruments of power at the disposal of the state are employed whenever constitutional provisions are violated by individuals or group of people. John Locke, a 17 Century scholar wrote, "Where-ever law ends, tyranny begins".[3] Sovereignty of the law of the land is imperative to prevent tyranny of ideology and invasion of the rights of the people by radicals and anti-democratic forces. In a pluralistic and secular society like India, it is unthinkable to impose radical religious or political ideology with a view to create cultural, political and economic fault-lines with an objective to secede from the state or create unequal societies on the basis of race, religion and political ideology. Thus the equality of all citizens under the law is a lynch-pin of the modern notion of the rule of law in a democratic state.[4]

In the emerging milieu, the threat is more to the "Idea of India" than to the physical structure of the state due to religious radicalisation and political dissonance on the basis of perverted communal and religious polarisation. India recognises the fact that disagreement, disputes, disengagement and disaffection are bound to happen in a multi-cultural pluralistic state due to rising political aspirations, quest for economic empowerment and historical social disparities. These aspects may have roots in the distorted perception of persecution and neglect by the state. Therefore, political philosophy suggests that, deeply disputed questions must find moral grounds to further social and political cooperation for grievance redressal of disengaged or disaffected section of society.

The primary objective of separatists and secessionist forces is to disable pluralism, fraternity, sovereignty and secularism. They often endeavour it by directly confronting the institutions of democracy and governance. India and Nigeria both are victims of these new threats. The challenges these modern irregular enemies of state pose are political subversion through surrogate organisations (that may appear to be benign), economic corruption and sponsored acts of crime and terrorism. The potent tools these organisations have employed in the recent past are exploitation of religion and weaponisation of ideology. The "underlying purpose" of the militants/insurgents is, "to provoke a violent reaction, or preferably escalation of violence, which could be used to show the people of Kashmir and global community how repressive Indian state is." As a result state must employ all instruments of power to defend and secure the idea of India and the values enshrined in the Indian Constitution.

Objectives of Counter Insurgency and Counter-Terrorism Campaigns

Eric Thor Olson a retired United States Navy admiral wrote that, "The best weapons in counter insurgency do not shoot". Kinetic force cannot possibly act as binding factor; rather it drives people away from the government. Killing insurgents is not the solution; suppression of violence has temporary impact and is unlikely to establish enduring peace. Professor Edward Luttwak a defence expert wrote in "Malpractices of Counterinsurgency" that, "The insurgents do not always win, actually they usually lose. But their defeats can rarely be attributed to counterinsurgency warfare."[5] It requires political intervention as early as possible for a coordinated, skilful execution and reconstruction program that is able to build trust and confidence with the people. That is the reason India's focus is more on WHAM operations than use of hard military power. Military should only be used to suppress the violence so that political intervention can take place. The objective of counterinsurgency operations is to disengage public from the insurgents and reintegrate the disaffected/disengaged section of population with the state. Reintegration certainly cannot be achieved by deterrence or force; it can only be achieved by deliverance of government and redressal of grievances.

Lessons from Seven Decades of Counter-Insurgency & Counter-Terrorism

India has dealt with multiple campaigns against five different insurgencies and terrorism mainly Punjab, Kashmir, North east, Left Wing Extremism and Tamil Tigers in Sri Lanka. All of them were distinct from each other, Punjab militancy was for establishment of Khalistan (Sikh Homeland). It was a brutal and a very violent militancy that had rocked entire North India. The Maoist insurgency is based on communist ideology and their objective is to capture state/political power through armed struggle. The insurgencies in the Northeast are predominantly secessionist movements for the establishment of separate homelands for people of different ethnic background. Kashmir is a case of cross border terrorism and proxy war by Pakistan where radicalisation has led to creation of local cadres as cannon fodder. India's engagement with Liberation Tigers of Tamil Elam in Sri Lanka was an insurgency that had the potential of spilling over into India's coastal state of Tamil Nadu for creation of Tamil homeland. All these insurgencies/terrorist movements had different objectives and different modus-operandi. Prof. Rajesh Rajagopalan of School of International Studies at JNU, has argued that India has "one of the world's most successful records in fighting insurgencies," noting that "it has not yet lost a counterinsurgency campaign within the country."[6] Thus the strategy employed against each of these insurgencies and terror movements has been different and not templated. Key lessons from India's counterinsurgency/ counterterrorism experience is given in succeeding paragraphs.

Keeping the Institutions of Governance Functional. Insurgents and terrorists create a perception of victory if they are able to disrupt administration, political process and paralyse the institutions of governance. Irrespective of the severity and nature of violence, the mandate of the local government to the administration and security forces is to ensure that the institutions of governance remain functional. Of course it was difficult in J&K, Northeast and even in Maoists infested areas to keep institutions of governance functional under coercion and threat, yet at no stage a situation was allowed where insurgents were able to paralyse institutions of governance completely. There were certainly setbacks but security forces with the assistance of local population were able to regain the control. Why it becomes even more significant is, because the engagement with the people remains unbroken if institutes of governance remain functional and that is the key to reinitiate development and redressal of grievances of disaffected population. These institutions are indeed a bridge to conflict management and conflict resolution.

Political Integration of Disaffected Population with the State. Integration and accommodation of insurgents in societal and political process is imperative for conflict resolution. However, it will work if there are sound plans for skilling, rehabilitation and reintegration of insurgent cadres. India successfully handled the insurgencies in Tripura and Mizoram, two North eastern States. The buyout and political incorporation of insurgents—has enabled India to keep a lid on a host of insurgent separatist movements in the seven states of India's eastern extremity, India's Northeast, since 1956.[7] This initiative gave indirect support to revival of political process in Assam, Manipur, Tripura, Mizoram and Nagaland. This arrangement led to secession of hostilities and engagement with the government except few groups that are based out of the country. However, in few cases this also led to spiralling of splinter groups that took advantage of cease fire and suspension of operation (SOO) to run extortion and conflict economy. India learnt two important lessons from this arrangement; first, even if the conflict is not resolved, engaging politically with insurgents can continue to allow institutions of governance to function effectively. Second, the political process will remain dysfunctional if skilling, rehabilitation and reintegration process are not executed in a structured manner.

Dedicated Counter-Insurgency/Counter-terrorist Forces. India has created dedicated counterinsurgency/counterterrorism forces to harness knowledge of terrain, culture, demography and intelligence. The military operations are focused to use minimum force so as to prevent collateral damages. These forces over a period of time have acquired the legitimacy of being sentinels of the geographic regions. For example Assam Rifles is synonymous with the acronym of "Sentinel of the East". Similarly, Rashtriya Rifles is a force that specialises in counter terrorism operations in Jammu & Kashmir and is fully conversant with the culture, vulnerabilities and sentiments of the people. Central Reserve Police Force (CRPF) is steadily growing as a potent and specialised force to deal with Left Wing Extremism (LWE). Such an arrangement has brought ownership, commitment and institutional memory to avoid committing operational mistakes. It creates a bond, interdependence and a trust between the people and the forces.

Avoid Overreaction and Focus on Employment of Just Force. For more than 150 years, Nationalist, Populist, Marxist and Islamist terrorists have all been remarkably consistent and explicit about their aims: Provoke the State into over-reacting to the threat they pose, and then take advantage of the divisions in the society.[8] More often the reaction of the state to a violent extremist action is to instinctively reach for the most coercive tools, in doing so, the State risks exacerbating the situation.[9] Such a response seems to be driven by lack of understanding of the true nature of the threat, an exaggerated faith in the use of force. This demonstrates lack of faith that democratic values are sufficiently flexible to allow for an effective counter-terrorism response.[10] Ultimate analysis is that no matter how grave the threat is; the response of the state should be application of just force because the focus is not to alienate but to conciliate. India has not used aircraft, artillery guns and any other lethal vectors to deal with the proxy war in Kashmir, LWE areas and in the Northeast. By violating just force code, state can lose the trust of the people and principle of conciliation.

Community Mediation and Role of Civil Society. Civil society has played a vital role in providing a platform for engagement with the insurgents and secessionist forces when official channels had ceased. The social organisations also played an important role in keeping the violence levels low by restraining insurgents as well as security forces. The cease fire with the Naga rebels of the North-east India is holding now for more than 22 years and Naga social organisations such as Naga Hoho, Forum for Reconciliation and Mothers Organisation has played great role in ensuring that cease fire is not violated especially by the insurgents. Similarly, Mirapaibies (Torch Bearers) of Manipur—a women's organisation have ensured social reforms even during the height of insurgency and acted as a robust channel of communication between security forces and the rebels. The role of social organisations in establishment of peace in Tripura (North eastern State of India) is invaluable; it was initiated by the Jamatiya Hoda, the Supreme Council of the Jamatiya tribe. The Jamatiya Hoda took a bold stand and resolved not to pay any kind of 'tax' to the terrorist groups operating in the State.[11] To reintegrate the disaffected population with the state, civil society should be incorporated as guarantor of peace and moderator as and when the differences do occur. The civil society will deliver if they are given respect, prominence and made accountable as guardian of peace. India has utilised the influence of community elders and civil society to manage the conflict and restore peace especially in the Northeast.

Operation Sadbhavna. Operation Sadbhavna (Operation Goodwill) has been a great bridge between people and the security forces. It has acted as a catalyst for counterinsurgency/counterterrorist operations in Kashmir and Northeast India. Government has been able to provide development and connect with the people through this path-breaking initiative. It is aimed at to meet the basic developmental needs of the people excluded from the main stream due to terrorism, tyranny of distance, lack of communication and lack of administrative reach. Operation Sadbhavna has provided connectivity between the government, security forces and people. It has been used by the Indian Army as an engine of perception warfare to disengage public from the separatists/secessionist and reintegrate with the state.

Neighbours do Matter. Neighbours do matter in dealing with internal instability especially when there are identical demography on both sides of the International Borders and conniving rogue organisations. India has been able to deal with the Northeast insurgency due to the significant role played by eastern neighbours of India. Bangladesh, Bhutan and Myanmar have contributed immensely by turning over rebels and insurgents from their countries. These countries have undertaken joint operations to flush out insurgents from their land and denied safe havens and material support to weaken the insurgents organisationally. Therefore, neighbours should be brought on board to deal with the internal instability with external linkages.

Way Forward

Focus on Anti-Radicalisation and Counter-Radicalisation Measures. The ideological fountainhead of Jihad and establishment of caliphate has been part of Wahhabi doctrine. It targets cognitive domain through radicalisation so as to create disaffection among the population with the state. Radicalisation is always associated with the violent extremism, however, it also creates dilemma of moral legitimacy of democracy in a pluralistic state. The objective is to destroy institutions of democratic governance. Such an idea is against the development of modern states and empowerment of people. Therefore, the states need to evolve a strategy to prevent radicalization of masses and de-radicalization of those who are willing to return or surrender to the government. The strategy for anti-radicalisation, counter-radicalisation and de-radicalisation should be different and specific to each individual. A sacrosanct model for all three stages is unlikely to work. The bottom line is that at no stage individual radicalised be demonised or victimised. Radicalised youths or those who are being radicalised should be given an opportunity to return back to the main stream.

Border Management. It is an old proverb that, "good fences make good neighbours." The porous borders lend itself to infiltration of terrorists, organised crime, human trafficking, drug and weapon smuggling. Border management is a complete system consisting of structural security, digital security, 24x7 surveillance system and quick reaction to land, air and maritime threat. There is a need to lay stress on incorporation of technology to convert border fence into smart fence that is capable of identification of intruders, warning of intrusion, able to impose physical restriction to cross fence and ultimately facilitate in elimination of armed intruders.

Battle of Narratives. Narratives are central to representing identity, particularly the collective identity of religious sects, ethnic groupings, and tribal elements. They provide a basis for interpreting information, experiences, and the behaviour and intentions of other individuals and communities.[12] Battle of narrative assists in shaping perceptions and deconstruction of misinformation and misinterpretation. It is a powerful tool of social communication and social media is a resolute platform to carry it to the desired audience. Important issue is that it is able to map the landscape and identify relevant actors who are working against the national interests. Care should be taken that it is credible, sustainable and carry irrefutable legitimate storyline. Target audience must be able to relate to the narrative put forward in an unbiased manner.

Preventing Terrorism and Insurgency through Inclusive Growth, Public Participation and Deliverance of Governance. State's failure to provide basic rights, services and security not only contributes to growing inequality, it also creates a vacuum that allows non-state actors to take control over State sovereignty and territory.[13] Most important facet of counter-terrorism and counter-insurgency is deliverance of governance, removal of inequality, promoting a rule of law, fight against corruption; enhancing participatory decision-making, increasing civic space at national and local levels; providing effective socio-economic alternatives to the groups at risk of the violence; strengthening the capacity of local governments for service delivery, security of state subjects[14] and initiate dialogue with the parties to conflict.

Countering Terrorism and Insurgency with Humane Face. "Insurgents do not always win, actually they usually lose. But their defeats can rarely be attributed to counterinsurgency warfare, as we shall see."[15] Out terrorising the terrorists or public is not a way forward. A state must display compassion and empathy towards people who are victims of violence from both sides. Respect for local culture, tradition and religion is in fact one of the potent tool to win the trust of the people. Human rights respect is of utmost significance. There is a need to maintain a balance between hard military operations and people friendly operations. People are centre of gravity in counter-insurgency and counter-terrorist operations. People friendly operations are a way forward to build trust and avoid human rights issues.

Transnational Terrorism and Proxy War Require Global Efforts. Global and regional efforts are required to deal with terror funding and cross border linkages of terror organisations such as Al Qaeda and ISIS. UN Global Counter-Terrorism Strategy (UNGCTS) has identified four pillars to deal with terrorism. These pillars apply to almost all forms of terrorism and insurgencies. The four pillars are, addressing the conditions conducive to the spread of terrorism, measures to prevent and combat terrorism (by a regional or global alliance), measures to build states' capacity to prevent and combat terrorism and to strengthen the role of the United Nations system in that regard and measures to ensure respect for human rights for all and the rule of law as the fundamental basis for the fight against terrorism.[16] Marshall Billingslea, President of the Financial Action Task Force, said that, while terrorist groups use funding to conduct terrorist acts, they also need it to maintain and grow their organizations.[17] These funds do not always come from domestic supporters. There is a long trail of terror funding from drug trafficking, state sponsored extortion, illegal sale of natural resources, and provision of mercenaries for a cost. In the light of the above, it is imperative that states not abiding by the UNGCTS strategy and continuing to use terror as a state policy must be penalised. Tools such as 'The Financial Action Task Force (FATF)' should be strictly implemented and sanctions against those who violate the UN Strategy be imposed.

Conclusion

There is a need to maintain balance between the threat posed by terrorism, and its human cost. Violence is the insurgents and terrorist's principal tool and it is used in such a way as to impact an audience far beyond the target of any individual attack—the choice of target therefore, tends to have a universal impact and quality.[18] If this be the objective of the insurgents and terrorists, use of violence to supress violence appears to be a wrong tool. It is falling into the "terrorist's trap" fully aware that violence perpetuated by terrorists and insurgents is aimed at to have symbolic value and is intended to terrify a wider audience than those immediately affected.[19] The objective of counter-insurgency and counter-terrorists operations should be to reclaim the disaffected individuals and population back to the society and redress all grievances by deliverance of governance.

NOTES

1. Community Perspectives on Preventing Violent Extremism: Lessons learned from the Western Balkans, News Overview, *Berghof Foundation*, May 15, 2019.
2. Hamid Ansari, In his final address as Vice President of India, at the annual convocation ceremony at the National Law School of India University, Bengaluru, August 07, 2017.
3. John Locke on the idea that "wherever law ends, tyranny begins" (1689), The Two Treatises of Civil Government (Hollis ed.) (John Locke), Accessed from https://oll.libertyfund.org/quotes/115 on September 20,2019.
4. John Locke on the idea that "wherever law ends, tyranny begins" (1689), The Two Treatises of Civil Government (Hollis ed.) (John Locke), Accessed from https://oll.libertyfund.org/quotes/115 on September 20,2019.
5. David Kilcullen, Edward Lutwik's Counterinsurgency Malpractice, Blog in Small War, Accessed from https://smallwarsjournal.com/blog/edward-luttwaks-counterinsurgency-malpractice on September 23, 2019.
6. Rajesh Rajagopalan, "Force and Compromise: India's Counterinsurgency Grand Strategy," *South Asia: Journal of South Asian Studies* 30:1 (2007).
7. Lawrence Cline, "The Insurgency Environment in Northeast India," *Small Wars and Insurgencies* 17:2 (2006).
8. Tom Parkar, Avoiding Terrorist Trap, World Scientific, Book Review, July 2019
9. Ibid.
10. Ibid.
11. Dr. Rupakjyoti Borah, Role of Civil Society Groups in Promoting Conflict Resolution in India's Northeast, A Paper prepared for the World International Studies Conference, Porto, Portugal, 17-20 August, 2011.
12. John De Rosa, Revising the Battle of the Narrative, *Small Wars Journal*, Accessed from https://smallwarsjournal.com/jrnl/art/revising-the-battle-of-the-narrative on September 30, 2019.
13. Preventing Violent Extremism through Promoting Inclusive Development, Tolerance and Respect for Diversity, United Nations Development Programme, UNDP 2016, p. 4.
14. Ibid, p. 5.
15. Kilcullen, N 5.
16. UN Global Counter-Terrorism Strategy, Adopted by consensus in 2006, Accessed from https://www.un.org/counterterrorism/ctitf/en/un-global-counter-terrorism-strategy on October 03, 2019.
17. Security Council Unanimously Adopts Resolution Calling upon Member States to Combat, Criminalize Financing of Terrorists, Their Activities, Accessed from https://www.un.org/press/en/2019/sc13754.doc.htm on March 28, 2019.
18. Parker, N 8.
19. Ibid.

14

Nigeria's Approach to Dealing with Radicalisation: Lessons Learnt and Way Forward

Dr. Fatima Akilu and Ramatu Jaji

Introduction

Nigeria's fight against violent extremism is often traced back to 2009; the year that Mohammed Yusuf, leader of Jama'atu Ahlis Sunna Lidda'awati Wal-Jihad, commonly known as Boko Haram, died in police custody and his followers took targeted action against the state and its institutions. However, while that was the year of the uprising in earnest, Yusuf had already established a following in the city of Maiduguri as early as 2002 preaching against the influence of colonialism and Christianity on the education system, amongst other things (Walker, 2016, pp. 144-5). It was no doubt on the basis of the recurrent theme of the erstwhile leader's sermons that the group was dubbed, Boko Haram meaning: "Western Education is Forbidden". In the last decade, the extremist group has been deemed the world's deadliest terrorist organization (Institute for Economics and Peace, 2015); seized towns in North East Nigeria; kidnapped thousands of people; and destroyed schools, hospitals and livelihoods. According to Council on Foreign Relations (CFR) Nigeria Security Tracker (NST), the insurgency has since claimed 37,530 lives among which 50 percent were Boko Haram militants, 45 percent civilians, and 5 percent state actors (Campbell & Harwood, 2018). While the initial response to Boko Haram was purely military, it soon became evident that despite the number of combatants captured or killed, the group continued to recruit and extend its influence in the North East. Shut out from jobs, quality education, feeling alienated and marginalized from community, the extremists have used the abundance of their imagination to carve a place for themselves. They have experimented with the formation of an alternative society, one in which they make the rules, using the manipulation of Islam as an entry point. Having identified the conditions that increase vulnerability to radicalisation, the Federal Government of Nigeria in 2012 broadened its counter-terrorism approach to include new laws, strategies, frameworks, partnerships and institutions.

Radicalisation in Nigeria

To appreciate Nigeria's approach to dealing with radicalisation, particularly Boko Haram, it is imperative to reflect on the history of radicalisation in the country. Radicalisation is understood as the adoption of an extreme ideology to the extent that one supports or engages in violence as a means to an end. It can be considered a process or a state of mind, which often precedes and indeed manifests as violent extremism or terrorism. While a number of groups have emerged and sought to realize their ideological goals by undermining the stability of the country, the most infamous revolt in Nigeria prior to Boko Haram dates back to the 1980s. At a time of intense political upheaval at the national level, a Cameroonian by the name of Muhammadu Marwa mobilised poor farmers and handymen from across West Africa. Based in Kano, his objective was to restore Islamic values and at the centre of the group's ideology was a rejection of colonialism and all technology and institutions it thought to be a product of the West. He was popularly known as Maitatsine, "the one who curses" and his supporters were referred to as 'Yan Tatsine. Similar to religious sects carved from the wider population, the group branded itself as true Muslims and anyone who did not subscribe to its beliefs and interpretation of the Qur'an was cursed. Initially involved in sporadic community violence, 'Yan Tatsine evolved into violent extremists after the death of Marwa's son (Walker, 2016, p. 120). In the pursuit of justice, the group clashed with the police, resulting in the death of thousands more, including Marwa himself. Every time 'Yan Tatsine would regroup, the military was sent in to quell the uprising until they were permanently defeated. Time and experience however have shown that ideologies cannot be fought with guns alone. In the intervening years and since Boko Haram, many other radical groups holding religious, political and economic ideologies have sprung up across the country. From the Movement for the Emancipation of the Niger Delta (MEND) to the Indigenous People of Biafra (IPOB), people are adopting violence to achieve their goals. As the Nigerian approach shows, anti-radicalisation efforts must attempt to win hearts and minds as well.

Government-led Interventions

Three years after the death of Mohammed Yusuf, the Boko Haram insurgency persisted, loss of life and property was on the rise, citizens' distrust of state ensued and the terrorists showed no sign of retreat despite military confrontation. It is in this context, coupled with the realisation that its response to extremism decades earlier was a temporary fix at best, that the Nigerian Government deployed resources to complement kinetic military action. First, laws that sought to check illegal activities related to terrorism were enhanced. The Terrorism (Prevention) Act 2011 was amended in 2013 to provide for the extra-territorial application of the Act, and strengthening of terrorist financing offences. Anyone within or outside of Nigeria who is party to the act of terrorism would be liable to conviction. Through the Money Laundering (Prohibition) (Amendment) Act, 2012 as well as the Central Bank of Nigeria Anti-Money Laundering and Combating the Financing of Terrorism Regulations 2013 (AML/CFT), financial institutions had to abide by strict protocols, curtailing the illicit flow of money, which often ends up in the hands of terrorists.

Another weapon of influence used by extremists is religion, or better yet, poor understanding of religion, so the restrictions did not end with financing laws. State Governments from Borno to Kaduna and Katsina instituted Islamic Preaching Boards, with a view to curbing the spread of incendiary rhetoric and ideology through the regulation of sermons and granting of preaching licenses.

Notwithstanding the strides being made by the government, it was apparent that unless the socio-economic and political factors that contributed to radicalisation were addressed, efforts to combat radicalisation would remain futile. As a long-term response to terrorism, government took steps to prioritise poverty alleviation and job creation in the country, especially in the North East where infrastructural and development deficit was most acutely felt. In line with this, a regional economic revitalization plan was developed. Previously known as the Presidential Initiative for the North East (PINE), it has since morphed into the Presidential Committee on the North East Initiative (PCNI) with an expanded mandate informed by The Buhari Plan. The mandate of PCNI is "to serve as the primary national strategy, coordination and advisory body for all humanitarian interventions, transformational and developmental efforts in the North-East region of Nigeria" (2017). Sequel to a law signed in 2017; the Committee has subsequently been subsumed as part of a more permanent structure called the North East Development Commission (NEDC), now responsible for coordination of all post conflict interventions.

Furthermore, the intensification of the conflict called for the development and refinement of national strategies. A Counter Terrorism Centre (CTC) domiciled in the Office of the National Security Advisor (ONSA) was created and in 2014, a National Counter-Terrorism Strategy (NACTEST) was launched. Additionally, the National Security Strategy was revised, the Nigerian National Safety Tips was developed, to enable citizens report suspicious activities and a National Policy Framework and Action Plan on Preventing and Countering Violent Extremism (P/CVE) was introduced. With ONSA as lead coordinator of counter-terrorism efforts, the strategy outlines the government's short and long-term strategic goals in the fight against terrorism and defines the roles and responsibilities of other ministries, departments and agencies (MDAs). Underpinning NACTEST—which was revised in 2016 under the leadership of the National Security Adviser, Major General Babagana Monguno (rtd) to include a monitoring and evaluation component that would track implementation—are five pillars ("NACTEST," 2016):

- *Forestall:* To stop people becoming terrorists or supporting terrorism.
- *Secure:* Strengthen protection capacity against terrorist attacks.
- *Identify:* Pre-emption through detection, early warning and ensuring that terrorists' acts are properly investigated.
- *Prepare:* To mitigate the impact of terrorist attacks by building resilience and redundancies to ensure continuity of business.
- *Implement:* A framework for the mobilization of coordinated cross-governmental efforts.

In addition to the aforementioned objectives, the strategy spans across specific areas of intervention such as border management, airports, seaports, cyber-security, as well as the importance of conducting thorough background checks on security personnel, enhanced documentation processes such as vehicle registration, birth/death certificates and driver's licences. Contained in the National Counter-Terrorism Strategy is the Nigerian Government's Counter-Insurgency (COIN) campaign, which "is a mix of offensive, defensive, and stability operations conducted along multiple lines. These other lines may be economical, socio-political, educational, religious and information lines of operations carried out by different government ministries, departments and agencies" ("NACTEST," 2016).

Adopting a civil-military strategy or a soft approach to counter-terrorism was no accident. It was a result of discussions with community members and detained Boko Haram associates, as well as extant research, which revealed that extremist groups often found a way to fill the gap where society and government have been deficient. Through persuasive messaging, they aimed at youth feeling disconnected, nursing a mix of grievances, feelings of alienation, poverty, substandard or little education, limited understanding of Islam, or simply looking for adventure. Together, these insights laid the foundation for the development of a more holistic strategy to fighting violent extremism. Known as Nigeria's Countering Violent Extremism (CVE) Programme, the approach was established in March, 2014 to stem the tide of radicalisation, reduce the incidence of violent activities, change the behaviour of violent extremists and counter the narrative of extreme groups while promoting core national values. Coordinated by the Directorate of Behavioural Analysis and Strategic Communication within ONSA, the CVE programme represents the nation's first attempt at a truly multidimensional response to combatting terrorism. To achieve these goals, three streams of the CVE programme were identified, with different layers of both state and non-state actors. These included:

- Counter-radicalisation Stream.
- De-radicalisation Stream.
- Strategic Communication Stream.

Counter-radicalisation

The counter-radicalisation programme was designed to engage vulnerable populations through education and economic intervention projects aimed at preventing radicalisation and recruitment. It was also designed to work both vertically and horizontally—i.e. across levels and tiers of government on the one hand and civil society, faith-based organizations and other non-state actors on the other—to create awareness of the threat of violent extremism. It sought to identify and strengthen credible voices in communities, collate data on religious figures, sects, places of worship and capture the kind of teachings or preaching in schools and worship centres. The counter-radicalisation stream also focused on the dissemination of counter-narratives through respected community members. By virtue of its whole-of-society approach, the counter-radicalisation programme was domiciled and implemented through an instrument set up by the Directorate called, Society Against Violent Extremism (SAVE) Project.

In the eighteen months that the SAVE Project was operational, the implementation team was successful in engaging communities across Borno, Kaduna, Kano, Kogi, Plateau and Yobe states with the purpose of building resilience against extremism. The team worked with community members and leaders at the grassroots level to restore their trust in

Chart 1: Counter-Radicalisation Programme SAVE

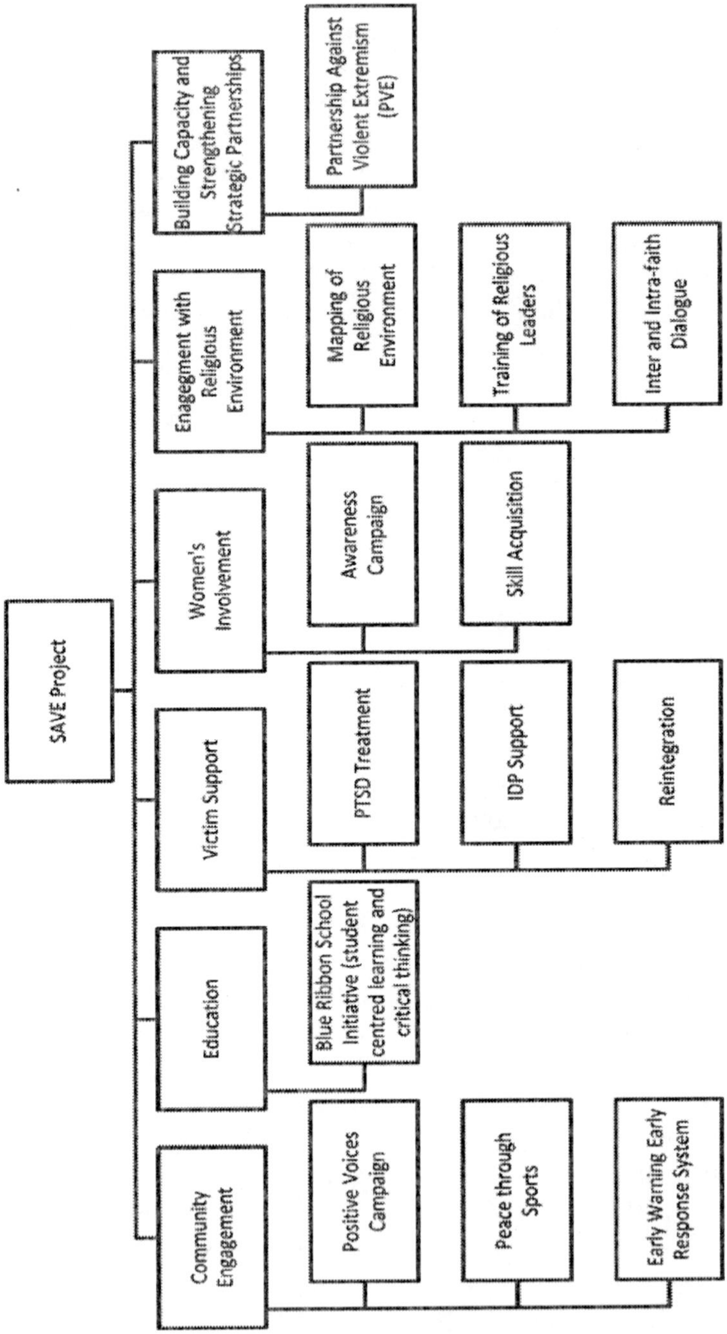

government and pave the way for collaboration in the fight against violent extremism; employed sports as a way of fostering tolerance and unity among hundreds of young people; and trained religious leaders on how to counter violent extremism through preaching messages of peace and tolerance. Finally, to encourage critical thinking, primary and secondary school teachers were taught to adopt student-centred learning.

The SAVE Project also gave rise to the first civil society security sector network known as Partnership Against Violent Extremism (PAVE). Comprising of multiple stakeholders, PAVE was set up to promote civil society buy in for counter-radicalisation initiatives, improve collaboration and increase the capacity of partners to support the CVE programme through a government-civil society network. It was expected that through PAVE, there would be greater understanding of the civil society environment and improved coordination of CVE interventions; all the while avoiding duplication of effort.

De-radicalisation

As stipulated in the National Counter-Terrorism Strategy, the de-radicalisation component of the CVE programme was designed to be a prison-based initiative driven by the Ministry of Interior and the Nigerian Prisons Service (NPS). It is important to clarify that the goal of the programme goes beyond disengagement from violence to ideological disengagement, therefore highlighting the need for the provision of adequate resources (Barkindo & Bryans, 2016, p. 6). Alongside the programme's objective, Nigeria's limited experience dealing with radicalisation necessitated the development of new expertise and frameworks to guide de-radicalisation interventions. With the support of the European Union Technical Assistance to Nigeria's Evolving Security Challenges (EUTANS), the government bridged the knowledge and skills gap by designing a basic prison-based de-radicalisation model; providing training to NPS personnel who were the majority of the programme staff; developing risk assessment and case management tools; and preparing a detailed de-radicalisation programme guide and training manual, which built on the Rome Memorandum on Good Practices for the Rehabilitation and Reintegration of Violent Extremist Offenders (Barkindo & Bryans, 2016, p. 6).

Having secured the required knowledge and competencies, ONSA and NPS first launched the de-radicalisation programme in January 2015 and commenced a pilot in Kuje Prison two months later. The de-radicalisation model itself was an iterative process that included engagement, risk assessment, needs assessment and interventions (Barkindo & Bryans, 2016, p. 10). Most, if not all personnel were prison staff who were trained to provide educational/vocational, psychological and other medical services, as well as religious guidance to the inmates. The multi-faceted approach to rehabilitation, of which, de-radicalisation is a major element, is crucial for successful reintegration.

Chart 2: Multi-faceted Approach to Rehabilitation

Under the de-radicalisation programme also are specific responses, which were tailored to address the needs of certain demographics with unique experiences:

- Women and girls in battle program—This was for women who joined the group and played various voluntary roles on behalf of Boko Haram, the only national programme that has ever existed for such women.
- Victims programme—This was designed for those kidnapped by Boko Haram, to support their reintegration and ensure they did not develop radical ideological tendencies while with the group.
- Programme for failed suicide bombers—Beneficiaries were mostly female.

Overall, the de-radicalisation programme has recorded some achievements including:

- Cataloguing of terror suspects.
- Development of a faith training programme.

- Training of prison staff and raising awareness on best practice in prison management.
- Training of psychologists, social workers, arts and sports instructors.
- Development of Nigeria's de-radicalisation curriculum.
- Development of a vocational skills programme.

Furthermore, the de-radicalisation curriculum has since been institutionalized and is taught in prison training schools across the country and the programme itself has been expanded to Aguata and Kainji Prisons.

Strategic Communication

The Strategic Communication stream of the CVE Programme was set up to produce a counter-narrative messaging system which presents subtle ideological/religious views as a way of countering the radicalized proposition of extremists. It is a stream built around promoting core national values and principles. The ability to institutionalize a coordinated national messaging system is a necessary tool in activating attitudinal and behavioural change among the citizenry, which instantly and consciously dispels contrary messaging by terrorists. The government's strategic communication approach to tackling the nation's security challenges were hinged on these key principles:

- Terrorism is un-Islamic—Extremists distort and manipulate religious texts to justify their actions. The approach seeks to counter their narrative through sound Islamic knowledge dissemination.
- Counterterrorism is not against Muslims—Specific messaging designed to carefully and tactically dispel the misconstruction that the fight against terror is a persecution of Islam.
- Muslims should be encouraged and empowered to speak out against terror—Capacity building and cooperation among mainstream Muslims countering terrorists messaging by exposing the true intent of government.
- Muslim-Christian relations should be cordial—Any intolerance between Christians and Muslims will be exploited by terrorists. It is therefore in our own interest that we foster unity through inter-faith cooperation.
- Counterterrorism is uninterested in politics—Terrorists are neither critics of a ruling party or apologists of the opposition. They are enemies of the state. There needs to be inter-party collaboration to ensure that political differences do not obstruct collective efforts.

Accomplishments of the CVE programme notwithstanding, there have been some changes with regard to focus, content and coordination. Some aspects of the government-led programme such as counter-radicalisation and strategic communication were completely discarded, while a comprehensive de-radicalisation programme was broken up into various parcels with different agencies having responsibility. The women and girls as well as the victims' programmes were completely stopped. Outside of the programmes listed above, there is a de-radicalisation, rehabilitation and reintegration (DRR) programme established as the vehicle to receive repentant insurgents. Known as Operation Safe Corridor, the programme is a major component of Nigeria's P/CVE efforts warranting a section on its own.

Operation Safe Corridor

Inaugurated in April 2016, Safe Corridor was designed to de-radicalise, rehabilitate and reintegrate insurgents who willingly surrender. In an interview with the Coordinator of Operation Safe Corridor, Major General Bamidele Shafa (2019), the process of surrendering was explained as follows: repentant insurgents can surrender through community leaders, the Civilian Joint Task Force (CJTF), non-governmental organisations (NGOs), or directly to the military, after which they are transferred to an investigation centre for documentation and then to Operation Safe Corridor. With the cooperation of 13 MDAs, Operation Safe Corridor, which has its facility in Gombe State, provides a range of rehabilitation services including psychotherapy, religious counselling, addiction counselling, and recreational activities such as sports, education and vocational training (Shafa, 2019). The programme duration varies between six and twelve months, depending on the individuals needs assessment. Re-unification is encouraged to ensure family support, as well as a sense of belonging among previous offenders. At release, the clients, as they are officially called, are allowed to determine where they would like to be reintegrated and the process is facilitated by the International Organisation for Migration (IOM) and the State Government. An integral part of reintegration is the acceptance of community members. As such, sensitisation is carried out to prepare communities for the resettlement of ex-combatants and associates. Furthermore, returnees are closely monitored by traditional leaders, CJTF and security forces. With over 2,000 former militants having surrendered (Nwankpa, 2019, the programme has certainly proven to be effective in encouraging terrorist defections.

According to Major General Shafa, 261 people have successfully been de-radicalised and 101 reintegrated, although the programme is not without challenges. For its amnesty provision alone, Operation Safe Corridor has been the subject of much criticism, further complicating the reintegration of ex-combatants and those associated with them. Another major obstacle identified by the Coordinator is the delay in transferring de-radicalised persons to their respective states of reintegration (Shafa, 2019). Should this persist, it could engender distrust on the part of the clients, discourage potential defectors and thwart the entire Safe Corridor programme. The other problem has to do with perception of victims and stigmatization against returnees. Many are of the opinion that there is more concern for perpetrators than there is for victims. A more general worry among citizens is that extremists are being rewarded for their actions with food assistance, trainings and stipends. To address the realities of the support provided to ex-combatants in the reintegration process, the government is working on an extensive sensitisation campaign to enlighten the populace about its CVE schemes for both victims and perpetrators and more importantly, the need for the rehabilitation of both groups and how it contributes to lasting peace.

Multinational Cooperation

From Cameroon to Chad and Niger, the impact of the insurgency has been felt well beyond the shores of Nigeria, thus compelling the Nigerian Government to respond in equal measure. Parallel to setting up a Multinational Joint Task Force (MNJTF) under the auspices of the Lake Chad Basin Commission, the first Lake Chad Basin Governors' Forum for regional cooperation on stabilization was hosted in May 2018. The forum, which held in Maiduguri, drew on extensive community consultations and high-level meetings with the goal of "strengthening coordination and collaboration on cross-border initiatives at the subnational level around the Lake Chad Basin" ("Report of the Inaugural Meeting of the Lake Chad Basin Governors' Forum"). While the MNJTF has been instrumental in ensuring the safety of citizens and property, the impact of the Governor's Forum is yet to be felt in the North East.

Role of Civil Society Organisations

Civil society organisations (CSOs) have been known to fill service gaps and with the Nigerian Government overextended fighting the insurgency and addressing the resulting humanitarian crisis, which has affected over 7 million people, the role of NGOs, faith based organisations and other civil society actors has never been more important. By virtue of their credibility across levels of society and at the grassroots especially, NGOs are well placed to co-design and implement P/CVE activities. Local/ national NGOs and groups such as the Federation of Muslim Women's Associations in Nigeria and Jama'tul Nasril Islam (JNI) were leading the way in CVE efforts long before the Federal Government sanctioned civil society involvement. However, with the launch of the National Policy Framework and Action Plan on P/CVE in 2017 came increased commitment, and enhanced cooperation between CSOs and various MDAs. Cognisant of the link between socio-economic conditions and susceptibility to radicalisation, emphasis has been placed on the provision of education, economic empowerment, but also psychosocial and reconciliation support for victims of the insurgency including former abductees, children associated with armed groups, and internally displaced persons. Local peace committees have been created where there were none, and strengthened in some other places. Neem Foundation, for instance has set up a radicalisation monitoring and response system. Committees consisting of traditional and religious leaders, youth group and women's group representatives, CJTF officials and the police have been created in the three most affected states of Borno, Yobe and Adamawa. Equipped with the knowledge of radicalisation signs and a mobile application, the committee members are able to report and respond to suspicious incidents before they escalate. Community members are central to this early warning system to ensure ownership and sustainability of the peace-building process.

Lessons Learned and the Way Forward

The rise of terrorism globally, necessitates innovation in the field of counter-terrorism and more so, underscores the importance of learning from what is being done across the world. The Nigerian Government's experience dealing with radicalisation can therefore serve as lessons for other governments with similar contexts.

The Nigerian response to radicalisation and violent extremism, though initially hesitant and slow, has tried to match the ambitions and the imagination of the terrorists in its understanding that a whole of government approach that includes all of society is needed to reclaim the ground that a decade long terrorist campaign had staked. Local Governments have been liberated and citizens have been rescued from Boko Haram, however we have still not defeated the terrorists. The following challenges double as lessons learned:

- **Lack of continuity and coordination**. Dismantling the coordinated CVE response in 2015 undoubtedly contributed to unsteady progress in the fight against violent extremism. Thousands of terror suspects remain in prisons around the country and in several military-run facilities and yet, no agency or arm of government knows the total number of suspects held by different agencies. More worrying, no one knows the number of people who have committed terrorist acts and returned on their own to various communities nor the threat level they pose. To consolidate the gains made in the fight against violent extremism, efforts have to be nationally coordinated and driven. While NGOs have done an incredible job filling the gaps, they cannot implement programmes on a large enough scale, only government can do that.
- **State action and human right violations**. In its quest to repel Boko Haram's attacks, the Nigerian military has sometimes detained innocent individuals during raids on territories occupied by the insurgents and taken other unlawful action against terror suspects (Amnesty International, 2015). Unsurprisingly, research such as the Journey to Extremism study shows that such egregious violations of human rights and lack of access to justice not only fuel recruitment into violent extremist organisations, but are in fact often the final push (UNDP, 2017). It is important to note however that in recent times the relationship between the Military and civilian populations have vastly improved.
- **Inadequate community preparation for reintegration**. Neem Foundation's work with communities in Borno State revealed that community members are ill-prepared to receive returnees associated with Boko Haram. This lack of preparedness undeniably leads to ill treatment and stigmatisation of returnees, who are left feeling like their place is with the extremists. Not only that, the situation perpetuates the cycle of extremism and undermines defection and rehabilitation programmes. For successful reintegration, it is worth drawing on peacebuilding models from other countries such as Rwanda and Sierra Leone to design effective conflict resolution techniques as all efforts to reverse the tide of violence would prove futile without forgiveness and reconciliation.
- **Lack of prioritisation by State Governments**. Despite the poor socio-economic indices in the North East, which have created the perfect breeding ground for radicalisation, State Governments have

been slow to make necessary investments in welfare development. Instead, they have continued to rely on international partners, whose immediate focus is humanitarian support. Improving equitable access to education, employment, and basic amenities should be a priority for all governments.

- **Lack of sufficient expertise to track, monitor and respond to radicalisation**. While the government and civil society have done an incredible job developing expertise required for the prevention of violent extremism, there is still a need to scale various programmes and ensure that victims and perpetrators alike can access them. For instance, the Transit Centre where released Boko Haram associates, including abductees and children are held is ill-equipped to attend to the number of people entering their custody every day. Government should collaborate with the private sector and civil society to continue to develop a whole cadre of practitioners in rehabilitation and reintegration. This should include psychologists, peacemakers, educators, social workers, humanitarian-development workers as well as researchers that will make this a life time career.

Ultimately, the success of Nigeria's anti-radicalisation initiatives is hinged on strengthening civil-government relations, building strong inclusive institutions, and implementing large-scale response. With these steps, tensions and grievances can be mitigated and violent extremism completely prevented.

REFERENCES

1. Amnesty International. (2015). *War Crimes Committed by The Nigerian Military*. Amnesty International. Retrieved from https://www.amnesty.org.uk/files/webfm/Documents/issues/afr4416572015english.pdf?javl0ewG5FpxZHPfucgy_PnBAYRDzytI
2. Anyadike, O. (2015). Unmaking Nigeria's Boko Haram. Retrieved from http://newirin.irinnews.org/boko-haram-road-to-redemption
3. Barkindo, A., & Bryans, S. (2016). De-Radicalising Prisoners in Nigeria: developing a basic prison based de-radicalisation programme. *Journal for Deradicalization*, 7(2363-9849). Retrieved from http://journals.sfu.ca/jd/index.php/jd/article/view/56/47
4. Borno State Establishes Board To Regulate Preaching. (2016). Retrieved from https://www.icirnigeria.org/borno-establishes-board-to-check-preaching/
5. Buhari Assents to North-East Development Commission Bill. (2017). Retrieved from https://www.premiumtimesng.com/news/more-news/247280-buhari-assents-north-east-development-commission-bill.html
6. Campbell, J., & Harwood, A. (2018). Boko Haram's Deadly Impact. Retrieved from https://www.cfr.org/article/boko-harams-deadly-impact
7. The Federal Government Printer. (2013). *Central Bank of Nigeria Anti-Money Laundering and Combating the Financing of Terrorism Regulations*. Lagos.
8. Institute for Economics and Peace. (2015). *Global Terrorism Index*. Retrieved from http://economicsandpeace.org/wp-content/uploads/2015/11/Global-Terrorism-Index-2015.pdf
9. Lake Chad Basin Governors' Forum. *Report of the Inaugural Meeting of the Lake Chad Basin Governors' Forum*. Retrieved from https://lakechadberlin.de/wp-eb6f4-content/uploads/2018/08/2018_05_The-LCBG-Forum-Report.pdf
10. National Counter Terrorism Strategy. (2017). Retrieved from http://ctc.gov.ng/national-counter-terrorism-strategy/
11. Nigerian National Safety Tips. (2017). Retrieved from http://ctc.gov.ng/nigerian-national-safety-tips/
12. Nigerian National Security Strategy 2014. (2017). Retrieved from http://ctc.gov.ng/nigerian-national-security-strategy-2014/
13. Nwankpa, E. (2019). As Boko Haram Tumbles Under Operation Safe Corridor. Retrieved from https://leadership.ng/2019/03/26/as-boko-haram-tumbles-under-operation-safe-corridor/
14. PCVE National Framework and Action Plan. (2017). Retrieved from http://ctc.gov.ng/pcve-nsa-book/
15. Schmid, A. (2013). Radicalisation, De-Radicalisation, Counter-Radicalisation: A Conceptual Discussion and Literature Review. Retrieved from https://www.icct.nl/download/file/ICCT-Schmid-Radicalisation-De-Radicalisation-Counter-Radicalisation-March-2013.pdf
16. Shafa, B. (2019). Operation Safe Corridor [In person].
17. Terrorism Prevention Amendment Act 2013. (2017). Retrieved from http://ctc.gov.ng/terrorism-prevention-amendment-act-2013/
18. UNDP. (2017). *Journey to Extremism: Drivers, Incentives and the Tipping Point for Recruitment*. UNDP. Retrieved from http://journey-to-extremism.undp.org/en/findings

Conclusion

The world has experienced a meteoric rise in the number of terrorist attacks in the last one decade. More than 100 countries are facing the threat of violent extremism across the globe. The attacks on Saudi oil facilities that disabled approximately 5% of the global oil supply have displayed the capabilities of non-state actors to cripple economies and threaten global peace. Such audacious attacks cannot be thwarted unless there is cooperation and collaboration among the nations and security agencies.

David Galula a French military officer and a scholar who was influential in developing the theory and practice of counterinsurgency warfare wrote, "Prompting disorder is a legitimate objective for the insurgent. It helps disrupt the economy, hence to produce discontent; it serves to undermine the strength and the authority of the counterinsurgent. Moreover, disorder-the normal state of nature—is cheap to create and very costly to prevent." The focus of counterinsurgency involves the attempts governments make to restore peace and rule of law. The aim is to minimize collateral damages and loss of civilian lives while strengthening the influence of institutions of governance. There are three stakeholders in any violent extremism, the victims, the perpetrators and the audience. The principle of counterinsurgency and counterterrorism operations are that victims and audience should be brought under government protection, however, the perpetrators should be dealt by the law of the land and those who are willing to return back should be given an opportunity to reintegrate with the society. India and Nigeria are victims' of violent extremism and both nations have handled terrorism and insurgencies with skill and focus on people friendly operations.

Counterinsurgent and counterterrorism efforts usually attempt to enforce values and rule of law that may not be aligned to the cultural, social and religious belief of the people. Though states may not have accurate understanding of the political, cultural and social aspirations of the people, but they do have broad understanding of larger good of the people. Ignoring the importance of cultural belief, counterinsurgent forces are incapable of resolving conflicts thus more often remain round pegs into square holes. The solution for unrest is usually political in nature, not military intervention, thus there is a need to create suitable environment for political intervention earliest.

The joint publication has assisted in documenting the lessons learnt by both nations that would assist counter-terrorist and counter-insurgent forces to handle the violent extremism in a more skilful manner. There is consensus among the authors of both nations on following aspects:

- Invest in identifying and understanding the factors of terrorism/ insurgency.
- Make no concessions to terrorists and states should not succumb to the dictate of terrorist/insurgent groups.
- Bring terrorists to justice for their crimes.
- Isolate and apply pressure on states that sponsor terrorism to force them to change their behaviour.
- Use just force to suppress violence and create conditions for engagement with disaffected section of population or parties to the conflict.
- Fundamental objective of counter-insurgency and counter-terrorism is to disengage public from the radicals and reintegrate them with the state. Thus it is imperative to initiate political intervention earliest to engage with the political dissidents.
- Constructive engagement of the youth to prevent radicalisation and recruitment.
- Involve cross-sections of civic society and community leaders in analysing the state of community vulnerability, setting policy priorities and platform for engagement with disaffected and radicalised section of population.

It is imperative to undertake such academic exercises jointly to develop doctrines, concepts and good practices for evolving grey zone and hybrid war. This is a bench mark study that will assist scholars and professionals to learn from each other's experience.

Index